Where Leopard's Cough

Trevor Frost

Dedication

Having been brought up under extreme financial difficulties and selfish beginnings on my part I would like to dedicate this book to my Mother. I hope in some small way I was able to eventually prove myself to you prior to your tragic death. I know you are out there somewhere watching over all we do. To my sisters who have always supported me in every way and inspired me to write my story, thank you and love you all.

To the late Mr. Bob Longstaff who turned my life around in every way for the better. If there were a possibility of having a second father, you were without doubt that person. I know you would have enjoyed my story as you were so much a part of the journey. For all the years I had the honour of working for one of the greatest men I ever knew, thank you so much.

To Mr. Basil Kinsey for his endless support to our junior golf which I believe was instrumental in changing my life for the better, he instilled in me the need to help others in a similar way in later life.

Acknowledgements

Editor

Monica Cromhout 083 453 0052

Proof Reading

Jennifer Frost

Penny Mitrovic

Alan Brown 082 770 8937

Typesetting

Daryl-Anne Leveton 083 988 2411

Chapter 1

For 5.00am it was hot. It had been a long night with little sleep.

In Rhodesia the sun shows its face early and, without compassion, it pours down its heat until eventually it disappears over the western horizon in a spectacular orange glow.

I climbed off my narrow camp bed, and avoiding the tent pole, stepped outside into the early morning sunshine of an African day. Two days earlier we had moved onto a site in a remote area of north-eastern Rhodesia and were busy setting up camp. Our contract involved drilling deep exploration holes into the ground to ascertain the possibility of a Madziwa Mine nickel ore-body continuing to the Mazoe River through the Ruangwa Valley. The Ruangwa River flows east, and joins the Mazoe River on the western side.

Geological maps and results from soil sampling and trenching had given positive indications, but there's only one way to prove or disprove exactly what treasure hides six hundred feet underground.

At nine feet intervals, the rig drills deep into underground rock formations bringing up cylindrical rock core samples about two inches in diameter. All core samples were geologically logged, together with a comprehensive report on the completed drill hole, compiled by the site geologist. Any interesting rock sections, better known as ore intersections, were sent to a geological laboratory in Salisbury for a full analysis. The core is split in half using a diamond saw to cut through the samples. Sometimes, prior to the lab tests, they are split a second time into quarters. Depending on the workload at the lab, it could be up to three weeks before results were made available to the mining house that had initiated the contract. To minimize expensive standing time for the drilling equipment, while waiting for the results, a new location for the next drill site was marked out and drilled.

The topography leading down to the Mazoe River and on up the Ruangwa Valley has some steep descents and ascents and is well known for being wild, remote, and teaming with game. Elephant, rhino and leopard are common, together with antelope varieties such as kudu, impala, duiker, and other smaller wild animals.

Our first area of interest was up on the plateau above an escarpment. The riverbeds were dry, stony, and hard-baked by the sun. The Mopani trees inhabiting the area were leafless. It would be about ten weeks before the rains came. In Rhodesia, now called Zimbabwe, the season of the rains is from late November to March. But it is not unusual for rain to fall in early September. Historically, this was not a good sign. Usually, early rains foreshadowed a dry season.

Cool, refreshing rain was appealing, but not desirable. We needed two months to complete our contract. Even in the dry season, the roads were almost impassable. If the rains set in while we were in the valley, the only way out would be by helicopter. But the company who employed us had no helicopter at their disposal.

Our contract involved the drilling of two holes on the plateau, then move down into the valley to complete the exploration project, and get out before being flooded in. Even in ideal conditions, completing five months of drilling in a maximum of twelve weeks was a daunting task.

In any drilling operation, before a contract budget can be calculated, the security of water supply must be known. The nature of the area in which we would be working required a pre-quotation site visit, mainly to ascertain the availability of water. Not only was water needed for washing, cooking and drinking, but also for the drilling operation which used thousands of gallons per day.

This time, our water source down in the valley was unknown. In the absence of any other source, we would pump water from the Mazoe River and cart it four miles to our sites. While drilling on the plateau above the valley it would have to be carted well over twenty miles each way, in 1,000 gallon water tanks.

In the work team were six people who would be working up to eighteen hours a day. Temperatures were in the high 30°C to mid 40°C, with little relief at night. Our accommodation would be canvas tents that by ten in the morning would heat to oven temperatures and only begin to cool late at night.

It was soon after my 20th birthday. I was proud to be on my first assignment operating a drilling rig on my own, in charge, and responsible for a team of workers in a wild, beautiful and remote part of Rhodesia called Ruangwa Valley. Although our purpose was to complete a drilling contract, we were also about to have unforgettable experiences with leopards, rhino, pythons, puff adders, crocodiles, hippo and a huge monitor lizard.

A few weeks earlier I had made a courtesy visit to the District Commissioner at Mount Darwin. I wanted to meet him, and let him know that we'd be operating in his area. I gave him the approximate duration of the project. I also needed a hunting permit, so that we could shoot for the pot. Obtaining a permit was a standard and necessary procedure. Being caught with game meat on site without a permit was a serious offence, leading to a charge of poaching.

When he handed me the permit, the Commissioner warned me about a herd of elephant that had been attacked by poachers, leaving one of the bulls wounded. This bull had since become rogue and was dangerous. I asked why he had not been put down, before he killed somebody. The Commissioner explained that there were no humans living in the area, and he wasn't suffering any longer. So he had decided to leave him to wander with the remainder of the herd.

He also mentioned that lately the rogue elephant had become a loner, and was mostly seen lagging behind the herd. He warned me to look out for him. What a pity I didn't remember that advice later. Little did I realise then what a deadly and terrifying reality that rogue elephant could be.

Chapter 2

In my early childhood I discovered that I only felt truly alive when I was outdoors, in the bush, and part of the great wilderness.

For a few years we lived in a town called Umtali in south east Rhodesia. It was often called the little Switzerland of Rhodesia. Our house was a double story with a magnificent view over a green valley leading through into Mozambique. There was no development in the valley and it was dense with trees. I used every opportunity that arose to escape into the bush with my best friend, Toby, a small brown, long-eared daschund or sausage dog.

Toby loved our excursions into the bush. We walked together for miles. He chased anything that moved, especially butterfly shadows. He never learned that they were illusive entities. He would tear after them, landing with both front paws triumphantly outstretched on the spot where he believed he had trapped a shadow. With long ears flopping forward he would carefully lift one foot at a time watching intently for what he had caught to come out. For the rest of his life, in spite his lack of success, he never let up on this obsession.

My Dad had bought me a pellet gun for my birthday and it accompanied me on our wanderings. One day I saw an advert posted in the gun shop window. It read "Anyone who brings in fifty varieties of bird wings pinned neatly on a board will be given a brand new Daisy pellet gun with 500 pellets." So I was on a mission to achieve this goal. While Toby chased everything that moved, I looked out for new and different birds to shoot.

Looking back, I am not proud of the destruction of birdlife which I caused. I was eight years old. I knew little about wild life and appreciated even less the wonders of nature. The sacredness of life meant little to me. All I could see was the Daisy pellet gun coming my way. I shudder at those needless killings, but I became a good shot and I learned about birds as I identified the ones I needed for my project. It was part of the learning curve of my life.

As carefully as possible, I cut off the wings of the hapless bird, salted the raw area, and pinned them neatly to my ever-growing board of bird wings. Not realising the cruelty, I was proud of the display board.

After removing the wings, I cleaned the bird by cutting it open and removing the insides. Over an open fire, I cooked the body of the bird, feathers and all. Between Toby and I, we ate the whole thing.

On one such excursion, following after a bird whose wings I needed for my collection, we ventured into a very dense area of the valley. Suddenly I heard a roar from somewhere in front of me. In fright, I thought: "Lion!"

The thick bush was impenetrable. The only escape route was to climb a tree – quickly. Scooping Toby up under one arm, with my gun slung over the other shoulder, I scaled the nearest tree as high as it would hold us without breaking. Under normal circumstances, without Toby under my arm, I could not have made that climb.

I wondered if the pellets shot from my gun would have any effect should the lion charge me. I decided that would annoy him all the more and increase the danger. Already he sounded angry.

I had never seen or heard of lion in the area. This was going to be quite a story to tell my Dad when I got home, assuming that I would survive.

There was another roar from behind me followed immediately by another one in front. There were two lions? This lowered my possibility for escape, and cut my chances of ever getting to tell my Dad about the encounter.

I was terrified, but didn't panic. I sat silently up the tree, clutching Toby, and willing him to be quiet. It was useless to shout for help. There was no one around to hear me and any sound from me would let the lions know exactly where we were. I sensed that they knew where I was anyway, so it was only be a matter of time. I was suspended in a surreal reality, a timeless space between life and death. Calmly, I waited. Gradually the growls died down to almost a purr, then a snigger, and then into hysterical laughter.

A flood of relief surged through me. I was not going to be eaten by a lion. Someone had played a foul trick on me.

I passed Toby down to a tall thin boy some years older than me and climbed down the tree to confront the two make-believe lions. They were brothers and introduced themselves as Reg and Jess. It was an auspicious beginning to an important friendship that would help mould me into a man. They regarded this bush as their territory and had been spying on me as I wandered around, unafraid, in their wilderness. Today they had decided it was time to put me through a test.

They slapped me on the back and laughed appreciatively as they shared their amazement at how quickly I had climbed the tree, carrying my dog and pellet gun. They were also impressed that I hadn't screamed for help or started crying. I had passed their test. They said we should all be friends and go around the bush together.

Their Dad worked on the railways. They took me down to their house beside the railway line. I had seen it before while I was exploring. It was a typical railway house, square and small with a corrugated tin roof. Twenty paces from their front door was the railway line.

We became good friends. They were a few years older than I was, and could teach me many things. Some of what they taught was useful and has helped me through the years, and in many ways. There were some lessons though, that were dangerous. One of these was free-riding the train. It was great fun and exciting.

As the train chugged its way towards Mozambique, at one place there was a steep climb and the train slowed down. If we waited close to the top of the rise it was easy to jump onto the steps leading up into one of the carriages. Using the hand railings, I mastered the art of train jumping, always with Toby under my arm, and my pellet gun on the other shoulder.

We travelled down into the valley and then the train began another climb. As we reached the top of that climb we jumped from the slow moving train. We spent hours exploring the new area. It was beautiful. To return, we repeated the train jumping in the opposite direction, ending up where we started. None of us ever mentioned our joy riding to our parents. We knew they would not be pleased or impressed. Our parents had no sense of adventure.

Reg and Jess had a younger cousin named Tony. He was a few months older than me. The two brothers decided that Tony and I needed to learn how to fight. They explained to us how, at school, or even at some stage in our lives, we would meet up with a bully. They regularly arranged for Tony and me to fight each other. We were evenly matched and had what we felt were tough, hard fights. After each fight our two trainers would sit us down and give us a run-down on what we had done wrong and how to correct it. Neither I nor Tony thought this was much fun, but it helped me later on, when I did come up against bullies.

My Dad often encouraged me to get into a fight and told me he would pay me for any black eye I brought home from school. This puzzled me, and I didn't ever manage to cash in on his black-eye offer because I knew how to hold a fist at bay, thanks to the valuable training from Reg and Jess, and about which my Dad knew nothing.

I quickly learned that when I stood up to a bully verbally, with a threat to beat him up, the jerk would back off and leave me alone. In school, I noticed that bullies got their kicks from scaring kids who were already scared of them. The bullies had something missing in life, and dominating some poor kid helped them deal with it.

My sisters and I all went to Umtali Junior School. It was probably a good school, because there were some clever kids around, including my three sisters. But I hated school with a passion. I had a best friend called Michael, and we took advantage of any opportunity to run away from school. We would leave the school and head off for the bush on foot. We were not very professional at this, and were often spotted before we even left town. There was one particular shop owner who took pleasure in reporting us to the school when he saw us passing by on the street. We were picked up and unceremoniously returned to school.

So we spent a lot of time in the headmaster's office - probably more time there than we spent in our classroom. The two of us helped relieve the tedium of his days spent running a school.

My early school life didn't set me up to be a top student in the future. I never did well in school, except on the sports field. Academically I was nothing to write home about. I didn't care about academics, and saw no sense in book work. What I did have was common sense. And I had a will to do well in everything I did - apart from school work. This attribute has helped me to get on in life more than being top of my class could ever have done.

Chapter 3

My Dad had a passion for prospecting for gold. In a practical and direct way, his passion contributed to my experience of bush life.

He dreamed of making a gold strike. He would become rich and we would all live in luxury for the rest of our lives. To fulfil this dream he spent many weekends on prospecting trips in the wilderness. He would take me along with him. We packed only the bare essentials, because we had to carry everything. We roughed it out there in the bush.

Prospecting is tough physical work. Where ever my Dad saw potential for gold, we panned in all the little streams we found in that area. He had designed a clever system for panning, using a steel trough with a series of compartments. We shovelled soil into the first section and then ran water through the trough. Each compartment led into the next one. The heavier materials were trapped in the first compartment with the lighter material being washed away. Ultimately we were left with just the heavier particles which we collected in our hand-held pans.

Our panning would prove, or disprove, the presence of gold. Panning involved filling a tapered hand-held pan with the mineral material collected in it. The pan was a steel container with larger top than base. Using flowing water from the stream we swirled out the lighter soil, leaving the heavier materials to sink to the bottom. Gold was the heaviest metal of all. Spotting the first sign of the yellow-gold tail was exciting. Then we continued the operation, working upstream to locate the source. This was strenuous, intensive work.

I loved those trips with my Dad. I learned a great deal of bush craft from him. I could not have known then that I was being set up for my future career in the drilling game. It was giving me the background I would need some twelve years later when my career opened up, and I was plunged into the experience of drilling on the Ruangwa Valley Project, which I relate in this book.

On one of these trips, we were joined by my Dad's good friend and prospecting partner, Garth Lear. We were way out in the wilds, and reached a point where my Dad's old Austin Cambridge could go no further. We climbed out of the vehicle, and carrying all the equipment and camping supplies, we set off on foot into the hills. We did some strenuous climbing in the hot sun, each carrying a heavy load. As we only had the Saturday and Sunday for these prospecting trips, there was no time to waste in feeling sorry for ourselves about the exhausting work we were doing.

Garth was an experienced prospector, and provided an extra back to carry equipment. He was also good to have around. He had a great sense of humour. When we really got tired and irritable, he could lighten up any situation and get us laughing. That also raised our energy levels.

Along the way, we stopped and panned at many little streams. My Dad chipped away at formations exposed by flooding water over millions of years. He gathered every tiny piece of rock, together with all the scrapings and the dust and sand that came away from the formations. We came across interesting and well-defined rock formations, close to the surface. My Dad was well experienced in this form of prospecting. He was able to recognise places where we were most likely to find gold, and he took chip samples from there. The larger pieces were crushed and added to the fine material collected from the chipping. This material would then be panned, using the water from a nearby stream.

We had had some promising results from the chipping and the systematic panning we had done. On a map my Dad and Garth carefully marked the exact points of interest. If the test proved to be as good as it looked, we would apply for a license to peg the area. Once we had an area pegged in our name, no one else was allowed to do any prospecting there within a certain time limit. During that time we would be expected to do follow-up work. If, by the expiry date, we had not done any work on the project and had not applied for an extension, our hold on the land would expire.

It was almost dark. Unexpectedly, we stumbled across a small dam. My legs and body were aching from climbing and carrying a heavy load all day. We decided to stop right there and spend the night alongside the water. We had not brought a tent, as it was too heavy to carry. Setting up camp was simple. All we had to do was decide where to throw down our sleeping bags for the night. We always carried a couple of fishing rods and a fully licensed .22 rifle, and a few tins of Bully Beef. But here, beside the dam, we could catch fish for our dinner.

We had no bait for fishing, so I went off and shot three bush doves. As a starter to our meal, we would each eat one, cooked over a fire. Their intestines were used as a substitute for worms, to help us catch our main course which would be tasty bream. If there ever was successful bait for catching bream, it was these intestines. In a short time we had caught enough fish, not only for a meal that night, but we also had a few extra to cook and take with us for eating on the following day.

It was not only the bream who took to the bait. I also caught a terrapin, which is a small tortoise that lives in water. I knew immediately on hooking it that it was not a bream. It gave more of a pull than a fight. But I had no idea what it was until I had reeled it in and pulled it out the water. We were all surprised to see what I had caught, but we had a problem getting the hook out of its mouth.

For protection a terrapin retracts its head into its shell and the front section of the shell, closes off completely. But this time, the terrapin was not protecting itself. We couldn't get to the mouth to remove the hook which had been swallowed into the shell. We considered cutting the line as short as possible and returning it to the water with a hook in its mouth that would one day rust away. But we weren't happy with that. It would cause suffering, and difficulties with eating.

If only he could understand that we were trying to help him. I felt so sorry for him and tried to explain in the best terrapin talk I could muster, but he wasn't interested and kept his shell tightly closed.

Garth had brought along a long nose pliers. With these he eventually managed to remove the hook, with very little damage done. We released him into the water, where he took off like a rocket. We got the message that he was not impressed with our treatment of him.

After the terrapin incident I was no longer interested in catching fish. I set about making the fire to cook our lavish dinner. We were excited about dinner as we had not eaten a thing since breakfast. Once the fire was ready, I took out a bottle of Coke from my bag. It was warm, almost hot. Garth and my Dad were both relaxed and enjoying a beer after the long, hot and thirsty day. In those days, there was no such thing as a screw-off lid. I always opened my drinks with a screw driver. I held the bottle with my left hand, just under the seal, placed a screwdriver under the cap, and with one hard flick against my top finger I could send the bottle top flying.

I bent over it and flicked the top. Being as hot as it was, the lid flew off with a loud bang like a firecracker. With the force of the explosion, the sharp serrated edge of the bottle top buried itself around my right eye and held fast.

Blood poured from my eye, and my Dad jumped up from the log he was sitting on to come to my aid. The Coke top had buried itself into the skin around my eye, and it held fast. With some gentle prying and pulling, once again using Garth's long nose pliers, the top was removed. We were all concerned about possible internal damage to the eye. I couldn't see with it, and was sure I had gone blind in that eye. We were out in the middle of nowhere, at night, with what could be a serious injury.

Among our things was a bottle of Detol. My Dad cleaned out the wound, and once all the blood was wiped away, he said it wasn't as serious as it first appeared. It was shocking how easily and suddenly an accident can happen. I took it as pay-back from the terrapin. We used toilet paper as a dressing to the eye to stop the bleeding.

Having sorted out my injury, we got down to cooking the bush dove first and then the fish. What a great meal we had. We all had another drink, opened with great care, and then climbed into our sleeping bags. We fell asleep immediately. I loved sleeping out in the open, and in spite of the throbbing pain in my eye, I slept well.

In the morning we cleared up the site, making sure there were no empty bottles or any other rubbish lying around. My Dad helped me clean out my badly bruised eye which had become stuck closed in the night.

We followed our tracks, heading back the same route we had come the previous day. We found the car, just as we left it. Although the areas we explored were remote and relatively safe, my Dad was never sure of what could happen to the car when it was left unattended for a day or two. We drove home all feeling that, apart from my little mishap, it had been a successful and enjoyable trip. I asked my Dad if we could stop at the first store and buy an ice cold Coke and to ask the shop keeper to open it for us.

We all laughed.

Chapter 4

My Dad was a short, very strong man. "Stocky" would describe his physique. As a youngster, he was an amateur boxer. His trophies were on display in our home. He had a high pain threshold, which was fortunate. He got to suffer a lot of pain.

He was mechanically gifted, and as good with his hands as he was with his fists. He understood machines and equipment, and was skilled in their repair and maintenance. In the mid-1950s, while I was exploring the bushveld with Toby, and learning from Reg and Jess how to fight, my Dad was employed by Central Mechanical Equipment Department, which constructed roads in near-impossible places to reach. The name of the department was shortened to "CMED."

Every week, between Monday and Friday, he was away from home. He worked with teams of labourers in the mountainous wilds of the eastern border territory between Rhodesia and Mozambique. He serviced various sites, driving heavy trucks, and working with heavy road-building equipment and stone crushers.

My Dad was not a patient man. He was driven by inner demons, probably arising from a deprived and abusive childhood, spent in poverty in the bush.

At the age of 16 he had lied about his age, and signed up to fight in the Second World War. The minimum age for enlisting was 18. Those were stirring times, and boys dreamed of adventure and of being heroes. My Dad spent the six years of the War serving in the army and the air force, much of it in Egypt. For the young men who returned, the wounds to their bodies could be seen, but not the wounds to their souls, or the damage to the families that followed.

My mother and two older sisters were afraid of my Dad. They took the brunt of his temper. Most of the time I escaped to the bush, and remained unaware of the gravity of family circumstances. When we were in the bush, he and I got along well. He taught me many things about surviving in the wild, which prepared me well for an adventurous career that lay in the future. When my Dad was in the bush, he was at peace.

He took out the worst of his anger and frustration on the most helpless of targets – the black men who worked for him. We all witnessed the horror of his violence. His powerful fists punched into faces, his feet kicked soft bodies, and blood flowed. The victims, who were often taller than he was, didn't dare protect themselves, let alone retaliate or even protest. There were never any legal repercussions, and no regret, remorse, or apology. That's how it was in Africa in those days. There were many men like my Dad.

Needless to say, his workers were terrified of him as opposed to having respect for him, the latter being far more humane and productive.

In 1956, a dreadful accident happened. The family got to hear of it two or three days after it occurred. Communication was almost non-existent. Where my Dad worked in the mountains, telephones were miles apart and unreliable. As usual, my Dad was away, separated from home by many hours of driving over rough tracks.

We had a telephone at home. On one particular day, when life changed for us forever, it rang. A distant panicky voice, so faint my Mom could hardly hear what was being said, told her that there had been an accident. My Dad's hands had been severely injured. It appeared that he had lost most of his fingers.

Three days before, at the end of a long hot day, one of the workers called my Dad to look at a problem with a stone crushing plant. It was almost time to knock off for the day, and the sun was low in the sky.

The crushing plant was driven by a large electric motor. My Dad turned it off, and reached with his arms deep into the jaws of machinery to fix the problem. The men stood by, watching.

Suddenly the crusher burst into action. The safety switch had been released. In a split second both hands were crushed. In that moment of desperation, and with no other option, he wrenched his hands from the machine, leaving behind four crushed fingers, three from his right hand, and one from his left. The bones of the remaining fingers were splintered and broken, and several were hanging by bits of flesh and skin.

The three workers fled screaming into the growing darkness. My Dad was alone in an isolated place in the mountains. From what remained of his hands, he was losing blood fast. The helplessness and pain he must have gone through are way beyond comprehension.

His survival instinct took over. He knew that about forty miles away, deeper into the mountains, there was a Catholic mission station.

How he managed to climb up into the truck and drive for hours over the rough mountain tracks, in the dark, we would never know. It was a nightmare that defied belief. He would have been in severe shock, losing blood, in pain, and unable to grip the steering wheel or the gear lever. The cab would have been slippery with blood.

The catholic nuns were surprised to receive a late-night visitor. Their shock at discovering the condition of the unknown driver of the truck is impossible to imagine.

My Dad tumbled from the truck and lost consciousness. The nuns rose to the emergency, called the mission doctor, and together they stabilized their unexpected casualty. As soon as it was possible, an ambulance was dispatched from a distant hospital. Reaching the clinic would have taken many hours of rough riding over the mountains, and the return journey would have been the same. My Dad was taken to the main hospital in Salisbury, a few hundred miles from the scene of the accident.

Only his stamina and determination to survive, and the skill and dedication of the medical staff, saw him through. But ahead lay months, and years, of physical and emotional trauma before there could be recovery.

Before the accident, the family was already decimated by fear and financial stress, and my Dad's drinking. My mother was a shadow. It was emotionally impossible for her to support him. During the months and months of recovery, he could do little for himself. His frustration and pain was unbearable. His fury at his utter helplessness and the pain of it, was unleashed on her, and on one of my sisters. Fear multiplied. I spent more time in the bush.

Surgery followed surgery, and more surgery, and then came painful physiotherapy. My Dad was in constant pain and frustration. It was a long road. The family disintegrated.

That he recovered, and learned to work effectively with his hands is astounding. On his right hand he was left with a complete thumb and a stiffened little finger. The three middle fingers were completely gone. The surgeons re-attached and repaired three of the fingers of his left hand. The middle finger was a short stump, eventually amputated below the first joint. His left thumb was in good condition. He was eventually able to write - fast and neatly - and even to return to working with his hands on machinery. He also got back to playing a reasonable game of golf.

But he was no longer able to punch a fist into a face. It would have been too painful. Pain and helplessness also changes a man. Later on in his life he built strong and respectful relationships with the black men who worked for him.

Chapter 5

On the Leopard Rock Hotel golf course, high in the Vumba Mountains which were part of the Eastern highlands of Rhodesia, my Dad introduced me to the game of golf. I was 10 years old. I am told that, from the start, I showed some promise. This meant that I managed to hit the ball more often than I missed it. I also fell in love with the game.

My dad was thrilled with my enthusiasm and talent and he was soon dreaming of the day I would be a professional golfer.

At this time, life changed dramatically for all of us. My parents' marriage ended. In those days there were very few families where the parents were divorced. My mother, three sisters and I, left the beautiful mountains and magnificent bush country of Umtali and moved to Salisbury, the capital city of Rhodesia. It was built on flat land, and was suburban and boring. I began a new school and made new friends. My academic performance remained dismal. I was good at sport and made the first team in both cricket and rugby, but golf was my great love. In high school, my teachers and headmaster forgave my lack of academic prowess for the prestige I brought to the school from my golfing triumphs.

Golf was an expensive game. Our Mom was raising us on a shoe-string budget. These days I often wonder how she managed from month to month. We all went without a lot of things. The only way I could get the money to buy balls and pay green fees was to caddy for the seniors at Warren Hills Golf Club. One of the advantages of being a caddy was that I spent time with good golfers. Associating with the best gave me the opportunity to learn what they did that made them the best. They coached me, and I learned quickly, gaining their support and respect as a reward for my hard work on the practice tee.

At that time, Rhodesia was renowned for the support given to junior golfers. The Foundation for Junior Golf was formed and I was one of the beneficiaries. The Foundation was championed by Basil Kinsey who became a real hero to junior golfers of that era. He was unwavering in his support for us. He found time to play with us on the course and to give us free coaching on the practice range. He gave us advice on the values of honesty both in golf and any other sport, and also in life. With his support and training, and my father's ambition, at a young age I was playing off a single figure handicap.

Basil had promised me a new set of woods when I got down to a single figure handicap. Being without money, this sounded like an impossible dream. The old and worn set of clubs that I played with had been dragged out of my Dad's garage and cleaned up. I played well with what I had, but I envied those young players who had beautiful new clubs. Basil's promise motivated me to practice my heart out, hitting hundreds of golf balls every day.

At the age of thirteen I was selected to play for the Rhodesian Junior Golf team on tour in Northern Rhodesia[1] in the colonial town of Mufalera in an area known as the Copper Belt. It was an honour to be part of the team and it was a great tournament. While on tour, my handicap was cut from thirteen down to a nine.

One day, just after arriving back from the tour, I was out hitting practice balls on the driving range. Basil came over and with a serious look on his face. He told me to stop hitting shots and follow him. I was bewildered and was sure I was in trouble. Like an obedient puppy I followed him back to the Pro Shop run by Joe McMaster, the golf pro who was reputed to be the best green keeper in the country. He was also a great guy and an excellent golf coach.

"Joe," he said, "let Trevor try out all the sets of woods you have in the shop, and help him choose the set that suits his swing the best. Put the cost on my tab."

Those were the most magical words I had ever heard.

A smiling Joe said, "Leave it to me Basil. We'll find something that will work well for him."

Laughing at my shocked disbelief, and my concern about the cost of the clubs, Basil said, "Well, I hadn't expected to do it so soon, but I promised you a new set of woods and now it's my pleasure to fulfil on that promise." I was stunned that anyone could do such a big thing for me. We settled on a set of Gary Player square toed woods. I loved those clubs and played great golf with them. That was the single biggest thing ever done for me by anyone. I have never forgotten it. It was playing

---

[1] Northern Rhodesia was part of the Central African Federation, and after independence became known as Zambia.

with those clubs that I got myself down to a scratch handicap and also achieved my biggest goal in golf – twice over.

At the golf club was a board displaying in gold letters the names of club champions. I aimed to see my own name listed there. In 1965, when I was 17, that happened for the first time. After winning the Club Championship at such a young age, I was selected to play an exhibition match partnering one of my golfing heroes, the famous South African professional golfer, Harold Henning. We teamed up against the two top players in Rhodesian golf at the time, Bob White and Willie Fulton. In spite of my nervousness, I managed to play well, lifting my game to match the elite company. In 1968 I won the club championships again. In 1965 I also won the Rhodesian Junior Golf Championship by seven shots clear of the runner-up. However, those two Club Championships meant more to me. They put my name on the Championship Board twice, and nobody could ever take that away from me. Even now, whenever I go to Salisbury – now called Harare – I play a game at that club just so that I can see my name on the board and remember the people who helped me get it there.

One of the ways that young golfers were encouraged was an annual junior tournament sponsored by a man called Mr. Mutch, who was very involved in the support and promotion of junior golf. This tournament did a lot to encourage the junior golfers at this time. The handicap system, regardless of the player's real prowess, was based on age. The younger the player, the higher it was. It was good system, but it did mean that some of us played off a much higher handicap than actual. With relative ease, therefore, I won the tournament five years in a row. While it was a real honour to be presented with the magnificent trophy each year, the handicap system made it a hollow victory. After winning for the fifth time, I was given the floating trophy to keep.

Check out the brilcreamed hair style and probably had my comb in my sock as well

Chapter 6

Lake Kariba is on the Zambezi River, about halfway between the river's source in north-east Zambia and the mouth, where it flows into the Indian Ocean on the coast of Mozambique, about 740 miles downstream from its mighty wall. It forms part of the border between what was Northern and Southern Rhodesia, now called Zambia and Zimbabwe.

It is the largest artificial lake in the world being over 140 miles long and up to twenty miles wide. This enormous mass of water is believed to have caused many earthquakes some of which were in excess of five magnitude on the Richter Scale. Sadly, during the construction of what is one of the largest dam walls in the world, more than eighty lives were lost.

Prior to the lake being filled between 1958 -1963, the existing vegetation was burned, creating a thick layer of fertile soil on the land that was soon to become the lake bed.

A number of fish species were introduced. A sardine-like Kapenta species was imported from Lake Tanganyika, and grew to support a thriving commercial fishery. Kapenta fishing was done from what became known as Kapenta rigs. Bright lights reflecting rays deep into the lake at night, attracted the Kapenta where they converged in massive shoals, they were scooped up by the thousand in nets. Game fish, particularly Tiger fish, indigenous to the Zambezi River, thrived on the Kapenta and were often captured together with the Kapenta. Fish eagles, cormorants and other water birds patrolled the shoreline for easy meals of fresh fish. Also on the shore were occasional elephant herds. Other inhabitants of the lake were the Nile crocodile and hippos.

There are many islands on the lake all of which had to be cleared of animals in what was called "Operation Noah." The lake supplied both Northern and Southern Rhodesia with power from the six large generators on the southern side and four similar generators on the northern side. Each power station was managed independently by the country concerned.

On the Rhodesian side, the town of Kariba was built to house construction workers working on the dam wall. On both sides of the river, other settlements developed to house people displaced by the rising waters.

I was introduced to fishing at a young age. I never missed a chance to go fishing, even if it was just down to the local stream where we could catch Barbel[2].

Colin Evershed was a good friend at school. His parents were successful farmers who owned a large piece of land about twenty miles outside of Salisbury on the road running north to what is now Zambia. On the farm were two dams. Both were teaming with fish. Colin often invited me to spend the weekend out there.

We would spend every possible moment fishing in the dams, or hunting for Guinea Fowl. The edges of the mealie[3] lands which, to me, appeared vast in size, were the favourite foraging areas for flocks of these large birds. They spent their days scratching for mealie kernels. We imagined ourselves to be great white hunters. As silently as possible we pushed our way through the towering mealie stalks. When we were lucky, we got really close and were able to shoot a couple of birds before the flock took off noisily, and mostly on foot as guinea fowl are not great flyers. It was a wonderful place for two young boys, and we felt free and without a care in the world. The fish we caught in the dams were not particularly big, but there were many of them. Eating fresh bream fried in a batter of flour salt and spices together with chips was one of our favourite meals.

One Sunday morning, as Colin and I tucked into the crispy bacon and eggs Mrs. Evershed had prepared for us, Mr. Evershed asked us if we'd like to join him and a friend called Rick on a fifteen-day fishing trip on Lake Kariba. We were speechless, for just a moment. Then, in unison, we blurted "Yes! Please!"

I couldn't wait to get home to ask my Mom if she would let me go on the trip. I was prepared to go to any lengths or to meet any conditions she imposed. I might have even volunteered to wash the dishes for a few days. In those days, at the age of fifteen, we were the main guys, with our slick Brylcreamed hair and a comb stuck in our socks. Nobody dared take us on. So offering help around the house

---

[2] Cat Fish

[3] Maize

would be a sign of weakness. But this was an opportunity of a life time, and my Mom understood immediately that this would be a good experience for me. She readily gave her permission.

On the day school broke up for the 1963 Christmas holidays we left for the lake, heading north. The diesel driven Peugeot pick-up was fully loaded with camping gear, and so was the Land Rover. Colin rode with his Dad and two farm workers, with a thirty-foot boat in tow. I joined Rick in the Peugeot. We had adrenaline rushing through our veins. For no other reason but to make them jealous, we had told all our friends about where we were going for the holidays.

In the early evening we reached Charrara, on the shores of the lake. Using a tarpaulin, we set up temporary sleeping cover for the night. In no time, there was a fire going. We cooked some meat on the braai grid, had a bath in the lake, and hit the sack for an early night.

Chapter 7

Before light we were all up and loading everything into the boat. It was going to be a tight squeeze with six people, supplies, fishing equipment, fuel for the boat, two boxes of fishing worms, six cases of beers, and three cases of Cokes. Our plan was to cross the lake from Charrara to Sanyati Gorge where we would spend fifteen days of solid fishing. In the gorge there was nothing but water, bush and wildlife.

We intended to leave very early, before the breeze picked up, but we weren't early enough. Initially the lake was calm and we made good time. About thirty minutes out from shore we hit some chop in the water. In just a few minutes the waves got bigger as the wind speed increased. The lake could be treacherous. The boat was overloaded. The captain, Colin's Dad, immediately turned east, heading for shelter among a group of small Islands about half-a-mile away. With the wind coming from the east, the bow of the boat pushed directly into the wind and the waves. We were still close to the shore so the chop in the water hadn't yet got high enough to be dangerous. But even so, the water splashed over the bow and into the boat. We were convinced we were going to sink and have to swim to shore. That would be the end of the fishing trip.

Our accomplished helmsman kept the boat going, and eventually we found refuge on the lee side of the closest island. The water was calm with small ripples on the surface. After beaching, we were instructed to unload the boat and bail out water while waiting for the lake to settle.

Within an hour the wind had calmed. In that time the boat had dried out and we re-loaded the cargo. Nervously we all climbed back aboard and set off once more for the Sanyati Gorge. The captain decided to take the long route, rather than head across the lake. We would sail close to the shore. The Lake is so large that from the middle of it, you can't see land in any direction. It would be foolish to push our luck. Our short but terrifying experience had sharpened our protective instincts. We cruised smoothly through a forest of hundreds of half-submerged trees. Eventually, in the mid-afternoon we arrived at the mouth of the gorge, safe and relieved.

Immediately, we unloaded the boat and began to set up camp. Colin's Dad and Rick would share one tent, Colin and I shared the smallest tent, and the helpers also had a tent to share. Our helpers from the farm were friendly, hard-working and tough. Their duties included making fires at night and in the morning, looking after the camp during the day. They also cured and smoked the fish we brought back after each day on the lake. They set off together to cut and gather poles and straight, strong branches to build smoking racks. They set them up on the downwind side of the camp, to spare us the smell of drying fish.

The responsibility of caring for the worms was given to Colin and me. We found a cool place in the shade, and wet hessian sacks which we laid over the worm boxes. We were also given a powder to spread underneath and around the boxes to keep ants at bay. Worms were more essential to a fishing trip than beers. Colin and I were too young to drink beer, but we knew the worms were important. The rest of the day was spent constructing a crude bathroom with cut-off branches, and we also got our fishing rods ready for the following day.

The next day, before sunrise, everyone was up and drinking coffee, reflecting on what the day might bring. The fishing gear and worms were loaded onto the boat, and we set off to catch bream and chessa among the half-submerged trees. For the first few hours very little happened. We caught a few small bream and some annoying baby Tiger Fish. However the old saying, "If you don't have a hook and line in the water you won't catch fish," had been drummed into us, and we kept on trying in different spots, and at different depths.

Then, as if set by a clock, feeding time came. I felt a slow, gentle pull on my rod, then again the same thing happened. I thought it must be another small fish, so I struck. Instantly all hell broke loose with my reel screaming as the fish ran with my hook in his mouth. Within seconds Rick struck with the same result. Colin and his Dad reeled their lines in to give us space to fight and play the fish without getting tangled in their lines. Eventually, using the landing net both fish were landed, onto the boat. Both were Mozambican bream close to 4lb in weight. We were so excited. We wondered if we had caught the only two fish that were down there. But for the next two hours, as fast as it was possible to bring them in, we caught bream and chessa, all of similar size. Although the bream are nicer eating and excellent fighting fish, they aren't a match on the strength of the chessa which swam with such speed that our fishing lines sang. We gave up the idea of reeling in when someone hooked a fish. Many times all four rods were bowed almost to breaking point with reels screaming, but not as loudly as the fishermen yelled.

By 11.00am the feeding frenzy quietened down. With all three keep-nets full we returned to the camp for brunch. Joseph was there, waiting to carry the fish. He was amazed how many there were. Laughing, with a flash of his beautiful white teeth, he said, "Boss if we are here for fifteen days we'll need to make more drying racks and get a bigger boat." With much laughter he turned and called for Nelson to come and help carry the fish.

After a meal of fresh bream fillets and chips, Colin and Rick decided to relax in the shade for a while. They suggested that we set off again for more fishing around mid-afternoon. Colin and I filleted our own fish for eating. We enjoyed the challenge of filleting for maximum flesh and minimum bone. We became quite proficient.

After cleaning up the dishes our two camp staff set about the unenviable task of gutting, butterflying, curing and hanging the fish over the smoking racks. Shallow holes had been dug under each set of drying racks for the fire. The racks themselves had been constructed about three feet above ground level. The open area from the ground to the rack was closed in with reeds to ensure that the smoke would be channelled straight onto the fish, and not drift away in the breeze.

Curing fish is similar to curing other meats, such as ham. The fish is salted, either with brine or rubbed with dry salt. Curing takes some moisture out of the fish, and at the same time adds salt and spices. After curing, the fish is rinsed with cold water to remove excess salt and seasonings. Then it's left to dry in a cool place until a glaze forms on the surface. The glaze keeps ash and other contaminants out, and seals in the remaining moisture. It also prevents the fats in the fish from rising to the surface and spoiling.

The smoking time varies from six to eight hours, depending on the size of the fish. It would take a lot longer, if we were fortunate enough to catch a large Tiger Fish, Barbel or Vundu.

With the success of the morning's fishing, we now had a concern. Had we brought enough sacks to store all the fish? Did we have enough salt for the curing process, and would there be enough space on the boat to load the dried fish?

Colin and I, young, energetic and enthusiastic, were ready to venture out in the boat once more, in the midday sun. Within half an hour we realized just how hot it was, and the fish weren't biting. We decided to return to the camp and rest in the shade. Colin's Dad teased us when we came to join them, saying we weren't as tough as we thought we were. The temperatures at that time of year in direct sunlight reach the high 40s.

Colin and I decided to help Joseph and Nelson prepare the fish for smoking. Although at the time it was a chore, we learned a lot from them – not only about cleaning fish, but about bush craft as well. They showed us how to make rope from bark, for securing the smoke racks. Once the bulk of work was done, they took us on a guided tour of the shore line and surrounding bush. They pointed out and identified animal tracks and droppings, and estimated the age of the animals. We vowed to spend our non-fishing time with them. They were chuffed to have an opportunity to teach two white guys. Neither of them could speak English so we spoke Fanagolo, which also improved in the days that followed.

In the late afternoon, we returned to the submerged tree forest for more fishing. By 5 o'clock we had filled two keep nets to the brim. This was turning into a bigger and more exciting adventure than any of us could have imagined.

Joseph and Nelson worked well into the night preparing the fish for curing and smoking. Over and above their normal rate of pay, Colin's dad paid them an additional amount for each full bag of smoked fish. The harder they worked, the more they earned.

The fires were stocked for heating bath water and one by one we took turns to bath out of buckets. There was no space on the boat for the larger tin tub usually used for this purpose. After we were all cleaned up, we shovelled red hot coals out from the base of the fire and placed them in area prepared by Joseph and Nelson for cooking. Sitting around the fire as darkness descended, we found ourselves in a surreal new world. We were in the middle of nowhere, with no other human, or habitation for miles. All that could be heard were the sounds of the night – crickets, night birds, frogs and insects, and the daunting sound of a lion's roar. Their roars and growls can be heard from six miles away and made the hairs on our necks tingle. The stars glowed brighter and filled the sky. Colin's Dad knew a lot of the stars and pointed out the Southern Cross and many interesting constellations. We were close to heaven.

The next morning, we were woken by the calls of the fish eagle and the francolin pheasant. By 6.00am we were fishing once again among the half-submerged trees. The fish were quiet. By 6.30am Rick was as surprised as the rest of us when he caught a two-pound Tiger Fish. Colin's dad had loaded two Tiger rods. After filleting the fish Rick caught, we set off to look for Tiger Fish in the mouth of the gorge.

When we arrived at the mouth of the Sanyati Gorge, the rods were made up with Tiger traces. The steel wire trace was two feet long, and attached to a swivel on the one end and a large hook on the other. This was firmly attached with a non-slip fishing knot tied to the line. The Tiger fillet was then cut into strips of about an inch wide. The hook was threaded back and forth through the fillet, and then a small amount of mercurochrome was poured onto it, to give the bait the appearance of a wounded, bleeding fish.

The boat was then set in motion just over idle speed and the lines were let out approximately a hundred feet behind by releasing the bailing arm on the reel. The boat then continued at that same slow speed dragging the baits of the two rods and this was called trawling. Back in 1963 there were no fancy lures so this was the most successful method adopted at the time, well to our knowledge anyhow. His Dad removed four match sticks from his box, broke two in half and asked us each to draw one. I was lucky enough to pull one of the short ones and Rick pulled the other. The prize being having the honour to let the lines out and man the rods ready for the first strikes.

We had hardly travelled more than five minutes and Rick's reel started screaming immediately followed by the most impressive sight I had ever seen.

This huge Tiger Fish broke the surface leaping high out the water shaking its head violently with spray flying in all directions. I sat watching spell bound at the sudden action. To ensure the lines couldn't become tangled I was urgently instructed to reel mine in. Rick with great excitement was shouting at the top of his voice for the fish to stay on the line. The minute the fish hit the water so the reel once again screamed as the fish took off on a long run. Using Pen Reels we had the luxury of one thousand feet of line. Many times the fish leaped into the air trying to shake the hook loose, but to no avail and after a great fight of some ten minutes or so Rick boated a beautiful twelve pound Tiger. Colin and I were amazed not only at the size of the fish but also the size of its teeth, they were huge and razor sharp! After successfully removing the hook from its lethal jaws, the process started all over again.

This time with Colin and I manning the rods my line took off. I was shocked at the power of the strike. However there was no jump, just the howling from the reel. Being inexperienced at the time I shouted back that as the fish never broke water I thought I could be stuck on a submerged tree. The boat however had been accelerated for a few seconds to ensure setting the hook and then shut down. Colin's Dad laughed loudly as my reel was still screaming with our boat standing still.

"I can tell you if that is a tree, man it certainly can swim fast!" followed by excited laughter from all. "The only Tiger that stay down this long are really big ones." Hardly had the words come out of his mouth when the huge Tiger Fish broke the surface, not really jumping, basically only the head broke the surface and then just kind of flopped over back into the water. "You have hooked a monster there give it one more hard jerk on the rod to ensure the hook is set." He never broke surface again and I eventually managed to land him with the help of Rick leaning over the side of the boat and gaffing it. He weighed in at eighteen pounds on our little hand scale, six pound bigger than Ricks and by far the largest fish I have ever seen. However, although a far bigger fish Rick's one certainly gave a better fight. Apart from the first run, all I basically had to do was reel him in. He was too big, fat and lazy to put up much of a fight. I couldn't resist looking down at the fish every ten minutes or so while we continued trawling for more such beauties. I felt like I was the only one in the world that could ever catch such a fish. Realistically I just happened to be holding the right rod at the right time.

Time was marching on, so we then called it a day with the Tiger and left for camp. After dropping off the two huge Tiger Fish and having a quick bite to eat we came straight out again to get stuck into the bream and Chessa. We had to ensure all our sacks were going to be filled with smoked fish to cover the expenses incurred by Rick and Collin's Dad for this wonderful adventure. To some this might sound like hard work, to us it was the opportunity of a life time and loved every minute of it. We both wished this dream would never end, however the days seemed to fly by.

On one of these afternoon sessions we stayed out late as the fish were still active. Eventually just as it was becoming dusk, we called it a day. Colin stood up, went to the front of the boat to untie it from the tree we were attached to. He looked a bit like a monk as he had a white sheet wrapped around his body to keep the mosquitoes away. Instead of pulling us slowly up to the tree to loosen the rope he gave it one almighty jerk. Well it was hilarious to say the least for the three of us as he pulled himself clean off the boat head first into the water. We weren't too concerned and casually looked over the side laughing our heads off. Funny how often we find other peoples dilemmas so amusing. However the laughter stopped when he didn't surface.

Rick was just about to jump in when this white sheet appeared on the surface of the water with Colin struggling desperately to get his head out from the tangle so that he could get a breath of fresh air. Leaning over the boat we quickly grabbed the sheet and pulled it up into the boat. There was Colin with his head now free from the water and the sheet, eyes bulging from holding his breath taking in huge gulps of air into his starved lungs. Reaching down Rick and I took a firm grip on an arm each and hauled him on board.

"What on earth did you think you were doing?" shouted Colin's Dad "Hell you could have drowned!" Colin in between spluttering and coughing water out of his mouth told us that when he hit the water the sheet flopped over his head. Tangled and disorientated he swam and struggled as hard as he could with the restriction of the sheet and eventually realized he was going down instead of up when he touched the muddy floor of the lake! He said he then pushed himself off the bottom as hard as he could with lungs almost at bursting point with panic and fear of drowning. Casually he then asked with a smile on his face. "Now that you guys have had so much fun at my expense do you think we could call it a day and go back to camp?" After the harrowing experience we all burst out laughing.

Once again the night passed peacefully. The new moon had grown considerably by this stage and shed a fair amount of light. The submerged tree area, where we had fished some three hours before, could be seen clearly. It almost looked spooky out there. This together with the constant smoke rising from the racks gave off a beautiful effect in the moon light.

Sadly the time arrived to pack up camp, the adventure was over. The bags of smoked fish were carried down and loaded onto the boat that evening to save time in the morning. In a short time the floor space was taken up and we started stacking the next row on top of the first.

Surprisingly we eventually loaded all the bags, all be it that it looked ridiculous. The top row of bags where now protruding well above the gunnels of the boat. The questions that immediately sprang to mind were, where would we load our tents and other camping gear and secondly where were we going to sit?

During our two week stay there Joseph and Nelson had manufactured long lengths of bark rope from the surrounding trees. Steel rings had been securely installed to the gunnels of the boat during manufacture. Using these together with the rope the sacks were tightly secured. I thought to myself. 'Great, the sacks couldn't now fall off, but surely being so top heavy the boat must roll over in the slightest swell!?' I really wasn't confident about the situation, but was assured by Mr. Evershed all would be fine.

Up even before the fish Eagles had chance to serenade us with their morning call we managed to have the camp completely broken down and ready for loading. The smoking pits were well doused with water carried in buckets to ensure there would be no fires after we left. The pits were then closed in with shovels and a general and thorough tidy up was undertaken. Colin's Dad rightfully stated that we found the area in pristine condition and should try to return it as close to that as possible. There was no room for beer or Coke bottles so these were buried in a deep hole and covered up.

The tents were semi folded and spread across the top of the sacks of fish for all of us to sit on. Gingerly we all climbed aboard expecting the boat to tipple over. All sitting at least three to four feet above the gunnels of the boat we must have looked like the hillbillies moving house. Even Colin's Dad and skipper had to lean right over to get to the tiller to steer and keep us on track. Eventually we set off slowly heading for Charrara and once again navigating the long route not straying too far from land. Any wind and waves would undoubtedly cause the overloaded and top heavy boat to capsize. Realistically we need not have worried as the boat was far more stable than we gave it credit for and after a good few hours of nervously plodding along, landed safely and with all cargo and passengers intact at Charrara.

Collin was taken straight off to the small medical clinic to have his finger seen to that had been badly cut open by a tiger fish and stitched with fishing gut by his Dad. We in the mean time, sorted out the unloading of the boat and loading of the vehicles. Some weeks later Colin's finger had healed beautifully. He told me that his Dad had made a really good profit from the sale of the fish caught. My immediate thought was, to make money and have that amount of fun, why farm? However you find in later years life just isn't quite that easy.

Chapter 8

While I was playing hard at golf and getting by in school, my country – Rhodesia - was in political turmoil. In the early 18th Century it had been colonised by white settlers, but had been self-governing since 1923. In 1960, British Prime Minister, Harold Macmillan, made his famous "Winds of Change" speech in which he stated Britain's intention to grant independence to British territories in Africa.

This was unsettling for white Rhodesians as it raised the possibility of black rule and a similar kind of chaos as had happened in the Congo to the north. Britain was unwilling to compromise on the policy of "No independence before majority African rule." Finally, on 11 November 1965, our Prime Minister, Ian Smith, took the unprecedented step of making a Unilateral Declaration of Independence (UDI). The white population of Rhodesia hailed him as a hero, but to the rest of the world he became a villain. Our country remained stable, with a strong economy. There was work, food and security for everyone. A real fear and threat to the peace and prosperity of Rhodesia were the events in the Congo to the North. Would their tragic circumstances be repeated in our country?

From July 1966 we became a country caught in a deadly civil war, fought mainly in the rural areas. It was either called the 'Rhodesian Bush War', or the 'Rhodesian War of Liberation', depending on your view point. It was a war between the official Rhodesian army and the 'terrorists' or the 'freedom fighters', according to your view point. People living in the cities and towns were not affected. Almost all the fighting happened in the bush.

Whatever the political ramifications were, the war affected me personally. It was compulsory for all white Rhodesian males, from the age of 18, to enlist for National Army training. So, when I left school at the age of 17, with no clear idea of what I wanted to do, other than professional golf, or becoming a game ranger, I decided to get my

National Army training over and done with as soon as possible. It would give me time to consider my options. Although the call-up age was eighteen and I still had seven months to go, I was in a position to modify this rule in my favour. The father of the girl I was dating was a captain in the army.

I would have to do my training in Bulawayo at Llewellyn Barracks. My contact, the captain, was friendly with the colonel there, who was a golf enthusiast and played off an eight handicap. A phone call from my girlfriend's father let the colonel know that I played off a scratch handicap, and that was enough to secure my training before the age of eighteen. I was ordered to report for duty on 22 February 1966.

So it was that on 21st February 1966 I boarded the overnight train for Bulawayo, along with the B Company's 81st intake. We were all excited and looking forward to having fun in the army, completing our training, and after that getting on with our lives. In the early hours of the next morning we arrived in Bulawayo, and were loaded onto army trucks for a twelve mile drive to Llewellyn barracks outside the town of Bulawayo.

Almost immediately, the prospect of having fun in the army was severely compromised. Long hair was the fashion of the day. The others had their hair cut before they left home. On arrival at the army base, as we climbed out of the truck, the Sergeant Major who was to be responsible for our training for the next few months, singled me out. I was ordered post haste to report to the barber like a sheep to the shearer. Hair flew and by the time the army barber completed his masterful exercise of scalping me, there was not a hair on my head I could grab with two fingers. My new-found friends from the happy train ride were greatly amused, and taunted me with "We told you so!."

One day, six weeks into the intense 1st phase training, a sergeant delivered an order from the Colonel for me to report to the first tee at the army golf course at 2.00pm sharp the next day.

"I'm sorry," I said, "I can't do that. Tomorrow we're going on a full-pack route march. I can't play golf with the Colonel."

"Private Frost!", barked the sergeant, "I don't give a shit about your plans. When you get an order from the CO to play golf, you play golf!"

I barked back: "Please tell that to my RSM. He's been riding me big time from the day I arrived. If I play golf tomorrow, my life will transform from this low level to hell on earth."

"You go tell that to someone who gives a shit, because I sure as hell don't!" he replied. "I'm passing on orders from the top. But I'm warning you, if you don't play golf tomorrow, you would rather be in hell."

With that, he turned and walked out. The other guys in the room all agreed I had no option.

On arriving at the golf course the next day, the Colonel introduced himself and invited me to tee off first. I knew that, regardless of how I played, I was going to be in trouble. I teed my ball up, had a practice swing and went through my routine of addressing the ball. Then he stopped me. "Tell me, Private Frost, have you been placed on charge yet?" he asked, seriously.

"No, Sir. But I have come close. The only reason I haven't is my Sergeant Major's obsession with torturing me personally" I said, with a half-arsed smile on my face.

"Well then, let me tell you something. Beat me in this game today and you'll find out what it's like."

It wasn't possible to know whether or not he was serious. So I stood there, driver in my hand, ball ready and teed up, and wondering what to do next. So much for my first impression of him being a nice guy. He burst out laughing and told me to play my heart out, which is what I did. On the last hole I missed a short putt to lose one down to him. Neither of us was really sure whether or not I missed it on purpose.

Every morning A, B and C Company would assemble in the main hall to discuss training programmes and be given orders. On the morning after my game of golf with the CO, my RSM took the stage and told all the trainees that he had an interesting story to tell them.

"Private Frost, please be good enough to stand up so everyone can see you," he requested, in an uncharacteristically pleading voice.

"Here we go," I thought, and stood up. He continued.

"It seems that things have changed somewhat in the army. Yesterday, while all my troops were out on a five mile route march with full packs, one of the trainees decided to do something different." He paused, for full effect, knowing the story had travelled around every barrack room anyway.

"SIR Private Frost here decided a game of golf was a better deal. Off he goes in search of the Colonel's Office, which as you know is off limits for us lesser mortals. Somehow he manages to get all the way to his office, knocks on the door, marches in and says, 'Hey, Colonel, how about a game of golf old chap?'"

I had witnesses as to how the order had been passed on to me, but that made no difference. The entire hall, including my witnesses, burst into laughter.

First phase army training is tough, extremely physical and disciplined to the extreme. Being mercilessly targeted by the RSM made mine tougher. I soon gave up letting it get to me, and knew that if I kept my nose clean I could get through this.

Then the Dunlop Open Golf Tournament was due to be held at the Bulawayo Golf Club..

A request for marshals for this prestigious tournament came from the host club to the army barracks. No guesses needed as to who was the first to volunteer to be a marshal. I was missing golf and needed a break from my friend the RSM. To my surprise he had no objection to this. Early on Saturday morning, along with eleven other trainees – none of them from my platoon – I was taken to the club. We were positioned at various places throughout the course to help with crowd control and to recover stray golf balls. Being a 72-hole tournament we would be there for two days.

I had played in the tournament myself a few times, so I was ready for ridicule from my golfing friends who were playing. They loved the sight of me wandering around in my army gear. Some of them had not yet enlisted for their army training, and I warned them that their turn was coming.

On our return to the barracks we were informed that all three platoons had gone for their TAB injection on Saturday and, due to possible side effects, they were given the weekend off. We were required to have ours the following morning. It was a mandatory injection for all trainees and we would be issued with letters from the hospital placing us on light duty for the day.

This was great news. Not only did we get out and have a good weekend at the golf club, but were going to have an easy Monday. Hey, army life was improving. Or so I thought.

Early the following morning, directly after breakfast, the twelve of us trouped over to the hospital for our jab. Whether it was because it was administered by a male nurse, or because it was just a painful injection, it was an uncomfortable experience. We were all given our letters and then marched up to the parade ground where all three platoons were doing drill. I walked over to my RSM, stood to attention and handed him my letter. He burst out laughing.

"If you think you can have a free weekend in Bulawayo and report back for light duty, you are mistaken. You will drill with the rest of your platoon. Collect your rifle from the armoury and get back here in double quick time."

"Sorry, Sergeant Major," I started. We were not allowed to call anyone Sir unless they were commissioned officers with one or more pips on their shoulders. "The doctor who gave me the letter said under no circumstances was I to do any physical work. He said it could cause serious side effects." I was confident that would sort out the problem.

The expression on his face changed.

"If you're not back here with your rifle within the next five minutes I'll place you on charge for insubordination. That means you spend a week in detention barracks. If you think you're having a hard time here, you have much to learn. Do I make myself clear?" He was shouting loud enough for all to hear.

"Yes, Sergeant Major, I hear you loud and clear." With that I spun around and at quick pace marched off to the armoury and returned on the double to join my platoon. We were drilled up and down non-stop for the next hour. I was starting to feel the effects of the injection and was relieved when we were eventually marched off to the armoury to return our rifles.

On arrival we lined up with our backs to the wall and filed through one by one. By this stage I was in trouble. My vision was blurred and I felt dizzy. I asked the guy next to me to be ready to catch my rifle if I fell over, and told him I thought I was going blind. Somewhere through the haze I could hear the RSM shouting. He called me names I had not ever heard of before. He was obviously close to me as I felt his spittle hitting my face. He was being downright derogatory.

His yelling made me determined not to fall down. With a bit of help from my friend next to me I managed to get to the open flap door and hand in my rifle. With his help I managed to get back to the barrack room and was relieved to lie down on my bed. My vision was coming back, but I had to hold onto the sides of the bed with both hands to stop myself being flung off. The room seemed to be spinning round and round. My friend assured me that all was fine, and slowly my head returned to normal.

During grenade training there was an amusing incident. With good reason, this part of the training was taken seriously, with an emphasis on personal safety. The precautions included going through the mock action of pulling the grenade out of the pouch, pulling the pin, throwing it over the wall, counting to five and then dropping down, while the grenade supposedly went off a few seconds later.

We went through all the things that could go wrong: throwing the grenade without pulling the pin, pulling the pin and accidentally dropping the grenade down next to you, watching where we had thrown it for too long and having our heads blown off by the shrapnel.

There is a clown in every group and ours happened to be Private Thomas.

"Private Thomas," asked the sergeant, "do you have any idea what would happen if the pin came out of the grenade and it exploded in the chest pouch of the webbing you are wearing?"

Without a moment's thought Private Thomas replied, "Yes, Sergeant. I would need to go and see the Quarter Master to get a new pouch. Then I'd be told the cost of the replacement which would be deducted from my army pay." We cracked up laughing including the sergeant.

There were many similar incidents. When we left the army those are the memories that remained, and the hard times faded away.

As our first phase came to an end we were given the option of being transferred either for Signals, based in Bulawayo at Brady Barracks, or for Artillery, based at the RLI[4] Barracks in Salisbury. Or we could remain in the Infantry at Llewellyn Barracks. Being a Salisbury boy with family and a girlfriend back there I opted for the Artillery. Once again, with the help of my girlfriend's father, I managed to secure one of the spots available. I was thrilled to be going back, but vowed before I left to have a private and serious talk with my Sergeant Major.

The night before we left, I went over to the Non-Commissioned Officers' Mess where I knew he would be. Luckily I spotted the same sergeant who had given me the golf message. He saw me and came over to see what I wanted. I asked him to tell the RSM there was someone to see him, but not to tell him it was me.

"Well, I'll tell him, but I don't know if he'll be interested. I don't know what you want to see him about, but it's probably not to say a fond farewell. Take care not to make the rest of your army training a worse nightmare than it has been already."

---

[4] Rhodesian Light Infantry

"Thank you for that. I'll take care. Can you call him for me, please?"

He disappeared, and soon after, to my surprise, my 'buddy' came through the door. I moved further back from the Mess to be as private as possible.

"Oh," he said on seeing me, "it's you! What the hell do you want? To kiss and make up, now that you're out of my hair?" He swaggered, with a smug smile on his face.

"You wish." I said. "I need to talk to you with no witnesses." I looked around to ensure that there was no one in earshot.

"You treated me like shit from day one. At least you made me feel noticed. However what you did to me that day on the parade square after the TAB injection, and the way you spoke to me at the armoury, including degrading my parents, is something I will never forget. I wanted you to know that one day your time will come."

He was shocked speechless. I continued."Here in the army you little shits live under a veil of protection from bits of coloured cloth stitched onto your shirt sleeves. Out there in the real world you are on your own." I turned around and walked back to my barrack room to pack and prepare to leave the following day. Surprisingly he was silent as I walked away. I never saw or heard of him again.

Chapter 9

Our new intake into Artillery went smoothly. I was happy to be there. I enjoyed the training and the difference it made to have an RSM who was a human being. RSM Erasmus was no pushover. He was hard and took no nonsense. But he was fair, had intimate knowledge of the training that had to be done, and he knew how to handle his troop. We had great respect for him. He was a dog lover and his beautiful Alsatian was with him at all times. In my eyes, just that, made him a good guy.

We trained on the 25lb artillery guns and learned to appreciate what valuable and destructive weapons they were. We went out on a few live ammunition exercises on a range some 40 miles out of Salisbury. Using smashed up old vehicles as targets, we put ourselves and the guns through their paces. These exercises included manning the OP (Observation Post) and we learned how, using radios, to instruct the unseen guns to adjust their aim. The whistle of a 25lb shell flying over your head and exploding as it hits the target is quite something to experience.

I was one of the drivers. We used Ford F250 4x4 trucks for transporting the guns, once they were set up in travel mode on their two large wheels. They were hitched to the tow bar and pulled from place to place.

On one of the exercises, everything was going well until it was time to pack up, load and drive back to the base camp. We were about 45 miles from our base camp. Then the heavens opened and it poured with rain. This was unusual. It was winter and Rhodesia has summer rains. We all got wet and were extremely cold. The drive back to camp was hazardous to outright dangerous. Of the six guns being towed, we were the only ones to get back to camp without slipping off the road or getting stuck in the mud. This made me a hero to the crew of my truck. We were the first to have hot showers and change into dry clothes. The others straggled into camp one by one, with the last truckload of men returning at four in the morning, cold and miserable.

I enjoyed the training and the association with the other gunners. Although it was a chargeable offence, with help from friends in the guard house, I managed to spend many nights at home. They let me out in the evening, knowing I would be back early in the morning.

In a lavish passing-out parade, throwing our beret's high into the air, we passed out as gunners. We were free to return to civilian life, having successfully completed our national service.

But I was still not sure what to do with my life, so I enlisted for another four-and-a-half months in the artillery. This time I worked as an instructor, including heavy-duty driving instruction.

I was proud to have been the only one in our original platoon to pass the heavy duty driver's test first time around. The real challenge in the test, where all the others had failed, was driving down the Salisbury Kopje[5]. There was a steep decent and the driving exercise entailed stopping the truck at the base. Sounds easy enough, except we had to assume the brakes had failed. This involved double-declutching through the non-synchronised gear box all the way down to first gear, switching the engine off, and under engine compression, coming to a halt.

One of the advantages of re-enlisting was that I made many new friends before finally passing out.

The compulsory army training at the time was four-and-a-half months. From the 82nd intake, this was extended to nine months. Voluntarily, ahead of that, I had completed nine months of army training.

As the Bush War intensified the army training for all whites of eighteen years and older was increased to two years. This was followed up with regular call-ups into the bush. This was disruptive to many young families as, tragically, the war dragged on for fourteen years, with the loss of many lives on both sides.

After my second stint in the artillery, I was now ready to start a new life. But I had no idea what that life would be.

-----

[5] A "kopje" is a small rocky hill

Chapter 10

One of my friends was employed by a Salisbury engineering company, on a five-year contract as an apprentice boiler-maker. He told me there was a vacancy for a new apprentice. With zero other prospects in my life I interviewed for the slot and was successful.

The trial period was six months, after which a final decision could be made by either party. I had plenty of common sense, worked well with my hands, and learned quickly. I enjoyed the work. I worked under an excellent journeyman who was proficient in his trade and he had a great sense of humour. I remember him sending me urgently to the stores section to ask for a long weight. Being new, enthusiastic, eager to please and, in hindsight, stupid, off I went. The store man listened to my request and told me to wait as he was busy. After fifteen minutes I became concerned about being away from the job for so long. I called the store man back to the counter and enquired as to how much longer it would be for him to get a long weight for me. He gave me a long, serious look and then burst out laughing. He said I'd had my long wait, and could return to my workbench. This was one of many pranks I was caught by, as the new appie on the floor.

All went well for five months. I decided to make boiler-making my career. The wages earned were pitiful, but once qualified this would change and I would be in a position to find a job anywhere. Hey, I could do this. I enjoyed the work and was going to make something of myself. But, in a flash, an inexperienced and naive young man can have a mental change of direction.

Another friend worked at the Salisbury Fire Station. He told me about a vacancy for a new fireman. He also mentioned what he was earning. It was four times more than I would earn in my third year as an apprentice, let alone what I would earn in the first year.

Another benefit was that he worked forty eight hours on and forty eight hours off, structured in a way that gave him every second weekend free. This would be perfect for me. It would give me time to play golf. I still had in mind that if all else failed I could try my luck on the pro golf circuit. This was assuming my back problems could be corrected. It had been discovered through X-rays that, at birth, my lower vertebrae were fused to my sacrum on the left side. This caused a kink in the spinal cord which was thought to be inoperable.

Bunking work for the day, I went for an interview for the post, together with eight other guys. I was successful and told to start work at the beginning of July 1967. When I handed in my notice to the engineering firm, my journeyman was disappointed, and so was my family. But I was on my way to become a Fireman.

I enjoyed the work - and the recreation - at the fire station. In the mornings we were thoroughly drilled in fire-fighting procedures. We were taught how it was possible with the use of two ropes firmly attached to a shackle in the roof and dangled all the way down to the ground to jump from a forty-foot high training tower in the station grounds. This was successfully achieved by attaching yourself to the two ropes via a spring loaded enclosed clip which in turn was firmly attached at stomach level to the harness you wore. Then with four people firmly holding each rope on the ground you simply jump out the window in what feels like a death defying manoeuvre. Quiet amazingly shortly before crashing into the ground the two ropes are pulled apart and your decent is instantly and smoothly halted and you are gently lowered to terra firma safely. We did ladder climbing exercises while carrying heavy fire hoses over our shoulders. We were also drilled, over and over, on the matter of cleanliness. We spent many hours cleaning the station and the trucks, until they shone like new. The next day we were instructed to do it all again.

We had intense first-aid training, not only for fire casualties, but we also had many call-outs to other emergencies. We had four well-equipped ambulances at the base. We were taught and regularly tested on topography. The urgency of getting to an accident or fire as fast as possible could not be over stated.

In between all of these activities, we had loads of spare time and spent many hours playing snooker, darts and card games. If there was ever a sure way of becoming proficient at any of these games it had to be working at the Fire Station. I played golf at least four days a week and made reasonable money at the end of the month. Hey. Life could be worse.

We were called out to many small to medium fires. There were also many false alarms, which were frustrating, and a waste of station funds.

I was also fortunate to be involved in call-outs to two major fires. On 4th Street, we fought a fire that set four shops alight. The second big one was a factory fire in the industrial area. When there was a real fire, the adrenalin rush was huge. High on a ladder with flames pouring out of windows, glass exploding all over you and thick smoke in your eyes, while aiming a high pressure hose at the carnage just yards away is an experience not to be forgotten. At those times we were thankful for those fire and safety drills.

I continued working as a fireman through to August 1968. By then I was a good snooker and darts player, and when it came to card games I was no push-over. Although I enjoyed the lifestyle, I knew that it would not be my lifelong career. Out there was something else for me. Eventually, with no alternative plan for the future, I resigned from the Fire Station.

Chapter 11

From a young age I had girlfriends. I put this talent down to growing up as the only male in a female household - my mother, my grandmother and my three sisters, two older and one younger. I was doted upon by all of them and in their eyes could do no wrong. This led me to expect adoration from all females.

There are many family stories about me, and girls. One of these was my first conquest - Sophie, who was one of Reg and Jess' sisters. I was unaware that she had a secret crush on me. One day, I gave her an apple. She treasured this gift from me by keeping it on her dressing table. It eventually turned rotten and when her mother threw it away she was inconsolable and her secret was out.

Another favourite family story happened in early primary school. In my class was a boy called James. He was the clever class nerd whom I had persuaded to do my homework for me. I protected him from bullies, and he liked being around me. He also had a crush on my girlfriend, Tanya.

One day, during break time, James and I opened up our sandwiches, packed by our mothers. I had egg sandwiches, but he had scrumptious looking tomato sandwiches. Knowing how he fancied Tanya I told him I was prepared to swop her for one of his tomato sandwiches. Not believing his luck, he jumped at the opportunity, giving me a sandwich before I changed my mind.

He was pleased with the heist he had pulled off. This made up for hours he had spent on my homework, and helping me get through school tests. Being an honest guy, I played my part and told Tanya about the deal. She didn't see the humour in the situation, and dropped me as her boyfriend. But she also wasn't interested in James. After the dust had settled, she forgave me and we made up. So, I got to have the tomato sandwich and to keep my girlfriend.

Throughout my growing-up years, I always had at least one girlfriend. In my late teens, according to my younger sister's memory, I was inundated with phone calls from girls, she remembers monitoring the calls for me. When the phone rang, she would answer. If it was a girl, asking for me, she would find out who it was. If it was a girl I didn't want to talk to I would go out the front door so that, in all honesty, she could say, "Sorry, he has just gone out the front door." She would never lie to anyone.

My impulsive attraction to beautiful girls often had me embarrassing myself. On one occasion my dad and I teamed up with two women to play golf in a mixed better ball competition.

Having tea in the club house after completing the first nine holes, a sexy blonde walked past. My dad noticed me giving her the once over and laughingly said, "Oh, that's Joan, a new member of the club. Believe it or not, you used to play with her when you were a small boy."

Without a moment's hesitation I blurted out, "Well, I'll tell you something, I wouldn't mind playing with her right now." The two mature ladies burst out laughing and I realised what a blunder I had made and I felt my face changing colour.

"Len," the two ladies concluded to my father, "I suppose he gets that from you. You have always had an eye for the ladies." By then even those at the table next to us were laughing, while I sat there grinning sheepishly.

A popular gathering place was the Epworth Quarry some five miles past the famous Salisbury Balancing Rocks. An enormous hole had been blasted out the granite rock. The resulting ballast was used for road construction. It was rumoured that it was a place of criminal activity and where stolen cars were dumped and discarded. It was also said that the bodies of a murdered couple had been dumped there.

But we were young and on the lookout for fun. Despite its dark reputation the quarry was the venue for some wonderful parties. Covering most of the base of the quarry was a deep pool of water. To my knowledge no one ever discovered the actual depth. Although nerve wracking at first we would dive off what was approximately a twenty five foot high cliff into the clear water. I believe this wasn't solely for the kicks, but possibly more likely to impress the chicks. In our late teens we had loads of things going around in our heads and yet feel it's not an exaggeration to say 95% of those thoughts revolved around girls!

Driving down the incline into the quarry led you out onto a flat section of rock surrounded on three sides by crystal clear water and large enough to accommodate up to fifteen vehicles. It was on this section that we held our parties, with music and dancing, and the inevitable sex orgy. Naked bodies could be seen all over the place on blankets, and in the water. It was here where many girls became women. There was a saying that if you couldn't get your way with your girl out there, it just wasn't going to happen and you should move on.

Organising these parties was a case of driving around Salisbury looking for chicks. On one such occasion I was driving a 1954 Humber Imperial reputed to be the same car in which the Queen Mother had toured Rhodesia in that year. It had long been abandoned. When my friend Neil took me to see the car I was surprised to discover that it was a nesting and roosting place for chickens. It was a mess. The guy who sold us the car wanted the old heap out of his yard, and we paid a meagre $20.00 for it. We jacked the car up, removed all the wheels and took them down to the garage to be pumped up. The car had been standing on flat tyres for years, yet somehow once pumped managed to keep the pressure long enough to tow the car to Neil's house some three miles away.

Then we got going with rebuilding the old girl. We stripped and cleaned the carburettor, and fitted a new set of points and condenser. We removed all the spark plugs, cleaned and reset the gaps to specification and as the HT leads looked okay we left them as they were. The oil showed to be full and clean. We fitted a fully charged battery, checked to ensure there was spark and spun the engine. It took a good few spins for the fuel to get to the carburettor and then suddenly she fired up. Not only was the engine running, but she purred like a contented cat.

This was too good to be true. We decided to go for a ride around the block to check gear box and general drive train. Although she still looked like a run-down chicken run, she drove like a Rolls Royce. The old banger was mechanically sound. Purely by chance we had stumbled onto something quite special and unique. We decided to put more effort into getting the car into good shape.

After many hours of rubbing down, we painted the bonnet, roof and boot area and the bulging mudguards black. Everything else was bright yellow. It was quite a car. It had three rows of seats with little reading lamps at the rear. Getting the seats clean entailed hours of hard scrubbing, but they were pure leather and came out looking great.

We all belonged to our little gangs back then. There were nine of us. We called ourselves and our yellow and black peril "Alcopone's Alcoholics." The name was painted on the back by one of our buddies, Doug, who was a sign writer.

We toured the city looking for women. The car was heavy. When cornering hard the body would lean over at such an angle that the front right or left edge of the bumper would scrape on the tar road throwing a trail of sparks. If the bumper never touched the road, Neil would shout that I was not going fast enough.

On one city tour, while approaching traffic lights, we came alongside a Mini with two really cute chicks in the front, neither afraid to show lots of leg and cleavage. While driving, I hung out of the driver's window in my attempt to chat them up and invite them to a party at the quarry. They showed interest, and while my mind was fixed on the pleasures to come, suddenly we came to a crunching halt. To my surprise the guy in front of us had stopped at the red light in his fancy Zephyr 6 and I had effectively re-arranged his back end.

He leapt out of his car and came running to the back to see what had happened. He looked to be in his late twenties, was a big guy and extremely angry. We were in for trouble and due to my negligence, rightfully so. Having a punch-up was the least of my concerns. Paying for the damage to his car however was a serious matter.

I climbed out the car and came around to the front to check the damage and to take my medicine for my irresponsible driving. His tail lights were smashed to pieces, and there was body damage to the boot just below the two fins. The two girls in the Mini were in hysterics about what had happened and eagerly awaited the confrontation.

He was about to fly into me with fists blazing. But then he saw eight rough, tough guys bundling out of the car. The colour drained from his face. Suddenly he was apologising for stopping so suddenly in front of us and offered to pay for the damage to our car. Relieved that I was not to be burdened with his repair bill, I generously declined his offer, shook his hand, and invited him to join us at the party. He politely declined the offer, climbed back into his car and drove off. The Humber was built like a military tank and had an enormous chrome bumper in the front. So, apart from a couple of small scratches, there was no other damage.

The girls were impressed with how we had managed the situation at the traffic lights. They promised to be at the party and to bring along some friends. Under clear, star-saturated skies we had a great night down at the quarry, partying, dancing - and everything else that went with it.

Chapter 12

My back problems persisted, and became something I had to live with for the rest of my life and it put an end to my hopes for a career as a golf pro. I didn't know what to do with my life, my future, I was at a complete loss and felt like a failure to myself, but more importantly to my Mom. Should I have stayed with boiler making? Hell, at least I would have had some form of qualification and a trade behind me.

For years, with very little money, my mother had struggled to get all four of us through school. My Dad had not been reliable in meeting his responsibilities with helping to support us financially. Life was tough for our Mom. My three sisters were more successful academically than I had been. One day, in desperation, after I had walked out of yet another job, she phoned my Dad and told him that she was at the end of her tether with me. She told him that he must sort the problem out as she was at a loss as to what to do next. By this stage I was really feeling bad and although I had no idea how I would ever do it, vowed to one day make it up to her and make something of my life.

My Dad worked in the industrial area of Salisbury, for a company called G. North & Sons. They supplied and maintained pumps and irrigation equipment. As I sat outside his office, waiting to talk with him, the owner of a large exploration drilling company was with him, taking delivery of spare parts he had ordered. He asked my Dad if he knew of any youngsters who enjoyed bush life, as they were looking to employ a learner-driller.

My father knew how much I loved the bush, and he felt the moving of a miracle. Without saying a word, he stood up, opened the door, and called me into the office. He introduced me to Mr. Longstaff who owned a Diamond Drilling Company and asked if I would be interested in working for him. It was a career I hadn't heard of before. I didn't know what to say. Seeing my hesitation, he told me it would mean living permanently in the bush. All I could say was, "When do I start?."

There was an instant, short interview consisting of two questions: "Do you like the bush?" and "Are you mechanically minded?" Mr. Longstaff wasn't interested in my academic non-achievements. My answer to both questions was, of course - "Yes.."

"Well, in that case, you can start tomorrow. Gus, the Managing Director, is going to Rasendie Mine near Umtali, where your training will begin. On the road, he'll give you a run-down on drilling and tell you about our expectations for drill operators."

I was to start on a salary of $50.00 per month with drilling bonuses coming into effect once I had completed the initial training and qualified as a drill operator. My hours of work would be from sun up to sun down. The Company shut down between 24th December and 2nd January, and that would be my annual leave. Accommodation would be a caravan or a tent, depending on availability and accessibility of the terrain. Food costs would be shared with the drill supervisor and operators. There would be a probation period of six months to allow either party to terminate the contract if not satisfied.

Although taken aback by the speed of things, I said "Yes." again. We shook hands to seal the verbal contract, and off I went home again, to pack and say goodbye to my delighted, astonished mother and sisters.

Chapter 13

Gus collected me at 6.00am the morning after my interview with Mr. Longstaff. We set off for the Rasendie Gold Mine about three hundred and fifty miles from Salisbury in the south eastern part of Rhodesia. The turn off to the mine is situated at the base of what is known as Christmas Pass which consisted of steep gradients with sharp turns left and right all the way to the summit of the mountain. Once reaching the top, travellers are rewarded with a view of the Switzerland of Rhodesia, the beautiful and quaint town of Umtali nestled below, in a fertile green valley.

I was excited to be returning to the area where I had spent my early childhood, and where I had first fallen in love with the wilds. Not only was it good to be going back, but I would actually be paid to be there

It was the end of September 1968 when we arrived on site and my introduction to exploration drilling. That afternoon I saw four labourers pulling down repeatedly on a ten foot pipe. This was in turn attached in the centre by a rope that ran through a pulley on the top of a thirty foot tripod and back down to, what I discovered later, was called a jar. This consisted of a thirty five pound, round hollowed out piece of steel. This in turn was installed over the pipe leading into the hole. Each time they pulled down on the rope, the jar flew up the pipe leading from the hole and with a solid bang it struck a steel jarhead screwed into the top of the pipe. I couldn't understand why they would be hitting it up, when actually trying to drill down?

Gus went over to the machine and spoke to the operator for a while. Fascinated with what was going on, I stood off to one side watching. After each strike of the jar the operator checked his mark against the casing obviously checking for movement. Gus came back to me and said, "That's the machine you will start off on. What do you think?"

In all seriousness, I replied "Well, if that's the way you get your pipes out every time, then I'm not too excited. I'm sure I can work out a more efficient way of doing it."

Gus burst into laughter. "Firstly, those pipes are called drill rods." More laughter. "Secondly, the reason we're jarring is because the rods are stuck in the hole." Hysterical laughter. "It's the only way we might possibly get them loose. If you think there's a better way - please, I'm all ears."

He took me over to where the workers were, and introduced me to Ken, the operator, who asked what the joke was. When he heard, he too cracked up laughing. By that stage even I was laughing. I wasn't sure what I was laughing at, but there had to be something funny going on, and it was a good way to start a new job.

On this site, I worked with Ken for the next few months. He taught me the basics of how to run a drill rig.

Chapter 14

My first drilling contract was at the Rasendie Mine near Umtali. It was also my first experience of living permanently in the bush. There was no telephone, and a severe shortage of girls. As often as I could, I returned home to Salisbury, travelling by train.

On some weekends my drill instructor, Ken, took me with him into the town of Umtali, and I made some friends. One of them was Eddie, who was also from Salisbury. He had found work at the Umtali sugar mills. At the end of each month we had time off from Friday night through to Monday morning. Sometimes we took the train trip together.

One Sunday evening after a great weekend in Salisbury, we boarded the train which would take us back to Umtali. While black smoke billowed from burning coal to build up steam to power the engine, the conductor came around selling bedding tickets. When only earning $50.00 a month everything was expensive. The bedding cost seemed high, but the convenience and comfort of having the bed made up for me on one of the bunks with crisp, clean linen and a warm blanket made me decide to pay for it.

Shortly after buying our bedding tickets a cute, sexy girl came out of her compartment and stood in the passage looking out through the window at the dark countryside rushing past. She wore a short red skirt, showing off two of the longest shapeliest legs Eddie and I had ever seen. Her white blouse left us with no illusions about the beauty of the treasures hidden within. Being two hot-blooded single men with needs, she caught and held our attention.

Eddie's face took on an "I'm-in-love" *look* - or was it an "in-lust" look.

"Wow. She's gorgeous. Why don't you go over and try your luck?" I said, though badly wanting to do that myself.

"Yes, sure," he scoffed, "you just want to have a good laugh when she tells me to get lost." He turned his attention back to the view of night countryside passing by, trying to distract his mind from the deep tingle at the base of his stomach.

I turned for a second look at the angelic vision that had come floating out of the next compartment. I was rewarded with a smile. I smiled back, and then felt foolish. She could be smiling at Eddie, or someone else in the passage behind me. Embarrassed I turned to see if this could be the case. Eddie was still gazing out the window and there was no one else around. Her smile was for me.

"Well," I said to Eddie, with great bravado, "if you're not going to talk to her, you have a good night. I'm going to make a plan."

"Sure, lover boy," laughed Eddie. "Let's see how long it takes before you come running back here with your tail between your legs."

"Well, if I come right, it will cost you a few drinks. On second thoughts, since you earn more bucks than I do, if I spend the night in her compartment, you can pick up the bill when I take her out for a meal."

Laughing scornfully at the challenge, he said, "No problem. You get your act together with her and it will be my pleasure."

I went back into my compartment, cleaned my teeth vigorously, pulled my comb out of my sock to comb my hair, which I wore long in those days, and with a squeeze of deodorant under the arms I was ready to go get my girl. "Eddie," I said smugly, "I'll see you in the morning," and confidently walked off in her direction.

"Hi. I hope you're not on your own. These trains are not safe on overnight trips." That was my introductory speech.

She gave me a smile that melted my knees. I held onto the railing for support.

"Yes, she said. "I am alone, and I appreciate your concern. But now that you're here I know I'll be safe." She offered me her hand, and introduced herself as Pam.

"I'm sorry," I said, taking her hand in both of mine, "shaking hands with a woman… it's not a man thing to do." I gave her a quick kiss on the lips and said, "Hi. I'm Trevor, and pleased to meet you." I fully expected to be slapped or at least given one of those sharp woman looks which mean "Get lost. I'm not interested." To my astonishment, she left her hand in mine, and was blushing furiously.

"Well, Trevor, that kiss was a bit impulsive, considering we've only just met this second. But I'm pleased to meet you too." She lifted her other hand up to her burning red cheek.

"I didn't mean to offend you. It's my way of saying hello to good-looking woman." As I moved in closer, she grew more attractive. "Tell me about yourself. What do you do? And what's a nice girl like you doing on this train, all alone?" As I said it I knew it sounded lame. I wished I could call back the words, knowing she would have heard corny lines like that many times. "*What a jerk I am*," I thought to myself. "Surely *I could have been more original*."

Pam gazed up at me with bewitching blue eyes. "My folks live in Umtali. My brother and I came through together to spend time with my aunt in Salisbury. We were both going back today, but my brother decided to stay on a few more days so. Here I am, alone."

"Well, to be honest, I'm not sorry that your brother stayed on in Salisbury. I'm a far better body guard. I promise to ensure your safety all the way home."

Had I made up for my blunder? It seemed so. To cut a long story short we got on extremely well and I not only shared her compartment, but her bedding as well. Sometime in the early hours of the morning I murmured, "I can't believe I wasted all that money on my bedding and never used it. I will have to ask the conductor for a refund when we arrive." We burst out laughing.

It was a wonderful night. I felt like I had died and gone to heaven and I told her I wanted to see a lot more of her, which I did. I was the only guy she spent a night with out in the bush in a caravan. With the help of Ken, we often managed to meet that way, before I left Rasendie Mine drill site for my Christmas break.

Chapter 15

About 20 miles from Salisbury, on the Shamva Road, was Mermaid's Pool, a popular weekend getaway. A large pool was fed by a stream flowing over a slope of smooth granite rock. The slope was made slippery by the continual stream of water. It was a perfect slide, down into the pool. http://www.panoramio.com/photo/45168846 taken in 1968.

We would either ride the slope, sliding on our butts - or we took a more comfortable ride on a blown up truck tube. The last twelve foot section sloped steeply, making the ride even more exhilarating. Instead of slowing down, we accelerated, eventually hitting the pool at speed and sending water exploding over everyone in the landing area. There was always the odd guy who, feeling brave and indestructible after a few too many beers, would attempt to take the slide standing up. Some were successful. Others were bruised and sore.

There was a good restaurant and a crystal clear swimming pool. The other attraction was a foofie slide which consisted of a steel cable securely attached high up on a tree on one side of the pool, drawn tight and fastened low down on the other side of the pool with a span of approximately forty yards. To this was attached a pulley with a handle. Holding on for dear life, we jumped out of the tree, and were sent flying over the pool, descending steeply and finishing spectacularly in a huge spray of water. Once again inebriated adventurers would let go half way across and come crashing down into the middle of the pool.

Adding to the excitement was a continual flow of live bands that pounded out their music all day. As one band took a break the next one took over, keeping a musical vibe throbbing across the pool, resonating off the rocks and through the acacia trees. Wherever there was a flat area, people danced - on the lawns, the verandas and cement pads next to the braai fire and even up on top of the rock slide. It was the perfect place for the young people of Salisbury to gather, have fun, meet old friends and forge new ones.

The first time I met Les, we were both at this magical place. While having a great time dancing and socialising, a good friend, Trevor Gombard, came over to me and said that a girl over on the other side wanted to meet   me. Never shy, I set off immediately to meet the girl who would eventually put all other girls out of my mind.

She was slightly on the plump side but attractive. I liked her immediately. She had a special and uncommon innocence about her. We got on well, and talked for hours. We had a wonderful day together. Eventually we left to head back to town, and made a date to go out with friends that night to a popular night club.

The only car I had at my disposal to impress my new chick, was my Dad's old grey Vauxhall Vellox. You could buy them in any colour you liked as long as it was grey. Being old wasn't the issue, but it was not in great running condition. I was terribly embarrassed. Firstly the car had the column shift gear-change which worked well when new. But age and wear over the years, were seizing up the complicated linkage system, transferring the movement inside on the gear lever to the selector in the gear box. The attitude of this was: "Can't do anymore: I'll just roll over and die."

Occasionally I would be lucky and change through all three gears without a problem, but most of the time, it was an impossible task. The linkage would jam up solid in whatever gear it happened to be in, but generally second was the main problem. The only solution was to pull over open the bonnet, ask the chick to hold it up for you to stop it falling on your head, as the metal arm support designed for this purpose had fallen off some time back. Then climbing up over the left front fender, reaching down at full stretch, I would juggle the linkage until it freed itself. To make this process really interesting, there was an oil leak on the left side of the tappet cover of the engine. This blew oil back onto the linkage making it messy. For this purpose I kept a pair of rubber hand gloves neatly folded in the boot. I checked to see if they were there and that they were clean. Les was a special person who had miraculously come into my life and I wanted to impress her. Oily hands would spoil my chances.

I had another contingency plan. I kept a full one-gallon petrol can in the boot, held in place with a rubber band cut from a car tube. Why, you might ask, would I need such a thing? Well, the fuel gauge, as with most of the other gauges in the car, didn't work. On many occasions, I had run out of fuel. To raise money to put fuel in the tank I would have to sell a shirt or similar article, or go to the golf course and caddy as many times as possible during the week. I was never in a position financially to fill the tank. Tonight of all nights wasn't a time to run out of fuel.

On my way to collect Les I was tangled inside with concern that the inevitable would happen. Funny things, our minds... They tend to dwell on all the negatives and not as it should be the positives.

This time, all my concerns were unwarranted. Not only did we have a great night out on the town, but the old Vauxhall obviously approved of my date and drove like a dream, or as close to a dream as an old *scorro scorro* can go. The gear linkage didn't jam even once, and we didn't run out of fuel. I shuddered at the thought of having to tell my gorgeous new date: "Sorry, we have run out of fuel." Generally translated this would be understood to mean: "I want to make out with you." Les's serene air of innocence had immediately attracted me to her, and I was not going to misbehave myself. At that age it took huge restraint. To be honest, it wasn't easy, but I succeeded admirably.

When I took Les home that evening, just after midnight, I invited her to come with me again to Mermaid's Pool on the coming Sunday, when the band, 'The Black Jacks', would be playing. Les's sister, Gill, was dating Jim Duncan the drummer at the time, so it seemed like a good idea. She graciously accepted. It was a great day and we had a great date, made all the better by driving out with a friend whose car was more reliable than my Dad's old rattle trap.

That evening, back in Salisbury, we went to the famous Nicks Café, a place frequented by most people at some stage of an evening's plans. The atmosphere was electric, with music blaring, people singing, playing pool, mini soccer, and at some stage of the night there would always be a good fight. On many occasions it involved my mates and me, in a punch-up against a bunch of guys from the other side of town. It was all part of growing up, so to speak. Fortunately on this special occasion everyone was well-behaved, and there was no hint of a fight at any time that night. I eventually dropped Les off at her house, kissed her goodnight, and told her I would give her a ring as I would love to take her out again.

Before I had a chance to make good on that promise, the unexpected and surprising offer of a new career came up and the excitement of a new life out in the bush completely absorbed my mind. All thoughts of keeping promises flew away.

Chapter 16

When home for my first December break I walked into the popular Le Coq d'Or night club in Salisbury, and who should I see sitting there with my good friend Trevor Gombard, but Les. She was drop-dead gorgeous, absolutely stunning. She had lost weight, her hair was longer, her eyes, still reflecting serene innocence, were more beautiful than I remembered. I fell in love there and then.

I was ready to take her in my arms and declare undying love. But on seeing me, the sparkle in her eyes turned cold. Her face registered surprise, annoyance and hurt as I approached her table. It slowly dawned on me what a fool I had been. I had not phoned or contacted her in any way since that incredible date some months back. I could not believe I had neglected so badly this most beautiful girl I had ever seen.

"Hi Les," I stammered. "I don't know what to say, but that I'm so sorry. I have no excuse. I will understand if you don't want anything to do with me and will leave immediately. "

"You know," she said coldly, "I expected that phone call and waited for days, then weeks, until I knew it wasn't going to happen. The last time we were together, I thought we might have had something good going, but I was obviously wrong." I realised I had really hurt her, as there was no doubt we had something going. Yet I, being young, stupid and wild, had not realised how much - until this moment. I was ready to do whatever it took to fix the situation because, in that moment, I knew I wanted to spend the rest of my life with her.

Slowly the ice thawed to some extent, and we finished up talking and dancing the night away. We spent the rest of my Christmas break together. By the time I needed to go back to my drill site at the mine and away from Les, I knew she and I would always be together. I made sure she understood how much I meant that.

On arriving back at Rasendie Mine I told Ken the same story. He burst out laughing. "As soon as we go into Umtali on our weekend off you'll grab the first girl who comes along and that would be the end of your relationship with Les." Surely I'm not that bad, I thought to myself.

"Ken, you're wrong. This time it's different. I have never felt this way about anyone before. You'll see." Still laughing, he wandered away to the machine, shaking his head.

I made him eat his words. Les and I officially went out for the next six months and then took the plunge and were engaged for six months. On 20th December 1969 we were married.

I learned a lot from Ken. In no time, he had me operating the machine, which left him free to do other things, including reporting for work later each day as he became more confident with my ability to operate the drill rig. He lived in Umtali so returned home each night. Looking back, he was being paid to teach me on site. However, at the time I was the learner driller and didn't think a thing of it. We hit it off really well and he had taught me a lot, in a short time. I was truly grateful.

I was young and cocky and thought I knew a lot about drilling, but, in reality, I knew very little. In my mind, I had everything under control and would, in the not too distant future, be given my own machine. Little did I know then that forty years later I would still be learning. Anyone in the drilling game will agree that you never stop learning. There are so many variables and possibilities for what can happen.

Fortunately, the formation we were drilling was solid. I put 100% effort into my work and succeeded in reaching similar production figures to what Ken achieved. The work involved filling the core barrel with core sample every ten feet, with as fast a penetration rate as possible, pulling it out and placing it into a core box. The contract at the mine eventually came to an end and all the equipment was demobilised and sent back to Salisbury.

I was ready to take on anyone in the drilling game. But I was heading for a wake-up call on my next assignment.

Chapter 17

I was transferred to a new site North West of Salisbury. This site was being run by an experienced driller by the name of Jack Rumbold, who was to continue my training in the drilling field.

At that time, Jack had been drilling for 43 years. Anything he didn't know about the drilling game was not worth knowing. He was one of the best, and most experienced drillers ever in Rhodesia. He was a hard man, pushed me to my limits, took no nonsense from anyone, but he was also a fair man.

He was running a drilling contract on the Gwelo side of Gatooma, a small farming community town about eighty five miles from Salisbury. Our accommodation was an old, but comfortable caravan that we shared. There was a small dam on the farm and the fishing was good. We had many good fish dinners.

I was young, fit, wide-eyed and if not bushy-tailed, I was enthusiastic about learning all I could from the best in the trade. On my first day on site, I wanted to start learning how to use all the levers and hydraulic systems on the new drill rig. Thinking I already knew just about everything and having operated a similar machine on Ken's site, I could see no problem here. The core barrel was full so I walked up to the rig and asked, "Could I pull the rods out of the hole?"

Not impressed, Jack told me to stay away from the machine until told otherwise. Surprised, I stepped back and said, "I have some idea of what to do as I was running Ken's rig. I'm keen to learn all I can from you and will do whatever it takes to become a driller."

"Well," he growled, "in that case, don't go anywhere near that rig until I tell you to do so. You little whippersnappers think you're tough and clever, yet within a few weeks you're running away with your tails between your legs, back to city life. "

"Right," I thought to myself, "I'm in for a fun time on this assignment."

"I don't give two hoots what you have done on Ken's or anybody else's rig." He was nowhere near finished. "Like it or lump it, but you're now on my rig and will do as I tell you. If you're not happy with that then you can pack your bags and bugger off. I'm sick and tired of all these kids they send out to me. "

I was getting the message loud and clear. There were long days ahead.

"Before you can even start to learn about being a driller, you need to learn how to be a spanner-man."

"Why, when there are good spanner-men to do that job?" I asked, trying to sound as clever as possible without being rude.

"That's exactly the answer I'd expect from a clever little shit like you." By this stage even his arms were going and I'm sure the other workers staff were enjoying the spectacle. "How the hell are you going to teach any new guy to do the work if you can't do it yourself?" he asked, this time with his hands on his hips and a look on his face that said: *Here we go again. What did I do to deserve these young upstarts?*

Not wanting to interrupt him I waited a few seconds before saying, "Hey, I'm sorry. I'm not trying to be clever, but I promise that I'll prove myself to you. I will do everything you ask of me, no matter how tough it may be. I love the bush life and I'm not afraid of hard work."

"Well," he growled a little more softly, "let's see what you can do. The last two little townies couldn't get out of here quick enough." I had heard about the last two learner drillers who had looked promising and hard-working, but had both failed. This made me more determined to learn all I could from this man. One day, I vowed, youngsters would be sent out to my rig to learn to drill and I would be in a position to teach them the same things I would now be taught.

For the next few months, I was put through the mill. I cut down trees to make drill rod stands, dug water sumps, greased and ran the drill rods out as they were pulled or lowered from the hole, cleaned the machine and water pump. It was hard work but was not doing me any harm. I felt fitter than when I completed my first phase in the army.

Once we reached the final depth required, all the equipment had to be moved to a new site which would have been marked out by the geologist. To me, at the time, this was a huge undertaking. Our only mode of transport was an old 1961 Land Rover belonging to Jack that, at best, battled to get itself to the site, let alone carry any equipment with it.

To digress... On one occasion, at month-end, Jack gave me the honour of driving us both to Salisbury in his pride-and-joy. It was the kind of car that only the owner could love. We were making slow, rattling progress, feeling every bump in the road. Just before reaching Que Que, we were pulled over at a police checkpoint. The white officer came over to check my driver's licence and was satisfied. But that was the only part we got right.

He ambled around to the front of the vehicle and signalled for me to turn on the windscreen wipers. Jack and I knew that for more than two years, these had not worked. We looked at each other and Jack leaned forward to hold the small hand-assisted lever on the wiper motor on his side, while I did the same for my side. Together we turned them back-and-forth to the shaking head of the police officer.

Next he asked me to blow the horn. From under the bonnet a tiny excuse for a honk squeaked out. He held his hand behind his ear as if to say, "Can you do that again?." I obliged, with the same result. He gave me his best cop angry glare, and all I could offer in return was a shrug of my shoulders.

Finally he called for the indicators. By the look on his face he already knew these would prove to be a problem. Jack could not remember if they had ever worked. All I could think of when he indicated to see the right indicator was to stick my arm straight out my side window, this being in a permanently open position due to the sliding glass section having fallen out some months back. With a puzzled look he then pointed to the left hand indicator. I stuck my arm out of the window once more, turning my hand in an anti-clock wise direction.

Jack, by this stage, was in fits of laughter, soon to be joined by the officer who told me, none too politely, to get the hell out of there before he took the vehicle off the road for good. I gave the officer a thumbs-up sign as a thank you, while pulling away, spluttering and farting down the road to continue our trip to Salisbury.

Returning to the topic of moving the drill rigs equipment without the help of a truck meant it had to be moved by four-man-power – three spanner men and myself. The moves were often in excess of half a mile.

We carried the steel sheer legs, consisting of nine sections, on our shoulders. These were manufactured using 6" steam pipe. To join and bolt them together they were flanged on both sides. They were twenty foot long and weighed around one hundred and fifty lbs each. Adding to the difficulty, the steel became excessively hot from the mid-day sun and even with cloth padding, our shoulders were sore and bruised by the end of the move. The exercise of moving the equipment left us exhausted having worked solidly from sun up to sun down. There's a saying in the drilling world that a shift starts in the morning when it's light enough to see the coupling joining the rods, and stops when it's too dark to see it anymore.

Fortunately, the machine is equipped with a winch specifically for pulling the rods from the hole. I was taught how to run the winch cable through a small pulley on the base of the machine and out onto the strongest tree we could find as an anchor-point, in the general direction of the new site.

Transporting the water pump and two railway sleepers was made easy by securing them, using an old hoist cable, to the rear end of the drill rig. With engine power driving the winch, all that was needed was to pull down on the winch clutch lever, take up the slack in the cable and like magic the rig would slowly pull itself on skids towards the tree with timbers and pump following like carriages on a train. This was repeated over and over until all the equipment was at the new site.

Once everything had been moved, the rigging procedure began. This involved digging sumps, cutting down trees to make the rod stands, and carrying enough drill rods from the old site to start drilling on the new site. The remaining rods were carried across as and when required. Hopefully the new hole would produce a good ore intersection. Having the contract extended depended on results. The higher-grade the intersection the more chance there was of finding enough ore to warrant the start of a new mine, or increase the ore reserves of a working mine. Either way, it was satisfying to get positive results.

I eventually passed my spanner-man apprenticeship. By this time I had gone from being new at the game with city soft hands, to actually operating the rig with hard calloused hands. The more I was left to operate on my own, the keener I was to become an experienced operator. Always close by, relaxing in the shade of acacia trees, Jack kept a watchful eye on every move. He was quick to point out mistakes. I had huge respect for him, and knew if there was any better training out there in the drilling field, it was not on this planet.

I learned about the rotation speeds needed to penetrate formations, which varied from 200–500 rpm, depending on the type of drill bit used. The friction caused by the rotation speed and pressure needed a continuous recycling of water. If, for any reason, the water was shut off, the heat generated became so great that it could cause the matrix on the cutting face to become molten, and weld itself to the rock. Drillers call this *'Burnt-in'*. The drill string becomes stuck in the hole – an expensive lesson. Regardless as to whether you are drilling deep or shallow holes, an alert, experienced drill operator constantly monitors water pressure. It has to be the most important gauge to indicate any in-hole drilling problems.

Drilling deep holes dramatically increases the danger of *'burn-in'*. It's possible through wear and tear to have a cracked or 'split-rod' which allows water to pass through. If this happens deep down near the bottom of the hole there are no warning signs, and the water pressure remains constant. In this situation the engine would start to labour and if remedial action is taken immediately to pull back on the hydraulics, to lift the drill bit off the bottom, a disaster can be averted. This was one of the many important reasons Jack pushed for me to be alert and present at the controls at all times.

We always tried to work closely and harmoniously with site geologists. Ultimately they were our client, our boss, and they often became good friends. We had a good relationship with John, our current geologist. When the time came for his annual leave, he left for a much-needed three-week holiday. He was replaced by a newly qualified geologist. He was the type who knows everything about nothing, and is never wrong. When proven wrong, he figured out a way to make himself look right. Jack, having been around in the drilling game for over 40 years, wasn't prepared to take shit from anyone. With all his experience, why should he? And with this newly graduated geologist, he had no intention of being any different.

The broken and fractured serpentine rock formations made production slow and difficult. These formations are usually green in colour, and have a greasy, waxy, silky feel. Often, serpentine formations are intersected by asbestos stringers, which caused blocking of the core in the inner tube. Not only were we forced to drill short runs and pull core to ensure 100% core recovery, but coupled with this, the hole was caving in and we had lost our water return completely. There were delays as we pumped water down the hole faster than it was being delivered to us. Our water was carted by tractor and trailer in a 1,000-gallon tank from a dam close by.

Because of the slow progress, Jack decided that, as we were about to down tools for the end-of-month break, it was a good time to grout the bad section of the hole. Our two days off would help ensure a successful setting of the grout mix. If this plan worked, the water-return would be restored, and with some luck the side walls of the hole would be stabilised. This would put an end to the drilling problems caused by what we call caving (falling rocks)

Grouting a hole entails first checking the core in the core trays to determine the depth at which we should try to set the grout mix. The last sixty feet of the hole had been drilled into solid rock, so grouting at that deeper section of hole was unnecessary. So we would have to insert a plug sixty feet up from the bottom of the hole. Jack wandered off to his Land Rover and returned with an old tennis ball. When I showed puzzlement, he laughed and told me to watch and learn.

By hand he forced the ball into the open mouth of the BX casing at the collar of the hole. Then, after scratching around in the tool box, he pulled out a BX reaming shell with a concave plate welded across the bottom. This was screwed and tightened to the end of the core barrel and lowered down the hole pushing the tennis ball down to the depth required. To ensure that the ball would be accurately placed, we had already set aside the number of rods needed for the operation. Then the rods were pulled from the hole leaving the snug fitting ball in place as a plug. The next phase was to calculate the volume of grout mix needed to fill the void from the tennis ball to the top of the bad section. Care was taken not to allow the grout to go as far up as the bottom of our casing as we hoped to extract it from the hole eventually, for re-use.

The correct gallon volume of grout was then mixed in split 44 gallon drums and pumped all the way down onto the tennis ball. For deep holes in excess of six hundred feet this procedure would be through drill rods lowered to thirty feet above the plug.

The rods were then pulled from the hole and flushed with clean water to ensure no grout mix would be able to set inside. For shallow holes, less than 300 feet, there was no need to pump through the rods and we could get away with pouring the grout mix through a funnel directly into the hole and allow gravity to complete the task.

A minimum setting time of twenty-four hours was allowed. In this instance we had two extra days for setting time as it was end of month and pay weekend. This gave us Saturday and Sunday off. This waiting time was generally spent cleaning the machine, pump, tractor, water cart and the site - including the camp sites. Jack was extremely strict, and grilled us daily on the need for this level of cleanliness.

After the pay weekend we lowered the rods slowly. The mix had set as planned. We then drilled through the cement using as fast a penetration as the water pressure allowed. The cement was cored and removed from the inner tube as in normal drilling.

A section of the core contained a lot of cave material from the unstable section of the hole. To the untrained eye the cement core could be mistaken for rock formation. Jack decided to show the geologist that he was not as smart as he thought he was. He placed the 18' long cement core amongst the other rock formation we had already drilled. When the geologist came to the site with his normal air of authority, Jack called him over to the core box and removed the piece of cement core from the core tray saying, "I've been in the drilling game for more years than you've been around, but I have never intersected a formation like this. Could you identify it for me so that I can add it to my core records?" The geologist studied the piece of core in great detail. He wet it to bring out the true colours. Using his Swiss Army knife, he scratched it to see how hard it was. (Isn't it funny how geologists always do that?) He even went as far a licking the piece of cement core. Eventually he came up with a complicated geological classification. In so doing he had an *'I'm such a clever boy'* look on his face, hoping to impress us with his amazing ability for identifying unusual rock formations.

Jack took the piece of core from him, and asked if he was sure he had the correct name, and requested the correct spelling, so that his records would be accurate. The confident geologist confirmed his analysis and slowly spelt it out, as if he were speaking to children. Jack burst out laughing and said, "Well, I'm not sure where you were trained as a geologist, but I think you should ask for your money back. This is just a piece of cement we drilled out of the hole today, with small bits of cave that had fallen into the cement." With that he sent the core piece flying through the air into the water sump and walked away, laughing.

Our smart geologist was terribly embarrassed. From that time on he became a normal down-to-earth guy and we all worked well together. Within a few months, with some degree of success, the contract was completed. Mineralization looked good, but lab results were not as promising as hoped for. They were not good enough to warrant continued drilling. The Mining House would have to regroup and decide which way to go with the project. The exploration game is an expensive gamble.

Chapter 18

I was moved to an interesting drilling project in the Gokwe area in central Rhodesia. I was pleased to hear my old friend and original drilling mentor Ken was the site supervisor.

The area consisted of loose sand with little ground vegetation. Drilling through the overburden which generally consists of loose sand, unconsolidated soil and small to large individual rocks and boulders was challenging. We had approximately 60 feet of sand, solidifying into sandstone with clay bands in some sections of the hole. We had on-going, expensive problems when trying to get our holes cased down to the correct depths. Without the correct casing emplacement in the hole the rods would get stuck. This was caused by water being pumped at pressure penetrating the clay bands causing them to swell and jam the rod string. With today's rod strings and drilling mud technology this is no longer such an issue, back then it was a massive problem.

After loosening many rod strings on the holes, I jokingly suggested that instead of mining coal in the area they should mine steel, as we had left a fair share down there, which would never come out again. Then we discovered quite by accident that, if left for a few days, the swollen clay would break up and the rods could be loosened. This didn't always work, but it did enable us to complete some of the holes.

I worked in the Gokwe area for a month, before being shipped off to operate my own machine. It was to be one of the most interesting and exciting experiences of my life.

When an apprentice driller was given his first opportunity to operate his own rig, he was put to work where there were other rigs operating already. There are obvious advantages to this.

Firstly, help is at hand. Any problems encountered can be rectified immediately with the help of experienced personnel nearby. There would usually be a drilling supervisor on hand to assist in the fine art of achieving optimum rotation of the drill head, together with controlled penetration rate using the hydraulic feed control. High production and bit performance were the goals. The supervisor would be responsible for ensuring adequate supplies of in-hole drilling spares and equipment, such as diesel, drill bits, reaming shell and core springs. He was also responsible for keeping meticulous drilling records, including drill sizes, depth drilled, amount of casing used, total loads of water carted, standing time encountered (always a contentious subject with the client), and all other aspects of the operation. Ultimately these records were sent through to head office in Salisbury, and the accounts department invoiced the client accordingly. The new guy did not have to be concerned with any of these responsibilities, and could focus on operating his rig efficiently.

My first solo assignment was far from the norm. The company had been awarded a new contract to drill holes in the North Eastern section of Rhodesia in an extremely remote area. I was earmarked to operate and run the contract, but because it would be my first assignment, and I had had very little drilling experience, there was some concern from management. All the other experienced drillers were out on other contracts spread around the country. None of them could be pulled out of those contracts without disturbing the project. Gus and Mr. Longstaff entered into a heated debate regarding my possible new posting.

For valid reasons they were uncertain about whether I could manage the contract on my own. I was interviewed at length regarding my confidence and readiness for such an important and difficult contract. I was born with abundant confidence. I always felt that, given the chance, I could achieve anything that was of interest to me. I assured them that I wouldn't let them down.

Because of the unusual circumstances, being my inexperience, Gus arranged for the most experienced crew available to join me on what would become a once-in-a-lifetime experience for all of us.

My assistant drill operator was a man called Thousand. He was one of the longest serving black members of the company. He was given the nickname of "Thousand" when he became the first black operator to drill one thousand feet in a month. Then there was Aaron, a powerfully built and likeable man, who made up for his lack of experience by being an exceptionally hard and productive worker. Then there was Clever, my faithful and honest cook and camp cleaner. He tried to convince me that the origin of his name was his abundance of knowledge. But his fellow workers were dubious, and the extent of Clever's knowledge was much debated among them. Kenneth was the spanner man, and he had a few years of training on the machines. He had an obsessive ambition to become a drilling operator, which no doubt would become reality. Elias had been temporarily employed by the company as a labourer. His contract was extended to include joining my crew. Last, but by no means least was my driver Piet.

He would be responsible for carting water to our drill sites with the old Bedford truck. Having been relegated to head office for the past few months, he was bursting to get out into the field again. Finally to cook, clean and provide all other services required by my crew, they themselves selected a woman by the name of Mudiwa, they were quick to inform me this meant 'loved one'.

I never questioned them on their choice, however mentally I had an accurate assessment of what the real reason for her joining us was.

Thousand, Aaron, Elias, Kenneth
My faithful crew in the Ruangwa Valley:
(Take note of the Personell Protective Clothing of the day!!??)
(Unfortunately I don't have a picture of Clever or Mudiwa)

I thanked Gus for his efforts in this regard knowing full well it would be difficult to find a more experienced and hard working crew. Just how well any of us would fare was left in the lap of the gods. Ultimately it would come down to our resilience under hard conditions, and our ability to improvise in a remote, out-of-contact place.

The mission: to establish the possibility that the Copper/Nickel ore-body from the Madziwa Mine continued on a West to East strike. Through the Ruangwa Valley, extensive geological sampling projects over the past five months showed promising signs.

The valley was part of the river system of the Mazoe River. The Ruangwa River is a small tributary flowing into the Mazoe River from the West. The river then went rushing down into the mighty Zambezi and eventually through Mozambique and ultimately into the sea.

Chapter 19

Before mobilising our equipment to the Ruangwa Valley project, we spent a few months on a farm not too far from the Madziwa Mine, drilling for limestone. Many of our drilling projects were on farms throughout Rhodesia. On several occasions we encountered well-founded resistance from the farmers. In some cases the correct procedures were not followed by the exploration mining company. Among other things, trenches were dug, roads made and trees cut down for firewood, without full and proper negotiations with the farmer. Understandably this behaviour didn't win favour from the farmers. By the time we arrived on the farm, therefore, we were in trouble before we even got started.

When starting out on this new project, my run-in with the farmer was one of the worst I had experienced. He chased me off his land with a shotgun, which he aimed through his vehicle window. I was accustomed to abuse by some of the farmers and responded diplomatically, and with understanding. However, this incident caught my attention more than most. It was only after much negotiation, which included our MD coming to the site, where he also received the shotgun treatment that we were eventually allowed back onto the farm. We signed a contract with the farmer for charges for firewood, sand, and water taken from his farm. These expenses would be passed on to the exploration company employing us.

In spite of this bad start, over the next few months, the farmer and I became good friends. As with most Rhodesians, he was a nice guy. He was also a good farmer. Had his approval been gained in advance, there would not have been a problem.

We bought all our supplies through his little farm store which was run by his good wife and, together with all the other charges he passed onto us for firewood, water, and sand, he was able to purchase a new BMW 2002.

Our friendship was mutually beneficial in many ways. If either of us needed help, mechanical or otherwise, we were there for each other. I was sometimes invited to dinner with him and his gorgeous wife, and we had pleasant evenings together. Sally was an amazing cook, and presented wonderful meals. I was not surprised that John was a touch porky, in spite of all the hard physical work he put in each day.

Back at the camp, all my cooking was done over an open fire. My cook would make stew for me in a pot and this, together with the sudza essentially consisting of finely ground maize mixed slowly into boiling water and stirred into a thick porridge, made a delicious meal. On many occasions he cooked a venison steak from a buck I had shot to provide meat for my crew. In spite of being basic, these meals were satisfying and filling and I really enjoyed them. However, it was something special to be spoilt every now and then with the roast dinners John, Sally and I enjoyed together at their farm house. To be honest, I envied John for his choice of a life partner, and believe me, it was not only for her cooking.

We were drilling for limestone on John's farm and were pleased for the time spent there as it helped toughen us up for the conditions we were soon to contend with. We worked on his farm and surrounding area for about five months before going down into the valley.

If the lime stone was found to be of the grade and quantity required it would mainly be used by the mine for the manufacture of cement. Another use is for masonry and architecture. Generally, drilling through lime stone was trouble-free. It was soft with high drilling penetration rates. The only real problem was the constant intersection of fissures. They appeared to be never ending, so maintaining a water return was close to impossible. We were informed by the geologist on site that generally regions overlying limestone bedrock tend to have fewer visible groundwater sources such as ponds and streams, as surface water easily drains downward through cracks in the limestone. Hence most well known natural cave systems are through limestone bedrock.

With the continued water loss problem it meant a continuous supply of water was required. The only means I had for carrying water was my old Bedford truck with a 1,000 gallon water tank mounted on the back. As we had two drilling machines on the site, there was a lot of standing time, waiting for water. Many times, I had to grout up our holes. In some of the worst cases I would pump as many as ten bags of cement down a hole that was only one hundred and fifty feet deep. Normally, in what we would call a tight hole, one bag of cement was sufficient to cover 30 feet of hole. There were times when we sent down drill rods to test the success of the grouting, to find that there was no evidence of the grout. All the grouting had been absorbed through the fissure we were trying to close up. We had no option but to continue drilling the hole with no water return, making production slow and rapidly wearing out drill rods as they rotated at 500 rpm against dry rock. Another way to seal minor fissures and restore water return is to use old, dry cow dung. The dung was gathered and transported to the site where it was ground up as small as possible. We slowly poured the ground dung into the hole and washed it down with water pressure from the pump. We aimed for the point where the hole intersects the fissure where the wet dung expanded and sealed off the fissure. When it worked, the water returned back up the hole ready to be re-cycled. It may sound rough-and-ready, but the dung was always available, providing an effective, cheap solution. When we had to make a plan, out in the wilderness and far from anywhere, we learned to improvise.

If neither the cow dung nor the grout procedure was successful, the only option left is to shut down the machine and wait for the precious liquid to arrive. We couldn't drill without the cooling effect of water passing through to the diamond bit.

John, being a helpful farmer and friend, had an old tractor and a 1,000 gallon tank mounted on a trailer. We hired this from him at a reasonable rate. Our production rapidly improved, as each machine was serviced with water, independently.

Under the circumstances, drilling progressed well. However, the on-site geologist from the mining house was one of those people who is never satisfied regardless. He was unpleasant company. Usually the geologists we worked with were good to have around the camp, but this one stretched our patience to the limit. Sometimes he had good reason, but many times he made our jobs difficult just because he could. The new hole we had started drilling was at a place that he said should be the centre of the lime deposit. He was convinced that it would produce pure lime stone. The other rig was set up on what he felt was the fringe of the deposit. This was the method he used to find the extent of the lime stone.

Before leaving for Salisbury for a few days, he checked all our levels, and the angle and direction of the drill mast and quill, to ensure we were rigged properly. He emphasised the importance of making accurate and precise depth markings on the core recovered. It was also important to keep the core clean. The quality and condition of the core sample was what the mining house was paying for, and was key to determining future planning. He repeated his belief that the hole would produce loads of lime stone, and stressed again that I should take extra care. I assured him that I always took care.

For a few months I'd had a hard time with his constant complaints about everything. I remembered what Jack had done with the piece of cement core when we had a problem with the graduate geologist. I decided that if his prediction was right, I would play a trick on him, to let him know enough is enough.

We started drilling the respective holes and, true to his calculations, the first hole produced beautiful white solid lime stone core samples. Also, true to his calculations, the other rig was on the fringe, drilling in and out of lime stone which, when intersected, was a brownish-white colour. I told the guys that, as each core box was filled to take it across to the other rig and to bring their full box to ours. We continued drilling the holes like this until the geologist returned a few days later.

He was speechless, and confused. These results threw out all his theories and interpretations of the lime stone deposits in the area. It just so happened that I was pulling the rods out of the hole to remove the core from a run he had observed. The hole had just gone through the base of the lime stone and so its appearance was like the core we had been bringing across from the other rig. He was baffled and bewildered, and told us to stop drilling immediately on both machines until he could decide what to do next.

The next day, the big bosses were coming out to the site, and he had already told them, in complete confidence, what they could expect to see. His normally sun-burned face had turned red with white blotches. I could no longer keep a straight face and began to laugh. He said he saw nothing amusing in the situation. I then told him what we had done and the reason, letting him know that he had been a total pain in the butt, and I hoped this might lighten things up a bit. Again his face was changing colours fast and I was a little concerned that he might have a heart attack. However, the shocked and angry shades slowly toned down, and a smile started to come through. Then he called me a whole bunch of things, using words I hadn't heard since my army days, finally bursting into laughter and shaking my hand. His relief was so enormous that from that day on there was never another problem. It goes to show that there's a happy solution to every problem.

Chapter 20

The contract on the farm was eventually completed and we set about restoring our drill sites and camp area. To the best of our ability we were required to restore it to as similar a condition as physically possible prior to the commencement of the contract. We could not leave until the whole area had been inspected and passed by John, the farmer. The upcoming project in the Ruangwa Valley area was linked to the lime stone contract in that it was also run and controlled by Anglo American. However the site geologist assigned to the new project was a man called Peter. He had many years of experience with Anglo and was a really nice guy.

I had received a message via the old party line telephone that all the equipment I had used on the farm was to be loaded and sent to a contract in Mavurodona some fifty miles north west of our position. Another operator was being sent there to run that job. I wanted to know what equipment I was to use down in the valley, if all my equipment was to be used elsewhere. I was told to return to Salisbury once all the drilling equipment was ready to go to Mavurodona and help with loading my rig and equipment. I then requested that Dave, the new operator for the Mavurodona project, come and help load equipment at the farm, for the same reason. I didn't want him going to the new contract and discovering that any odd bits of equipment were not on the truck. He needed to be both satisfied and responsible for what he was taking with him. The following day he arrived and between the two of us we had everything loaded and ready to leave late that same afternoon. He left with his Land Rover to follow the truck to the new site. After saying farewell and thank you to John and Sally, I too set off to Salisbury to sort out all my new equipment.

As I would be on the valley project for the duration of the contract, Gus felt I should be in Salisbury to ensure all equipment required would be loaded onto the truck.

I arrived home on a Saturday afternoon. I was given the Sunday off to sort out my personal things, and was expected at the workshops first thing Monday morning to start loading.

It was good to be back in civilization again, after being out of it for three months. I had a great weekend. I called a few friends and, together with Les we all went out to a night club and let our hair down. We spent the next day at Lake McIlwaine, a popular place for young people to gather and have fun.

Lake McIlwaine is a man-made lake and was the fourth largest lake in Rhodesia. It was formed in 1952 on the Hunyani River some 37km southwest of Salisbury. It's a popular lake for recreational purposes with good fishing, water sports, game viewing, tea-rooms, picnicking and braai area. It was also the main water supply reservoir for the city, and the source of irrigation for downstream farms. It has an impressively high spillway along the dam wall. At the height of the rainy season the water plummeted spectacularly over the top, causing a misty spray to rise, with Cat Fish (Barbel) trying to swim up the flooding waters. That weekend we had a great time in the sunshine, fishing, braaing and relaxing.

Come Monday morning, I went in to the office at 6.00am and we started loading the truck. knowing how isolated we would be, for at least three months, I had to make a comprehensive list of requirements, and all other possible extras such as a welding plant and a generator to run it and also to provide lights we would need to run the eighteen-hour shifts envisaged to have any chance of completing the contract in the time frame stipulated.

By the Tuesday evening I was happy that everything I needed was loaded. We were ready to leave first thing on Wednesday morning.

To mobilize the new rig we had to transport all the required equipment from Salisbury to the site. We used an eight-ton Morris truck. The drop sides were almost bulging from the load. Access to the area would be difficult, and we had to ensure that everything we needed would be on the first load. A second load under those difficult conditions was not an option.

The truck handled the situation well, considering it was not built for those rough and narrow tracks. There were many tricky parts of the road where I could easily get through with the Land Rover or the Bedford, but the loaded, top-heavy eight-ton truck was a different matter. With my heart in my mouth, I navigated some tight sections. When the wheels of the heavy truck sank into the crumbling mountain road, we had to back-fill gullies with soil and rock. Sometimes the truck tipped at impossible angles, ready to topple. That would be hard to explain to the boss: all his equipment, along with his truck lying in a tangled mess at the bottom of the cliff with a seriously injured driver. That was not the way to work my way up in the company.

Slowly, and as safely as possible, we wound our way closer to our destination. Not too far from the site was a steep climb. To be safe, I tied a strong chain between my vehicle and the truck and with the use of low range 4x4 helped to pull it up and over the top. Half-way up I knew that if things were to go wrong and the truck toppled off the narrow, rocky road, the driver would have no control and would go hurtling down the side of the mountain taking me and my vehicle with him. But we successfully negotiated the precarious climb. At the top we stopped to remove the chain. Going down the other side, the driver was on his own.

I instructed him to engage 1st gear to give as much engine braking as possible, and regardless of how slow it was, he was to stay in 1st gear all the way to the bottom. Then with me in the front in my vehicle, keeping a close watch on proceedings through my rear view mirrors, we made a slow, descent down the other side. There were some scary tight turns, but we reached the bottom, safely and in one piece. The remaining section of the road we traversed without incident, eventually arriving at the site around 5.30pm. Off-loading began in earnest. The truck had to leave at first light the following morning and head back to Salisbury where it was needed for moving other rigs and equipment around the country on other contracts. That driver earned every cent he was paid each month.

We were left with my old Land Rover and an even older Bedford truck. These two vehicles would have to see us through the contract above the valley. Once the two wild cat exploration drill holes had been successfully completed, the Morris truck would return to load and transport all the equipment down the escarpment to complete the contract in the valley.

We set up camp and cleared an area around the perimeter as a fire guard. Although the veld around us was sparse as far as leaves and grass were concerned, the vegetation was dry after a long rainless winter. Any spark could set off a fire. Although we were over twenty miles from the nearest farm, a fire would be devastating for the wild life.

I managed to get the drill rig into the area marked out by Peter for our first hole. We were now in the TTL's (Tribal Trust Land's) with no farming for miles around. The peg surveyed in by Peter our Geologist was on the slope of a small granite *kopje*. (*A hill too small to be a mountain*) Extensive excavation was therefore required to level the site. I left the guys digging in the drill platform to enable us to set up the rig and marked out where I needed the water sump to be excavated. This would take the best part of the day, so I left with my driver, Pete, to collect our first load of water from John's farm, some fifteen miles from the site.

Our journey in had not been easy, quite the opposite, it proved to be a real mission. Due to lack of maintenance coupled with no traffic passing over them for many years the roads were badly rutted. They were worn by weather, rain and erosion. There were steep climbs on extremely narrow tracks. Seeing the conditions, and knowing that we hadn't even started on the escarpment yet, made me feel grossly under-equipped. The five-ton Bedford I had was a two-wheel drive. A four-wheel drive would have made the trip a lot more manageable. However, the faithful old truck coped adequately. The rounded mudguards rattled and banged around badly, but as long as I had spare bolts, a roll of wire and a welding machine, anything could be kept together in one piece. The engine, which ran on diesel, had done well in excess of 160,000 miles and somehow it just kept on going. Back in those days, they made good, strong and reliable vehicles.

Chapter 21

Piet and I were on our way to the farm to fill the water tank. We had travelled about one mile when I noticed a small trickle of water coming down the side of a large granite hill just off the road. Had I not been looking in the right place at the right time I would have missed it. I told Piet to stop and to come with me to investigate the source of the water. We climbed the rocky ledge and on a flat section of rock was a small pool of water being fed by a trickle coming down from higher up. By the time we had climbed to the source of the precious liquid we had passed three more pools. Each of these had to some extent blocked up with old dry leaves and dead sticks restricting the flow considerably. The source was undoubtedly a natural spring of water. I was both surprised and excited about it at the same time.

The view from the top was quite something to behold. We could see for miles over the scrubby bushveld and surrounding granite kopjes, on down into the valley we would be moving into at a later stage. Heat waves rose like ripples of water from the solid rocks, each wave dissipating as it rose, to be replaced by a new wave. It was a reminder of the heat we would endure for the duration of the contract. Standing there above a dry landscape spreading around as far as we could see, we knew a miracle had happened. By pure chance, we had found a spring of sweet water.

It was probably the only natural source of water for miles in any direction. If only Neil Armstrong knew how much more excited I felt at that time than he possible did taking mankind's first steps on the moon. This discovery of water may not sound as spectacular as his achievement, but in our desperate need it was miraculous, and I will take with me to the grave that intense feeling of gratitude and satisfaction.

The only drawback of this life-saving spring was that the flow at the source headed off in two different directions. Somehow, I needed to bring them together into one stream, and feed them into the same pool at the base of the kopje. This would double the volume of water catchment. I sent Piet back to camp to fetch one of the labourers, two bags of cement, and a pick and shovel. While waiting I climbed back up to the source to work out a plan to get both streams of water flowing together down the same route.

When he returned, I sent Piet on to the farm to fill the water tank, as we had originally planned. In the meantime, the labourer and I set to the task of attempting to dam up the water. The sun beat down relentlessly. It was hard, thirsty work. But we had sweet spring water on tap. We crouched down to drink like animals do at a water hole.

Once we had completed our dam wall, we climbed back up to the water source to put into action my plan for joining the two streams.

Where the second stream ran off in the opposite direction we shovelled loads of soil in a curve to divert the water in the direction of the other stream, where they could flow in one single flow down the rock. This worked well, so we set about mixing cement and stone and built a low wall behind the temporary soil wall.

Once the soil had washed away, this would take over as a permanent wall and we could collect all the water flowing from the spring. The original trickle became a strong flow down through the three higher ponds and into the little dam at the base.

Once we had put all the rocks in place we grouted between them and left it to set, having temporarily bypassed the stream. Not only was this water source available for our drilling activities but it was also good drinking water. Some hours later Piet returned, together with 1,000 gallons of water from the farm. This would certainly get us up and running on the drill site until the cement dam wall dried allowing containment of the flow from the spring.

Very soon, small game, like the klipspringers and other small buck, smelled the new water source and came to drink. It was not long before we had kudu joining in as well. Hoping this might happen I had gathered a lot of dry bushes and placed them around our little miracle dam, leaving place for the animals to drink on the outflow side so they would not contaminate our drinking water.

Checking the dam some days later, to my surprise I found leopard spoor there. Knowing that other game would visit often, I quietly hoped leopards wouldn't use the dam as an ambush site. I quickly banished the thoughts from my mind, remembering that leopards don't kill for sport. They kill for survival, and to feed their families.

Chapter 22

One thing in life – especially life in the bush – I could not live without was a dog. When we originally moved out to John's farm I never had a dog nor could I find a suitable one for the conditions we would experience. I asked my father to keep his ear to the ground and if there was a good dog available to let me know. I felt sure being out there on my own without man's best friend would certainly drive me crazy.

At the end of the month I went to Salisbury to get drilling supplies to carry us through the following few weeks, before additional supplies could be sent down. On my arrival my father said he had found the perfect animal for me. It was a huge, well built dog called Major, a cross between a Bullmastiff and an Alsatian. His fawn coloured fur had a beautiful shine to it and with his rippling muscles and extremely wide and impressive head, he was one of the most beautiful and powerful animals I had ever seen.

Being a dog lover and never afraid of animals I walked over to him, calling to him at the same time. The owner of the dog, Mr. Diamond, who just happened to be my dad's boss at the time, shouted an urgent warning for me to keep back. He told me that the reason he was looking for a home for the dog was because neither he nor anyone else he had tried had ever been able to handle the dog. He was aggressive and would growl if you came anywhere near him. He had already bitten quite a few people so would be a real handful and he would understand if I was not happy to take him out into the bush with me. I felt sure if I didn't take him he would be put down and he was far too beautiful for that to happen.

I had never been bitten by a dog. It was my firm belief that I never would be, no matter how vicious the animal was. Mr. Diamond and I set about coaxing Major into the front seat of my old Bedford truck. He wasn't happy with the idea, but after a few bribes of biltong left on the seat, he did eventually leap into the Bedford and scoffed down the bait.

Thankfully he then settled down on the passenger seat, hoping for more biltong. I was given all his blankets and large packets of dog food. All I needed now was to coax myself to get into the front seat next to Major. I didn't need a biltong bribe, just the balls to do it.

I climbed into the truck slowly without making eye contact with him at all. Even so there was a deep low growl that sounded like it started somewhere down in his tail and worked its way up through his throat, mouth and bared teeth, vibrating all around the steel cab which was void of upholstery. I joked with Mr. Diamond, asking him what tooth paste he used on Major as his teeth were a beautiful white and he really was enjoying showing them off to me.

Cautiously, I managed to get into the driver's seat, and closed the door. I was trapped in the front of the old Bedford with an unfriendly animal that looked more like a lion than a dog. I turned the ignition switch on and cranked the engine. I hoped that when it fired up it would not backfire as it normally did. What would Major make of that - in this small space? For once, the engine fired into life with the normal old diesel rattle, black smoke billowing from the exhaust pipe, but no backfiring. My new canine friend was unconcerned. He lifted his ears and made himself look impressive sitting next to me. Our close bond was already forged – well, on my side anyway. Major was to become my best friend, the most protective and loyal friend a man could have. We would spend our first few months together, working down in the Ruangwa valley.

Major and I bade farewell to my Dad and Mr. Diamond, and spluttered our way down the long driveway out onto the road. I talked quietly to my new friend, trying to settle him down. Whenever I turned my eyes in his direction, that deep growl came rumbling up through his throat. Slowly but surely that sound became a lot less vicious than it did at the start of the trip.

Was he starting to enjoy the trip? Or was he just getting me settled into a false sense of security? I figured that if I gave him a few of his favourite biscuits he would concentrate on them and forget about me for a while. Ever so slowly I put my hand into the packet already opened and ready for this moment. I pulled out a handful of biscuits, all the while talking to him in as soothing, caring, and loving voice that I could muster. I moved the handful of biscuits over onto the closest edge of his seat without looking directly at him. From the corner of my eye I saw that he looked down and was interested in the food. But, being a male, he was not going to let me off that lightly and refused to eat. We settled back into our routine of me talking quietly to him and he growling back when I looked in his direction, though far more quietly.

I drove on up through Motoko and out into the open bushveld on the way to the site. Major was becoming restless and kept standing up and sitting down, trying to tell me something. I realized he needed us to stop so he could get out. When a man's gotta go he's gotta go, it was no different in the dog world. I was in a similar situation, but had been holding out, dreading what Major would do when he was let out of the Bedford. I had a vision of him tearing off into the bush, trying to get back home. After an hour-and-a-half together in the truck we had made some progress on bonding with each other. It would be devastating to me and disastrous for him, if he were to run off.

His behaviour in the front of the truck together with this disgusting smell wafting around the cab gave me the message loud and clear that either I stop, or he makes a smelly mess on the front seat. I pulled over to the side of the dirt road and stopped. My main concern when letting him out was the possibility of another vehicle to come screaming by and frighten Major causing him to run off into the bush surrounding us on all sides. Although a dirt road, it was the main road that led to Madziwa Mine making possible traffic a reality. Ten miles from here we would turn off and head down what could only be described as tracks on our way to site and hopefully Major's new home. Seeing any traffic on this section would rate somewhere between slim to nil.

I climbed out of the vehicle, closed my door and walked around to his side. I had asked whether I should have a lead for him and was told he went berserk and could possibly attack me in his frustration of the collar around his neck.. So, here I was about to open his door, knowing full well that once he was out, I might not ever see him again.

I had taken his water bottle and dish out of the truck and made sure he could see me filling it. It was another extremely hot day so I was sure he was as thirsty as I was. Gingerly I opened his door. He half climbed and half jumped out of the truck, right in front of me where I stood by the door. For a moment he stopped and observed me, with a bemused look on his face, and then wandered off the road and squatted. I couldn't believe it was possible for one dog to make such a mound, but there it was. I was relieved he had done it off the road as a 4-wheel drive would be needed to get through it. I joined him, to relieve myself. When he eventually completed his relief exercise, he kicked sand over everything and ran over to the water dish to drink like a dog possessed. When the dish was almost empty I walked over with the water bottle and refilled it, with my hand almost touching his huge head. He was okay with that and drank some more. I took out his food dish and half filled it with biscuits. Putting his pride to one side, he got stuck into it straight away. I could almost hear him thinking, "Hey, this guy's not so bad. I might stick around for a while and see what happens next."

This was the turning point in our friendship. Once back in the truck he was completely relaxed. He lay down on his seat with his head right next to me. I put my hand out and began to stroke him. That was that. From then on, we were inseparable.

Major and I on the drill site in Ruangwa Valley

Chapter 23

Two holes were to be drilled. The first hole was to be at an angle of 45°, and about 450 feet deep. The geologist set the rig up on a bearing using a compass at the exact direction he required the hole to be drilled. At an average of 30 feet per day, completing the hole would take about two weeks. Back in 1969 we were still drilling what is called the conventional BX method. Every time the core barrel was full, or blocked, we had to pull all the rods out of the hole to remove the core. Impregnated bits were still to be invented. Penetration rates with surface set diamond bits were slow. However, at that time we knew no better. The wire line systems used today were introduced many years later.

This new source of water managed to get us through with only one extra load being required from the farm house. Not only was this convenient but was also a huge saving in carting water all the way from the farm over bad roads. There was also the significant reduction in diesel consumption. Diesel was another scarce but essential commodity.

The drilling of the hole progressed well, without any real mishaps. However about halfway through the drilling, our water pump for filling the tank from our little dam broke down. Without spare parts I was unable to repair it. We would have to carry more loads of water from the farm until repairs to the pump could be completed.

To collect our first water load, I had to drive the truck myself. Piet, the driver, was ill. I had given him the day off. Our only first aid and medical supplies were headache pills and a bottle of disinfectant. There always was the possibility of illness, drilling injury, and the threat of wild-life injury, which included snakes, scorpions and spiders.

Having experienced firsthand the intense pain of a scorpion sting, these little critters were more of concern than the elephants and leopards in the area. It was essential before sliding your foot into your boot in the morning to turn it upside down, tapping it on the floor to shake out unwelcome visitors. If any of us had a serious health problem or injury, we were many hours away from medical help. With today's health and safety rules, this sounds crazy, irresponsible, and even stupid. But, at that time, we didn't give a thought to those possibilities.

As I mentioned earlier, the area was well populated by leopards. I saw many of them. One day, as I drove out to collect water, there was one spectacular incident involving a baby leopard lying close to the road. I had seen it from about 150 feet away, so turned the ignition key to shut the engine off and I coasted down to where the cub lay. I pulled up right next to what can only be described as one of the most beautiful animals on earth. Being as young as it was, its colouring was vivid with the sharp contrast between the yellow and the dark spots.

Surprisingly, he didn't run away. He just lay there, licking his paws and every now and then, he looked up at me in my old grey Bedford truck. If there were such a thing as a digital camera, I would have taken some spectacular shots of him. Even more surprising was the presence of his mother, who lay some twenty yards off the road in the shade of an Acacia tree. Although keeping a close watch on us, she was content with what was going on, and continued to enjoy her small patch of shade. She sent us a mild warning, with an occasional swish of her tail. The incident was calm and unthreatening. The cub looked so cuddly I felt I could climb out, pick him up, and scratch his head. I marvelled at how safe these animals felt. In this remote part of the country they had not learned to fear man.

When it comes to rating my best animal sightings, this one would be near the top. In those moments, I was wrapped in a magical world. It felt like hours. As much as I wanted to stay longer, I needed to get to the farm, fill the water tank and head back to site. I shook myself out of my trance. I turned the ignition key and the engine fired up into its normal clattering diesel life with black smoke pouring from the exhaust.

As I pulled away the baby got up and strolled off to his mother. I imagined him telling her of the wonderful experience he had just had, seeing a vehicle with a real live person inside. There were a lot more leopards in the area than people or vehicles, so in fact, as crazy as it sounds, I was a rarer sighting for him than he was for me.

Chapter 24

On another occasion I collected the load of water together with more supplies from the farmer. I also filled the old five-ton Bedford trucks diesel tank together with three 45 gallon drums with diesel, and set off back to the site. The trip back was eventful and tragic.

Grinding my way back to the campsite, I came across the geologist's Land Rover standing in the middle of the road with the engine running. That was strange. I wondered if he had shot a duiker or something else to take back to camp for food. I pulled over, switched off the engine, and Leaving Major in the truck I climbed out.

As I walked up to the vehicle there was a sharp whistle from high up on one of the granite kopjes. It was the geologist, standing on one of the gigantic granite rocks. He called frantically for me to come up there with Major, and my .22 riffle. I turned off his ignition switch. With heat in the high 30s, we were in the unforgiving direct sunlight. I ran back to my truck to get my rifle and let Major out. Together we headed up the kopje to see what was making Peter so excited.

"Come quickly! I just shot a leopard," he shouted down to us, as we struggled up through thorny scrub and granite boulders.

"Why did you do such a stupid thing?" I yelled back, appalled and shocked. Breathing hard in the scorching heat, Major and I reached the top of the kopje. "Okay, so where is the leopard?" I asked.

"I thought it was going to attack one of my guys who was up here checking a beacon marker. I'm sure I hit it, but it's not here. " He was in a panic. Sweat poured down his face.

"Do you realise how dangerous a leopard can be, let alone a wounded one?" I was shattered to hear what had happened.

"I know it was wrong to shoot. But it could have killed Johannes. But let's deal with the problem. We must find the animal." He was in shock.

We all were - Peter and his two local workers, one was Johannes whom he had thought to be in danger, Major and me - were now in a seriously dangerous position. We scanned the scrub and rocky area around us, apart from a bush dove cooing there wasn't a sound nor movement, no indication that the animal was anywhere nearby. Suddenly Major barked, picking up the scent of the wounded leopard, and ran off into some knee-high grass.

The next thing, there was what I can only describe as the most terrifying sounds I have ever heard. The leopard was about sixty feet away, terrified and in pain from a badly wounded front leg. If Major had not been with us, we would not have found her. Leopards are hunters, and remain quiet and still for hours, waiting for their prey. Now, with Major attacking her, together with her painful broken leg, she let out a growling scream. She reared up at Major slashing out with her good foreleg. Realising it was not going to be effective, she spun around and ran further up the Kopje on three legs, with the crippled one flopping around and hindering her escape. Not far up she found a crevice deep enough between the rocks to escape into. She turned to face Major, in what would be her last stand.

She was making an even more terrifying scream than before. I'm not sure if it was sheer terror or if the sound was magnified by the crevice. Major was trying to get to her, but was hindered by the narrow entrance and her slashing claws, from one good front leg.

Feeling dreadfully sorry for the leopard, I was now also concerned for Major. Regardless of how powerful he was, and the leopard handicapped with only one front leg, she was still capable of killing him. All she needed was a firm grip on his throat, and that would be the end of my faithful companion. Her rage and terror were fuelled by her pain.

I ran up, followed by Peter, to where this horrific scene was taking place. I knew Major would not allow the leopard to harm me, even if it cost him his life. I managed to clamber above the crevice and called to Peter to come up to see what, if anything, he could do from the other side, as there was an opening leading down to where the enraged leopard was now trapped. I was almost overcome by the spine-chilling sounds coming from within. Peter had his 30/06 rifle, the one that had caused this disaster in the first place.

"I can see it, I can see it!" he cried out and fired off a round. All we got in return was even more heart rendering screams from way down in the crevice. Once again he shouted, "I can see it again!" He fired off a second round with the same result.

I was confused. "What the hell are you shooting at? You can't possibly miss from this range," I shouted. Things were really getting out of hand. The leopard was beyond angry. She could come flying out of there, and who knows what injuries she could inflict on all of us. From where I was, I was still unable to see her. It brought back memories of climbing a tree as a child to get away from what I thought to be lions. But this was no prank, no nightmare, just real terror.

Peter replied, "All I can see is its tail swishing." This was becoming more bizarre by the second. Speechless, I moved from my position and climbed up onto the top edge of the crevice. There through a small hole I could see the leopard, no more than six foot below.

I thrust my rifle into the opening and shot it right through the top of its head. Although I had only a .22, from that range, with a direct shot into the brain with the lead hollow nose bullet the animal dropped like a stone. An enraged Major immediately rushed in and buried his huge jaws into the already dead leopard's throat and started shaking it around like a rag doll. To see that kind of strength was hard to believe. I had one hell of a strong and protective dog as a companion.

I was devastated, swore at the geologist and, beside myself with fury, I attacked him, holding him against a tree, and threatened to knock his head off. "Have you any idea what you have done?" I roared, still in shock and confusion. "That was not only protected game, but also one of the most beautiful animals you will ever see. This will have to be reported to the District Commissioner. I don't give a shit about what happens to you, as a matter of fact they can lock you up and throw the key away as far as I'm concerned!"

"I'm sorry. I was stupid and cruel. But please believe me, at the time I believed Johannes was in danger. If you report the incident to the authorities together with all the repercussions that could follow, it will not help to bring the leopard back." He was pleading, worried about what he had done and was still in a panicked state.

"I'm disgusted. There's no way in the world to rectify your mistake." I let go of him and he slumped onto the ground against the tree. "I'm now going back to the drill site with my injured dog," I continued. "I'm too angry and shocked to think right now, I don't know what to do about this incident. You do whatever you want with the leopard."

Calling Major off the leopard we clambered down the kopje together, and climbed into the truck. I drove around Peter's Land Rover, and as we trundled down the dust road I blinked back tears. This would be a day etched in my memory for all time.

I had loaded the broken water pump and taken it with me to the farm. John kindly loaned me a spare pump, and promised to order the spares I needed for repairing the broken one. He said we could keep his pump on permanent loan, so that we would always have a spare pump. His kindness helped to get us going again. No more waiting for water. John was a one-in-a-million guy.

While I had been away from camp, the rig had been cleaned up. It was almost dark, and I was feeling down. I gave everyone the night off. First light the following morning we started drilling again with our new load of water from the farm.

The following day Peter came to the site - more to see me than to see how things were going. I was not interested in talking to him. "Please, can we move away from the noise of the rig and talk? We can't get through this contract in silence," he said. "Tell you what," I said coldly, "why don't you come back some time when I'm not so busy. Like maybe in a month or so when I might have settled down a bit. We just lost a beautiful animal through your stupidity."

"I have already said how sorry I am. Believe me, I regret what I did, and all the consequences that come with it."

"Yeah, sure." I said. "Go tell someone who cares. I don't give a shit." My anger was rising again. I lit a cigarette. "Actually, don't just tell someone who cares. Go and explain it to the dead leopard's life-long mate." I took another puff and inhaled deeply. Blowing the smoke out I continued, "This is something I will never forget. Never! Now, please, I'm busy and angry. Come back tomorrow."

He was right we had to sort out our differences. We were the only two white people within one and a half hours drive in any direction. Once we were working in the valley the distance would increase to four hours.

Peter turned and, without another word, walked over to his Land Rover and drove away in a cloud of dust. The following day he returned and we talked the whole thing through and shook hands. After getting over my anger, I am able to shake hands and let go of the past. I had thought about what happened long and hard. There could have been merit in his reason for shooting the luckless leopard. There was no doubt that he was feeling bad. He started to say what he was going to do with the leopard's skin, but I stopped him. I just didn't want to know.

Chapter 25

For the next ten days, we continued drilling. The hole was eventually stopped at 480 feet. All that remained was to survey the deflection angle of the hole. This was performed using what was called "acid bottle tests."

A mix of 60% hydrofluoric acid to 40% water was poured into the bottom half of a glass test tube and tightly sealed off with a tapered rubber plug, this in turn was inserted snugly into a steel container and with the use of the drill rods lowered to the required depths. The chemical reaction of the hydrofluoric acid etched a ring around the top of the mix at the angle of the fluid surface. This gave the geologist, using a standard universal scale, for calculating the exact angle of the hole at each test. Ultimately this would give an indication as to exactly where the hole was at completion and if required be used for planning purposes at some stage.

We were drilling through solid granite which is hard. There were no obvious or visible ore zones. But Peter was going to take back to Salisbury for full analysis what he felt, was an interesting section, between 360 and 375 feet of the core. Before leaving for Salisbury he took me around to the other side of the hill to show me the new site and put in the line pegs for us to rig up on. This entailed first setting the hole collar peg into the ground, then pacing to around sixty feet away and using a compass, setting the exact direction the hole would be drilled in before inserting another peg, which we called the back peg. The front peg, on the same line, was then put in. Now, Peter was free to go to Salisbury, while we moved the rig to the new site and set it up according to those pegs. Once again the hole was to be drilled at 45°. Although in the reverse direction of the first one, it was on the exact same bearing.

I joked with Peter saying, "I assume we stop this hole once we intersect our first hole drilled in from the other side of the hill."

"The chances of that happening," he said, "are in the region of one trillion to one. But it would be great if we could achieve that, as, ultimately, it would be the perfect result to tell us that both holes were lined up 100% and neither hole deviated." He laughed, knowing this would never happen. He then loaded the core with the help of the guys, and left for Salisbury.

This second hole also required a fair amount of excavation and levelling. Although it was at the base of the hill, it was still on a slope, similar to the first one. We were not expecting rain for some time and the flow from the spring was down to 60% of what it had been. I decided to use the time they took to level the site, to get another load of water from John's farm.

Digging a sump was time consuming so, in order to save on a lot of digging, as there was no chance of rain, I told the guys to use the bottom of the small stream next to the rig as part of our water sump. This is something I would never do normally, because if the stream did flow it would flood and that would be the end of the water sump needed for recycling the water and other drilling fluids.

Leaving the driver to help with the extensive preparations, I set off in the Bedford truck with Major sitting next to me on the passenger seat. He enjoyed a ride in the truck and sat on the seat with an expectant look on his face, hoping to see something exciting along the way. This particular one would certainly prove to be worthwhile by his standards.

The trip to the farm was slow and rough, but we travelled without a hitch. The Bedford truck ground its way down the dirt roads, until we came to within yards of the spot where I had come across Peter's vehicle with its motor running, and the tragedy of the leopard began. Right there, as if designed by fate, the right back wheel punctured.

I climbed out of the vehicle to jack up the car, remove the wheel and fit the spare. I had a weird feeling that I was being watched. Was it the spirit of the fated leopard looking down on me from her Kopje of death? The chances of having the puncture right there had to be 10,000 to 1.

Was there a hidden meaning in this - for me? Because of the terrible events of that day, was I to suffer a similar fate, possibly dealt out by one of the dead leopard's family? The terrible memories of killing the leopard at this place were raw and unnerving. I felt vulnerable and alone in the silent, motionless vastness of wild bushveld. I also had a strong, prickly feeling of accusing eyes that sent chilling tingles down my spine, and threw my mind into a spin.

It was late afternoon. If I was going to spend the night in the truck this wasn't the best place. I urgently needed to change the wheel and drive away, free from the silent, menacing watcher.

Taking the jack out from behind the driver's seat, I went around to the back and placed it under the rear axel. Every sound I made jarred the silence of the wilderness, calling attention to me. All I wanted to do was quietly slink away from this haunted spot.

I was relieved to find that the jack worked well. I jacked up the truck until the wheel was almost off the ground. I took a good look around to make sure there were no visitors stalking me, and fetched the wheel spanner from under the passenger seat. I rushed back to loosen the wheel. To be safe I put two rocks in front and behind the left back wheel so there would be no chance of it rolling either way off the jack, once the wheel had been removed.

The wheel nuts were really tight, but after a lot of swearing and jumping up and down on the handle I managed to eventually loosen and remove all of them.

Driving around here on my own with just Major to help me was not a great idea. An extra pair of hands to help with a problem like this would have been welcome. The sheer weight of the wheel made getting it off the wheel hub bolts heavy work. Eventually, the wheel was off. The hollow feeling in the pit of my stomach grew. By this stage I was convinced that I was in a serious situation. There was, for sure, something out there watching every move I made.

After the struggle to remove the rear wheel, I still had to bring down the spare and fit it to the truck. It took a huge amount of energy and I struggled to align the heavy wheel with the studs. I was in a desperate hurry. I was lifting, pulling, and even pushing the top of the wheel with my head. I realised eventually that I was trying too hard to get the job done quickly. I told myself to relax, that all was fine, and to concentrate on the job at hand and not imaginary things. It helped. Focussed concentration always helped me achieve more, in less time, and with less energy.

Eventually after a mammoth physical struggle I aligned the studs and pushed the wheel into place. I was swearing at the top of my voice. Whatever was out there must have heard me. I swung my head from side to side in an almost 360° circle to see if I was being charged by anything. All was quiet. My guilty mind was playing tricks on me.

A fast as I could, I hand-screwed the nuts and then using the wheel spanner tightened them. Once the wheel was fitted I rolled and heaved the punctured wheel under the rear of the truck, fitting the lifting plate attached to a chain into the hole through the middle of the wheel. With the help of the lifting handle, I pulled the wheel up into position.

Perspiration poured from my body. I had been smart enough to bring a one gallon bottle of water with me. I gulped over half the liquid down my burning throat. The remainder I poured into a bowl for Major who drank it down thirstily. He had not been interested in anything other than trying to stay cool, and had been lying panting in the shade under the truck. Even though it was late in the afternoon, the heat had not abated. The drink of water was reviving. At least, if I happened to be eaten out here, I would not die thirsty.

Relieved that the puncture had been repaired and the spare wheel safely secured in its place under the truck, we could get away from this eerie place of tragic memories and unseen watchers. I opened the door and called for Major to jump in.

Chapter 26

As I was about to get into the truck I caught a small movement out of the corner of my eye about sixty yards off the road. I closed the truck door to prevent Major escaping to go after it. Intrigued, I climbed up onto the back of the truck to get a better view. I had a deep urge to know what the movement was. I was astounded to see a young leopard get up and slowly walk away, turning his head every few paces to see what I was doing. It was in no hurry and appeared to be disinterested.

It struck me like a bolt of lightning. Was this the cub I had seen with its mother a few days before, close to here? Could it be that we had killed the mother and left this beautiful young animal to fend for its self? The thought sent me into a state of panic. I wanted to run after it, pick it up, take it back to camp, and care for it. I could not leave it here on its own. It was too young to hunt. It would starve to death. The cub had been the silent, accusing watcher.

Climbing off the truck I began, instinctively, to stalk the cub. He knew where I was, and continued to wander off towards the kopje. I matched his slow pace, and watched to see what he would do. Did he want to come with me? Had we bonded the last time we met? He had shown no fear when he lay there next to my truck licking his paws and looking up at me. Was that kind of bonding possible? I would not have had those thought if he now ran off into the bush. But he ambled along, tempting me to follow. Was he asking me to take him away and care for him? My hot and exhausted brain was not running on all eight cylinders, and weird and wonderful ideas came flowing through my head.

I continued to walk towards the cub, with the sun beating down from a cloudless, deep blue sky. A flat horizon circled all around. So bent was I on making up for the horror of the memories of this place, that the thought never crossed my mind that this could be another cub altogether. It didn't occur to me that its mother could be waiting nearby.

All I could see was a baby leopard cub in desperate trouble needing help, and I needed vindication. I took a few more steps in its direction when out of seemingly nowhere came a flash of yellow and black spots racing towards the cub. With dust flying everywhere she turned around and gave a terrifying hissing snarl. I froze and just stood there, not because I thought if I stood still I would stand a better chance of survival. I simply could not move a muscle in my body.

Thankfully, blood gradually started flowing back into my legs and brain. After the initial shock, my heart began pumping. I felt the artery in my neck pulsating like a machine gun. My brain was telling me I was about to die a terrible and lonely death.

Major, having seen everything that had happened, was growling and barking louder and more high pitched than I'd ever heard him bark. He could not get out as the window was half closed – not because I had half closed it, but because it was jammed in that position and had been that way for as long as I could remember. He was snarling and clawing at the window in a frenzy to get out and protect me.

I hoped Major's commotion would unsettle the leopard and persuade her to stay with her cub. Slowly I turned around and walked back towards my truck, trying to float rather than walk, wishing I could grow wings and fly. I didn't look back, remembering my Dad telling me that in this kind of situation never to look an animal in the eye.

My concern now was that, if I were to make it to the truck alive, the passenger door was the closest point. But if I opened that door and took a leap, Major would certainly fly out of that door before I could stop him. This was an angry, dangerous leopard mother. As strong as Major was she would kill him in a few minutes. I would have to take the longer route around the front of the truck to the driver's side, and hope that Major would stay on his side of the truck, absorbed by my angry friend.

For just a second, stupidly I hesitated and glanced behind me. Snarling loudly the leopard immediately charged for me. I ran around the front of the truck heading for the driver's side, convinced I wouldn't get there before I felt claws digging in and tearing the flesh off my back.

I did make it. Leaping into the truck, I slammed the door so hard I thought the concussion would throw Major's door open. The leopard stopped about forty feet from the truck. Like waving goodbye she slashed the air with a paw, with claws extended. Then she turned and walked back to her cub with an indignant tail swinging from side to side.

Major saved my life that day, with all the commotion he made inside the truck. He caused the leopard to hesitate, delaying the charge and giving me precious seconds to escape to the safety of the truck.

If I had sweated earlier from the hard work of changing the wheel of the truck, I was sweating a lot more now. Fortunately my seat was worn from years of use, with the odd spring showing through worn areas. Perspiration gathered in a pool and trickled through a hole in the seat. I was desperate for water to drink, but after the wheel-change, Major and I had drunk all we had. I made a mental note to myself that in future I would be sure to always carry extra water in the truck. Being without food in this heat would not be too serious, but not having water would be fatal.

I started the truck and watched as the two leopards disappeared into the scrub. Although badly shaken, I was relieved to know that the cub was in good hands and would grow into a beautiful adult. Major was still in one hell of a state and was trying his best to get out of the window. Being inside the vehicle with him brought home to me again how terribly vicious he sounded, and if pushed, could become. From the heat in the truck and the energy he was burning up, he was also loosing body fluids. His muscles rippled under his shiny wet coat. The only way to calm him down was to drive away as quickly as possible from this site where we, together, over the last fortnight had shared three memorable experiences with leopards.

By the time we reached the outskirts of the farm, Major had settled down and so had my own heartbeat. With a more regular heartbeat, a peace came settling over me – the peace of vindication, of being forgiven for my part in the tragic death of the leopard. It had certainly been a remarkable day, and since we were both alive and unharmed, I can say that I would not have missed it for anything. I doubt that Major felt that way. He had been so frustrated by the limitations to his protective instincts.

Chapter 27

It took all day to move all the equipment, level the drill platform and dig the water sump at our second site. At first light the following morning we began the heavy work of setting the machine up on the timbers and cementing in the dead men bolts. These are round bars, three feet long and ¾" in diameter, threaded on both sides. They go into holes drilled through the timbers using a hand auger.

The bar is pushed through the timber and into a hole dug four foot, large enough to accommodate an old plough disc, and attached with the use of a ¾" nut and large washer to hold it in place. Then a cement mix is poured into the hole, grouting in the plough disc, making an effective anchor point for stabilising the rig when drilling was in progress. Once the cement has set, to complete the operation, the short piece protruding through the top of the timber was tightly fastened and locked in place with a second ¾" nut.

The two front shear legs leading away from the machine were placed approximately twenty feet apart, in line with the hole. Where these met, some forty feet behind the machine, they were joined, using a top bolt and clevis, to the back shear leg at the pivot point. The shear legs are then lifted as high as possible by hand and placed on an empty 45 gallon fuel drum. This was done to ensure that the pivot point kicked up when pulling through the winch and cable to the rear of the back leg. The new ¾" non spin hoist cable was run through the sheave wheel attached at the pivot point, and back down to the rig ready for use once the shear legs were up.

Aaron was my right-hand man. He was just over 6' tall and after a lifetime of hard labour, was blessed with rippling muscles. He pulled out the cable from the bottom pulley of the machine and attached it to the end of the rear shear leg. I made sure the spread of the front shear legs were well positioned. Once this was done, the labourers and I set about installing the old drill rods across the two front legs. One just below the half way point with a second one three quarters of the way up. The hole was to be drilled at a 45° angle, and these were used to support the drill rods when they were pulled or lowered from the hole.

Using a fourteen-pound hammer, we securely knocked the umgwalas (old drill rods, cut off into 3' lengths) into the ground, in front of each leg, to act as an anchor.

The next morning, once the cement had set holding the dead men bolts firm, everything would be in place for simply pulling on the winch cable, leading to the back leg and the shear legs would be pulled up into position.

Last, but by no means least to minimise water loss in the sump through seepage, we splash cement up the complete inside right up to the surface. By this time it was dark, we were all tired, hungry and desperately needing a bath.

Aaron and I climbed into the front of the Land Rover, and the others clambered into the back, and together we drove around the Kopje to our camp. Heating water for our baths was done over a fire, using five gallon oil drums that had been well scrubbed. These worked well and cost nothing, as they came to us filled with oil and once used up turned into outdoor hot water geysers. After a day on the machines it was wonderful to climb into a steaming hot bath and relax. My bathroom was an open air arrangement next to my tent. I lay in my bath tub, soaking in the hot water, and looking up into a cloudless African sky with millions of stars. We each had a bath in our little tin tubs, sorted out something to eat, and went to bed.

In the morning around 5.00am, we surfaced from a deep sleep, and started the day with a cup of coffee before setting off to the rig. We checked the results of our hard work of the day before, ensuring that everything was safe before pulling the shear legs up. The shear legs are used basically as a platform to pull the rods out of the hole, hence the importance of the pulley at the apex of the shear legs being straight in line with the drill hole. Similar to a tri-pod with a pulley at the top with rope sheaved around the pulley to help lift and load equipment

Happy, I slowly took up the slack in the cable leading to the rear leg, through the mechanical winch on the rig. Once all the slack was taken up, I pulled down on the clutch lever on the hoist with the engine set just over the idle mark, so that it wouldn't stall as the legs started going up - but it was also slow enough to control them until they were safely up.

Keeping a close watch on the front anchors was important. If the force exerted on them by pulling the legs up lifted them out of the ground, they would fall sideways. This could be dangerous. They would damage anything they fell onto, including the shear legs themselves. Great care was needed throughout the whole operation. Fortunately, they held fast. I continued pulling until, looking through the bottom of the quill shaft, I could see either the cross-piece or, even better, the sheave wheel. I was lucky. The sheave wheel was close. To line up perfectly, we needed to dig down the front left leg slightly.

We were ready and equipped to begin drilling the hole with a 4 9/16" short starting barrel. Once the pump was started this was drilled in to a depth of ten feet. This was normally deep enough to case and make safe the overburden with 4" casing, or stand pipe, as we called it. This is a straight forward procedure normally completed in one hour or so.

However, we were rigging on the edge of the stream which had over many years undercut the bank and deposited loose sand and rocks up to 10' deep. Drilling down to that depth with the use of the starting barrel with 4 9/16" bit and shell connected on the bottom was not a problem. Or so my inexperienced brain thought. Penetration was fine and initially water and sand freely pumped out the top of the hole. Some 6' down the water return ceased. I figured just carry on down to 10' and then pull and slide the 4" casing in and the surface loose sand would be made safe. To say the least this presented serious difficulties. The starting barrel became tight in the hole and ultimately we had to use hydraulics to reverse drill it out. The loose sand and rocks closed the hole off. It was impossible to lower the casing, as the hole was virtually closed from 3' down.

Once again I drilled down to the 10' mark, in the hope that cleaning it out again might just do the trick, but the casing was not going in. The problem with the caving of the hole was made worse by the 45° angle at which it was set. Fortunately I had two ten foot lengths of 4 9/16" casing on site for just such an eventuality. However, Gus had told me to use it only if there was no other way. After wasting the whole of that day trying to get the casing down to ten feet, I felt that the time had arrived. Continuing with what we were doing would only destabilize the top section to a greater extent.

I tightened a 'casing shoe' *(Drill bit designed to remain attached to the casing for the duration of the hole)* onto the 4 9/16" casing, then lowered it into the hole. With the use of 24" wrench spanners together with a water swivel rod lowered into the top of the casing with pump running at full pressure to help wash it down. This washing action worked well as loads of sand and stone were washed out through the top of the casing. Eventually, after three hours of struggling I got it down low enough to go under the chuck, and I could use the drill rig to drill it down to the twenty foot that I felt sure was required. However, to join the second ten foot section, I would need to drill with what I had in the hole down to twenty feet. As the casing head would be 10' below ground level, with loose material above it, the chances of getting stuck were high.

About six feet down the inevitable happened, it got stuck. I tried pulling and pushing with the hydraulics on the machine, continually washing up the side of the casing with the pump. It wouldn't move, and couldn't be turned.

The geologist had passed on a message to me that Mr. Longstaff, the owner of the company, would be coming out to the drill site the next day to see how things were progressing. Well, he was not going to be happy. The drilling business is all about production. At that stage, on this hole, it just wasn't happening.

The immediate problem was that the casing was stuck. The only way to get it out would be to dig down to the casing head to free whatever it was that was holding it so tightly. This was going to be time consuming, but we had wasted enough time already. We had no option but to bite the bullet and get on with it.

I take my hat off to the guys on site. They got stuck in with the picks and shovels and in a few hours we were down to the problem and managed to pull the ten foot section up to enable us to join on the second piece. Using the Land Rover lights to see, as by this stage it was getting dark. To my surprise, with some turning, pushing and swearing, we managed to get the casing string to the bottom of the hole

It was the end of the second day, on the second hole. I had only managed to get down to twenty feet! The big boss was arriving tomorrow and suddenly the fun we were having was fading fast.

Chapter 28

In the drilling world, Mr. Longstaff was a highly respected man. All his working life, he had been in drilling and, much like Jack knew everything there was to know in the drilling game. We used to say '*things they had forgotten about drilling the majority of us were still to learn.*'

He was a fair man, giving generous praise and support to his employees - as long as production was up to speed. But he was also a hard man who expected results. When expected results were not achieved, he had a short fuse. This would undoubtedly be one of those times.

The imminent arrival of our boss turned up the pressure. He would have been driving for several hours from Salisbury, negotiating some of the worst roads in Rhodesia, suffering scorching heat of around 40° Celsius, with no air-conditioner in his vehicle. Something told me tomorrow would be another long, hard day. How could I explain that for two days we had all worked our butts off, but had only produced a hole of 20'? I knew how I would feel if I were in his shoes.

The next morning, before 5.00am, we were all at work, anxious to get as much done as possible before the boss arrived. I managed to drill in the NX Casing to 30'. Late that afternoon, while lowering the casing into the hole, along came the Land Rover. The boss had arrived. We were secretly hoping he had changed his plans, and that he'd give us a few more days to get the hole up and running properly.

Mr. Longstaff climbed out of his 4x4 and walked over to the rig. As he passed each of the guys he gave them all a pat on the back as he greeted them.

"Hi, Trevor, how is it going?" he asked with a smile. He had a great smile and I decided to try and keep that picture of him in my mind, when the inevitable storm broke.

"Hello, Mr. Longstaff, I hope you had a good trip? That road coming in here is really bad," I said, trying to smile back. "Yes," he beamed, "it was not a lot of fun, but seeing a beautiful Kudu bull and four females on the way helped." It struck me that, he was looking amazingly fresh for someone who had just made that trip from Salisbury."I see you're lowering casing. Have you lost your water return?" he asked, relaxed and interested.

"Well, Mr. Longstaff, we have had huge problems on this hole," and I began to relate the standpipe problem to him. Before I could finish he butted in abruptly."How deep is the hole?" His smile was receding fast.

"I was trying to explain what our problem was. We had major problems with the stand pipe," I began again.

"Trevor, the question I asked was, how deep is the hole?" There wasn't a hint of a smile on his face.

"The hole is only 30' deep and we . . ." I couldn't finish before he exploded. "Are you telling me you have been on this hole two days and have only got down to 30'?" he shouted.

"No, Sir. It has actually taken us three days." I said, remembering I had been taught that the truth is always best.

"Jack assured me you were ready to be sent onto a contract like this. He said you were one of the best learners he had ever had. He was confident you would manage!" He was way beyond angry.

"Please, Sir, if I could explain to you the problem we encountered at the start of the hole..." But once again, I was shut down.

"You don't have to tell me what the problem is. I can see what the problem is. You're not capable or ready for this. If Jack was here, he would have been half-way through this hole by now. I should never have let him talk me into sending you out here. "

By this stage, his anger was being replaced with concern over how he was going to solve the problem of having an inexperienced operator on a contract as remote as this. I plunged into the space of his hesitation.

"Yes, Sir. I learned everything I know from Jack, including how to go about trying to get the surface casing through loose sand and boulders. That was the problem with this hole." I took a breath. He allowed me to continue with my story.

"The river has undercut the banks, so below this top layer of soil all there is, down to around 12', is sand, loose stones and boulders. Have a look at that pile of rubble over there that we've had to wash out of the hole to get the surface casing in." I pointed to the evidence. I was not going to be stopped now. I had reached the stage knowing I was going to be fired anyway, and would tell him the story whether or not he wanted to listen.

"It's possible that Jack, or some other experienced driller, might have got through the problem a bit faster than I have, but I tackled the problem in the best way I knew. Although it took three days to get the stand pipe down to 20', I solved the problem. The hole is now safe and should be completed in a few weeks."

"The first hole I drilled was completed in a short time, and the site geologist was pleased with the progress we made. But that hole wasn't started in a river bed, so I didn't lose three days at the start." I was on a roll, and when I get like it's easier to stop a run-away train. It didn't matter any more how angry Mr. Longstaff had been.

"To be honest, I don't believe there's a driller anywhere who could have got that casing in any faster than the guys and I have done, under these circumstances. I'm also not too sure how many drillers would have discovered and developed the water source I've been using only one mile from here." Surely this had to be a trump card to help get me back on some kind of decent footing with the boss.

"Had I not been lucky and observant enough to find the water source, we would have had to go the expensive and time-consuming route of carting water from the farm. You'll remember that was our original plan. Had that been the case we would still be struggling on the first hole, with the slow turn-around time to the farm and back. This would have been hours of rig standing-time, while we waited for the water to arrive."

Mr. Longstaff was actually standing quietly and listening to me. That gave me confidence and courage to continue.

"You have just come in on that road. You know how bad it is." This was no way to speak to my boss for whom I had utmost respect. But make me or break me, I tell things the way they are and don't say what the other person wants to hear. My boss stood there with his hands on his hips and a stunned look on his face.

I knew this must be the quiet before the real storm. In my head I was getting ready to be out of there by morning. To be honest, in that moment, thinking of how hard we had all worked, of the long hours we had put in, and the conditions we were working under, neither I nor the guys would have minded one bit getting out of there. A few of the guys had already expressed concern for the remoteness and the abundance of wild life. All they needed was an excuse like this to climb into a vehicle and get the hell out of here.

I had a terrific crew. Not only were the conditions extremely tough, but we all knew that once this hole was complete we'd be moving down the escarpment to an even more remote and wild area called the Ruangwa Valley. The geologist had warned us there were loads of elephant down there and a greater chance of spotting leopards. The area was barren of human life, and even hotter than it was where we were. I fully understood the apprehension of the men.

Chapter 29

Thousand, who was working with me on the site, was an experienced local black operator. He had been with the company for ten years. He started, as we all did, as a labourer. When he showed promise and aptitude, he was taught how to operate and drill on the machines.

He was a really good guy to have around, not only for the help he offered on the drilling side, but as someone I could sit with at a fire at night, and share stories. He couldn't speak English. Nor did I speak Shona. So we conversed in the universal language of Fanagolo or better known in Rhodesia as Chilapalapa, which we both spoke fluently. It is basically a mixture of languages made up mainly of Zulu, some Xhosa, a little English and an even smaller mix of Afrikaans. It is extensively used throughout Southern Africa in the mines.

Mr. Longstaff walked off to his Land Rover calling for Thousand to follow him. I didn't know what else to do, so I called my crew together and we continued lowering the NX casing down the hole. Once it reached the bottom, as best I could, I sealed it off. We began to prepare the BX core barrel we would use to complete the hole.

I was about to pull the core barrel up into the tripod, ready to lower into the hole, when Mr. Longstaff returned, still not smiling. But at least he was more relaxed than he was fifteen minutes ago.

"This water story you told me about. Tell me more." His voice was calm.

"We are all extremely excited and proud, firstly that we discovered the water, and secondly of what we made of it. If it's okay with you I'd like to show it to you." I was also a touch more relaxed.

"Well, what are we waiting for? We don't have all day to drive around. There's a hole that has gone nowhere for three days, and needs to be drilled and completed." It wasn't my imagination. There was a trace of a smile on his face. "Thousand, we won't be long. Please could you lower the core barrel into the hole and make sure everything is ready to start drilling before we get back," I ordered.

Climbing into Mr. Longstaff's Land Rover, we set off back the way he had come in. "I must say," he commented, "driving in for the first time, I'm impressed that you got that loaded Morris Truck to your site. This access is as bad as I've seen anywhere. "

"Yes. It was difficult and dangerous. It took us the whole day to cover the 20 miles from the farm to the site. There were whole sections of track we had to repair with picks and shovels, so that we could get through." I was getting back on a roll.

"On a few occasions I was worried that the truck would topple over. That would have caused major damage, injury and delays. I would not have been able to get my vehicle back to get help. There were those huge boulders on one side, and the sheer drop on the other side." I was now relaxed and enjoying being allowed to relate our adventure into the area.

"At times I wondered how I was going to explain to you how your favourite truck and equipment got to be lying upside down in a deep gulley." I laughed, trying to lighten. Just a little, Mr. Longstaff joined in,

"Thankfully, all went well. Your truck arrived safely back in Salisbury. Now, in spite of some drilling problems, we are drilling our second hole." I knew he would have to be impressed.

"Yes, Trevor, I'm sorry about earlier. I was not in the best of moods after the long, hot trip. That, together with my expectations of how deep your hole should have been, made rational thinking difficult."

He paused, and then continued in a serious tone, "As you saw, I spoke to Thousand. He told me you are doing one hell of a job, as well as looking after your crew well. He says that if I take you away from here, the whole crew would want to go with you. "

I took that as a compliment. After what we had been through earlier, this was a relief. As I have said, I had the utmost respect for Mr. Longstaff. I looked on him as a second father. If there was anyone I wanted to do something right for, it was my boss.

"Thank you, Mr. Longstaff. I hope that means I'll get another chance to complete this contract. I really thought I would have to be out of here by tomorrow morning. I want to stay in drilling and have always given 100% to everything I have done for you." I was now bursting with confidence.

"If there was ever a contract with extreme conditions to prove myself on, it's this one."

From that moment I would be on a mission to do whatever was required to successfully complete the contract before the rains set in. I would prove to Mr. Longstaff that he had not made a bad decision, and I'd show him I would never intentionally let him down.

We arrived at my little gem of a 'water mine'. We climbed out the truck and walked through the scrub to the little dam with its crystal clear water.

"Have a drink," I offered. "It's good sweet water."
He cupped his hands and drank the liquid gold. To us, it was worth more than gold. "How did you find this?" he asked, genuinely surprised and impressed."It was my turn to get lucky. I can't begin to explain how excited I was when I saw the trickle of water coming down the Kopje." I went on to explain the process involved in getting the water to flow into the little dam.

He said he would like to climb up to the top to see the work we had done up there. The look on his face on reaching the top and seeing what we had achieved, made me proud to show it off.

"Trevor, not only could an experienced driller have drilled the hole any better than you did, but you were right when you said not many of them would have made this kind of plan. Well done! You have convinced me that if you keep this up, you won't be leaving this area until the contract is done."

Hearing that from Mr. Longstaff made me feel that I was not on the top of a kopje in the middle of nowhere, but was actually standing on the top of the world with my head held high. Yes, it felt good hearing those words from this man for whom I had so much admiration.

We went back down to the bottom and, after another drink from the dam, we drove back to the site to get the hole up and running.

Chapter 30

Thousand, in his efficient way, had everything ready. We started up the water pump to get the circulation pressure up, and began the drilling. It was late in the day, and sun was almost gone. I called for the guys to check the oil and start the generator to get the lights going. Mr. Longstaff interrupted."It's been a long day for all of us. No one is working into the night today. Let's just fill the core barrel to see what the formation looks like, and then call it a day."

As we shut down the rig, we were all happy to have the night off. We were at a good stopping place. Although the hole was shallow, the 10' run was already into good solid formation. The staff went off to their camp. First thing for all of us was a bath.

A little later Mr. Longstaff and I sat under the stars and enjoyed the cold drinks he had brought. He had a beer and I had my usual Coke. I only had one camp chair, and gave it to him. I sat on a five-gallon tin. He had not only brought drinks, but also cigarettes and bullets, and some good steak. We cooked it over the fire and life could not have felt any better. We had one more drink each and decided it was time to hit the sack.

My tent was small. We would not both fit into it for the night.
"I have brought a stretcher with me and will sleep outside under the flap in front of the tent," said Mr. Longstaff, with finality.

"I can't sleep in the tent and let you sleep outside," I insisted.

"One of the things I enjoy most when visiting the sites is sleeping out in the open. It will be a lot cooler out here, anyway." He had made up his mind.

"Then Major will sleep outside with you, and you'll be safe. He's the best protection you could have." I gave Major a pat on the head. As if he had understood every word, Major walked over to Mr. Longstaff and flopped down next to his chair.

I marvelled again over my dog, realising just how much his companionship and presence relaxed me out in the bush. He gave me a complete sense of security. I could sleep with the flaps of the tent open, allowing the cool night air to blow through. Except for the sounds of the bush, the night was quiet. We, all three, slept well.

As usual, we were up at first light. Clever had water boiling on the fire in a tin kettle. I made coffee for each of us. By 6.00am, we had checked the rig over, using a standard check list, and had started another day's drilling.

After all his years of being involved in drilling, Mr. Longstaff was an early bird. Regardless of how late we had worked, or stayed up the previous night, he would be up and about by 5.00am walking around without his shirt on until he'd had coffee, washed and shaved. He was a short, well-built man and looked good, considering his age. There was not a hint of a beer belly.

I was just twenty at the time, and hoped that when I got to his age, not only would I still be alive but that I would be in a similar shape to him. He was always active and a keen and excellent gardener. His home in Salisbury had a beautiful sculptured garden that had taken much manual labour to get it that way. Most of it he had done himself.

I drilled another two runs of 10' each. The core remained good and solid. Mr. Longstaff was happy. "Everything seems to be going well here. I'm going to leave now and head on up to see how things are going on the contract up in Mavurodona." I didn't envy him at all travelling along those roads in the heat of the day. "Thank you for coming out here, and for bringing supplies. I hope you have a good trip. Give my regards to Dave when you get to his site. Thank you for your support. You have no idea how much it helps." "Keep up the good work, Trevor. Even with that thug you have, who looks more like a lion than a dog to protect you, be careful out here. There are many wild animals, snakes, scorpions, spiders and heaven knows what else."

We shook hands and he left waving goodbye. As he disappeared around the corner with dust drifting off over the Mopani trees in the light easterly wind, I was sorry to see him go. But I had a happy heart. We had passed the test with flying colours.

Chapter 31

As with all cultures, black Africans have many superstitions and fears that can be traced back to ancient tribal myths and legends. They treat most reptiles with respect and fear, keeping well away from them. They're particularly afraid of chameleons. One myth regarding chameleons was that the gods sent various animals with a message to all the tribes around the world. In those days, everyone was black. The message was that there was a secret pool that, when bathed in, would turn skin white.

It was the work of the chameleon to deliver this message to the peoples of Africa. Since the chameleon moves slowly, it took a lot of time reaching everyone with its message.

The hare had been sent to the people of Europe. Being such a fast animal, they got their message first, bathed in the pool and turned white. By the time the people of Africa got the message and found the pool, the water had all been used up. There was nothing but a puddle left into which they could dip their hands and feet. That is why their palms, and the soles of their feet, are white.

The second myth explains how death came into the world, or rather, why death was not prevented from coming into the world. The gods sent a chameleon to the peoples of earth to declare: "Let no man die!" As is the way of the chameleon it moved slowly, lingering and dawdling. Long after the chameleon had set out, the gods sent a lizard, the blue-headed gecko, with a different message. It was to declare: "Let men die!" The lizard, as is its way, ran straight there, wasting no time, made its declaration and returned.

Much later the chameleon eventually reached its destination and dramatically declared: "It is said, Let no man die!" But the people had already accepted the word of the lizard, and could not hear the words of the chameleon. These myths helped to explain the extreme fear of reptiles held by my crew.

Two days after Mr. Longstaff's visit, our driver, Piet, returned to the rig in an agitated state. He had been to collect water. I saw him talking to the others, gesticulating wildly. He was excited about something. I went over to find out more. Downstream from our dam he had seen a giant snake, bigger and longer than our casing he said.

While the pump was filling the tanks, he had wandered off downstream to relieve himself, and spotted this monster with half the length of its body in the water and the other half stretching way out to the other side of the stream. He said it was an *umtagate*, a creature that casts an evil spell, and must be avoided. For him, the end of his world had arrived.

I asked Thousand to take over the controls on the rig, while I went with Piet to have a look at this frightening creature. It was the hottest part of the day, and Major was fast asleep under the drill rig. He looked so peaceful and cool I decided to leave him there.

On arriving at the dam Piet refused to get out of the truck. He pointed downstream to where the monster snake was. Carrying my .22 rifle, I climbed out and followed the stream of water coming from the spring. Suddenly, I stopped in my tracks, spellbound by what I saw. It must have been one of the largest pythons in Africa. Now I understood Piet's excitement. It was a spectacular being. It had just slithered out of the water, and was wet and shiny, its golden and black markings vivid, iridescent. He was a beautiful sight, lying beside the stream with an air of owning the world, knowing that nothing and no one would mess with him.

I had brought my rifle, in case we found a black Mamba or a large cobra, both of which could be dangerous. If it was one of those, none of the guys would come near to the pool to collect water, until it was proved dead. But this magnificent creature was neither poisonous nor aggressive. I couldn't shoot it. I called for Piet to come and join me. He refused. I walked back to the vehicle and ordered him to get out and come with me, threatening to pull him out and leave him with the snake while I returned to the rig.

I assured him that as long as the python was left alone it would not harm him. After some hard coaxing he got out of the truck, and I locked the door behind him. He was ready to run off into the bush.

"Piet, don't do that. The snake could have a mate. It could be anywhere out there." Terrified, he pleaded with me to let him back into the truck. He clung to my arm. "Come now, Piet. Do you think that I'd do this if the snake was dangerous? Come with me and see how harmless he is." I needed him to do this. If we didn't sort this out, I would have to come and collect water myself from now on.

Slowly but surely, we both got to within 20' of the Python. I was not convinced myself that we were perfectly safe, but what gave me confidence was a huge lump in his stomach. What on earth could he have eaten that was so big? How could something of that size fit into his mouth, let alone go all the way down into his stomach? The lump gave me courage. I knew he would be docile in that condition, and would be looking for a safe place to sleep while he digested his catch.

He was not interested in us. Apart from lifting his head and coiling it back, a little flicking of his long tongue in and out, he was calm.

This was not the case with Piet. When the python lifted its head Piet tried to pull away from my grip on his arm, wanting to run and never stop running until he reached safety. He, like the python's prey, was so terrified he couldn't move. It was a good thing the Python was so satisfied. Around here, it would be hard to find a good replacement driver.

Assuring him once more that there was no danger, I took him two paces closer to the reptile. This bothered the snake, and slowly, majestically, he slithered away effortlessly, disappearing into the long grass near the stream. I was awestruck by his size.

I spoke to Piet in soothing tones. "Calm down, Piet. We haven't harmed him. From now on he will protect this area from other dangerous snakes." I waited for this prophesy to sink in.

"The reason I took you so close to him was so that he could get a good look at you, and recognize you in the future. That way, he'll look after you, each time you come here. There's no need for you to ever be scared of him again, or any other snake in this area." He became notably more relaxed, gave a weak smile and thanked me. I continued, making up the story as I went along. "These are rare snakes, but very lucky snakes to find, as long as you don't harm them. If you do hurt or kill them, they put a bad spell on you forever." I didn't want anyone telling the geologist about the snake. He would have gone looking for it, to shoot it for the skin, which is worth a lot of money. I told Piet about this and said if you or any of the others guys tell the geologist about the snake we were all going to be doomed.

When we returned to the site he raced off to tell the rest of the team about his adventure, and about how lucky we were that this snake had come along. They all seemed to believe this little story, and the site settled down to the productive sound of the rig drilling its way down into the depths of the earth. The next time Piet went to collect water he took one of the guys with him. "Just in case," he said. Not seeing any sign of the snake, from then on, he was confident to go on his own. We never did see the python again. Good luck to him and may he be around for many years to come.

The African Rock Python's life span is 20-25 years. They can grow up to approximately 30' in length. The female will lay on average about 40 eggs, but have been known to lay 100. Up to 50% of these are generally infertile. To supply the heat required for incubation and protection she wraps herself around the eggs. Incubation period is approximately 3 months with hatchlings of 18-24 inches long. Unlike most reptiles she will guard her nest constantly only leaving for short periods.

They will eat anything from the size of a rat to a goat depending on what they can catch and kill through coiling their powerful bodies around the prey and effectively squeezing the life out of them. If cornered they are aggressive and although not poisonous will bite, readily inflicting a nasty wound.

Chapter 32

Drilling progressed without any major delays. Most things we were able to repair on site. The hole was almost complete.

I was possessed by a need to complete the current hole and make up for the lost days. Being so preoccupied, I had given no thought to our meat supply. We had been without meat for a few days. The rest of the crew were feeling a need for meat, which was more important to them than it was for me. Thousand eventually plucked up courage to talk to me about it.

"Please, Baas," he said, uncomfortably, "the guys are complaining about there being no meat. They say they can't work these long hours without eating properly."

"Hell, Thousand. Tell them I'm sorry! I've been thinking so much about getting the hole done, I forgot about getting meat." I felt bad about my absorption with the job. My selfish motive was to impress the boss, and there was no time for going out to shoot for the pot.

"Tell them they'll have a feast today!" Thinking about it set my own meat-craving hormones alight, and suddenly I was hungry too. I longed for a fresh venison steak.

"We have done well with the hole. You can take over pulling out the rods, once we've filled the core barrel. Then Clever and I will go hunting for food." I had let the guys down. They worked hard and were dedicated to the job, but without food in the belly they were like a car running out of fuel. We worked really long hours and it was definitely time for refuelling. It took another half-an-hour to fill the barrel with core before handing the machine over to Thousand to pull the rods, remove the core and lower the rods back to the bottom so we could continue drilling on our return.

Clever, Major, and I climbed into Land Rover to go to the camp to collect my rifle. Clever was the lookout man, and had established himself as my hunting partner. He stood on the back of the Land Rover holding onto the light roll bar just behind the front cab. The higher elevation gave him a better view than I had from the driver's seat. There was also little room in the passenger seat which was always taken up by the huge and powerful Major.

Unless he was asleep when I went out he would not allow me to go anywhere without him. He seemed to know what we were setting out to do. He sat there, alert and looking out through the windscreen and side windows for anything exciting. As soon as Clever saw something for me to shoot he would tap lightly on the roof to let me know. It worked well. Once I had shot whatever presented itself, if there were no passage to drive in, we would drag it back together to load onto the vehicle.

So that he felt part of the hunt, Major was let out of the vehicle. He always knew exactly where the animal was and ran up to it, grabbed hold of it by the throat and give it a good shaking to make sure it was really dead before we got to it. Once we arrived he would let it go and stand back proudly to show off what he had caught.

I had been driving for some time and was surprised that we had not seen anything yet. The area was teeming with game. Suddenly, instead of the light tap on the roof, there was an almighty and urgent bang, bang, bang that almost got me jumping out of the side window. I came to an abrupt stop and jumped out of the cab to see what the panic was about. Clever couldn't speak, but was pointing off into the bush. I was unable to see anything in the direction he was pointing so climbed onto the truck to have a better view over the scrub.

I was caught by surprise. A huge rhino was standing about 300 yards off the road. I understood why Clever was so excited, and a tinge of excitement ran through my veins as well. I didn't know there were rhino in the area. I joked with Clever, keeping my voice low.

"If you think I'm going to shoot that for the pot you've lost your mind. Even you guys couldn't eat all that meat" We both laughed softly.

It was thrilling to come across the Rhino. I wanted to get closer. I had heard that they were almost blind, so if you stayed down-wind it was possible to get close. I suggested to Clever that we climb down and walk slowly towards him, to get a better view. The wind was light in a south-westerly direction, putting us directly downwind of our horny friend.

Well, Clever didn't think it was a good idea. He suggested that we move off fast, and while we were still alive, return to our assignment. I smiled at his fears.

"Come on, this is exciting. We'll move slowly." I climbed off the vehicle, feeling excited and eager to get up as close as safely possible. Clever was happy to stay where he was.

"Hey, my baas, I didn't come into the bush to get trampled on and stabbed by that horn. My spirit would be cursed for being stupid. My family wouldn't mourn my death. They'd be angry with me. I should have paid more attention to his reasoning!

"Clever, you know I'd never do anything to endanger your life." I spoke in a persuasive tone. "Your family and friends will be so proud when they hear of your bravery in going close to a rhino." I made my face as serious as possible. "When they hear your story, they could be so impressed that they vote you in as the new chief of your village."

This idea gave him courage. "Please, if I die and you survive, you must promise me that you will tell my family I died trying to save your life." His brain was in overdrive, wanting to prevent his spirit and his memory from being cursed for all time.

"I promise," I said, "if that happens, which I can guarantee won't, I will tell your family you are the bravest person I ever met. However, if you don't come with me I will have to think of another story to tell them, and also the guys back at camp. Believe me they will laugh at you for the next few weeks. Also, when your time comes, who knows what might happen to your spirit, having shown yourself to be such a coward?" This got his attention and, reluctantly, he climbed off the back of the truck and stood next to me.

"Now, Clever, stay right behind me. When I move left you move left and when I move right you move right. That way he will have less chance of seeing our movement. If he sees us, we will look like one object from where he stands," I instructed.

"Don't worry, my Baas, I'm behind you. If you die, I'll speak of how brave you were, and I will protect your spirit." He gave a sheepish, nervous grin. I stifled my laughter. My rifle was left in the truck. If something went wrong, it would be of no use. If I shot the rhino, it would just annoy him. What I really needed to shoot with was a camera and, of course, didn't have one. Crouching low, we stalked the rhino. The few dry, leafless trees and small bushes weren't great for cover, but we were getting closer and he didn't seem to notice. When we were about 50 yards from the truck, we began to feel more confident. My back was feeling the strain of our stalking position, and we began walking a little faster in a more upright stance. It was a mistake.

Was it that? Or did the wind change? Whatever it was, in a flash and a cloud of dust, the rhino spun around to face us. He nodded his head sharply, making the large long horn above his nose look even more dangerous. I wasted a split second wondering why he had done that. By the time I had my brain back in gear and turned to run back to the vehicle, Clever was more than half way there.

I ran as fast as I could, not knowing whether or not I was being chased, and was not looking back to find out. My only thought was to get to the vehicle and to safety. Clever had leapt up onto the back and was urging me to run faster. My feet left the ground and flew into the driver's seat. For obvious reasons, Major had been left in the truck. He cocked his head to one side, quizzically. "What's going on?" he was asking. I looked back to see what the rhino was doing. My heart sank. He was charging towards the vehicle. Then, as abruptly as he had spun around earlier, he veered off to his right, still at full speed. He was flattening bushes, with dust and loose dry leaves flying everywhere. It was an impressive sight and although my pulse rate had increased considerably I was enjoying the moment. When he reached the road he turned away from us, and continued towards the escarpment. His scary charge was to frighten us, not to attack us. Clever and I were impressed.

Being young and stupid, I had not yet had enough. I set off in the Land Rover, following the rhino. From close up, it was massive. It was running at speed, with his stomach swinging from side to side. We chased after him for about half a mile. I being in awe, and Clever was in a panic, standing in the back holding on, yelling for me to stop.

As we arrived at the brim of the escarpment there was a hollow in the road with a clearing off to the right side of about 12 feet running into the side of the mountain. It was originally opened up many years before, when the track down the escarpment was cut through. It led down to the Mozoe River and a dead end. There nothing down there. I had asked the geologist about it. He was equally surprised by the mystery.

The Rhino ran down through the hollow and turned off into the small clearing and then had nowhere to go. Behind him was the sheer cutaway into the mountain. Being so close behind him and so fully preoccupied with all the action I was caught unawares by his sudden movement off to the right. He came to a dead stop in a huge cloud of dust that hid him from view. We couldn't see which way he was facing. I could not stop. On the one side, within a few feet, was the sheer drop at the edge of the escarpment. At a similar distance on the other side

116

was the rhino. A nudge from his powerful, horned head would have sent us careering off over the side.

I shot past him, so fast we could have been air borne, and came out to the other side of the hollow. The rhino hardly knew what had happened. I continued for about one hundred yards and stopped to assess the situation. There was nowhere to turn on the way down so I didn't want to go too far. I climbed out of the vehicle, confident he would not follow us. In an instant Clever leapt off the back and was sitting in the front passenger seat. Suddenly there was room for both him and Major.

"Hey, Baas, I should not have come with you to shoot for food. We will soon be dead." He was in shock. "We have made that thing angry. He will never let us back up. He will wait, and attack us when we try to go back."

I tried to reassure him, but he became more hysterical, "No, no, no, my Baas! You have already told me that we would be safe, but he nearly killed us when he charged the car. Then when we get a second chance to live, you chase him with this *scorro scorro.* " he shook his head violently from side to side.

He was rightfully upset, and I was responsible. He had never before seen such a terrifying animal. This crazy situation was beyond his comprehension. I was starting to feel the same way.

"Okay, I'm sorry, Clever. But you must settle down. He will go back into the bush where he feels safer." I was trying to convince myself, too. "We'll wait a few minutes and then reverse back up the road so that we can turn around at the top. From there we can go back to find food, and then head back to camp."

"We must stay where we are," declared Clever. "He can't get to us from here. The mountain is too steep. If he comes down the road to get us we can at least drive away, all the way to the bottom."

"So," I snapped, "you're saying we should sleep in the Land Rover for the night?" I was now getting a bit agitated with Clever, and was confident we were safe to return to camp. "Well, I'm driving back up. If you want to sleep here on your own that's your choice."

With that I climbed into the driver's seat and selected reverse gear.

"Clever are you coming or staying? I'm leaving right now." He gave no answer, and sat there shaking his head with sweat pouring from his face.

I started reversing up the short section. As I thought, the Rhino was gone. I reversed into the clearing to turn around, and Clever jumped back into the passenger seat. As we travelled in the direction of the camp, to the huge relief of both of us, the rhino was nowhere to be seen. When we passed the spot where all the drama had started, we looked at each other and laughed. It felt good to laugh, and to hear Clever lighten up and laugh.

Fate was on our side. About a mile or so further on, a duiker ran across the road and stopped to look back at us. I grabbed the .22 rifle and shot through the passenger window right in front of Clever's nose. We were so close. It was a perfect head shot and the duiker dropped like a stone.

We climbed out of the car to pick it up, and to my surprise, Clever jumped neatly onto the back of the vehicle.

"Come on now, Clever. I need your help to carry the duiker. You can't hide up there like a coward."

"No, my Baas. I just want to look around from up here to make sure there are no more funny things around for you to play with." With that we both burst out laughing again.

"Okay, smart arse. Come help me down here." Still amused with the whole episode we ran at a trot to fetch what would be enough meat for all of us for the next few days. Clever would skin the duiker and cut it up into steaks and thin strips for hanging on a wire to keep it fresh.

Chapter 33

When we returned, after off-loading the duiker at the camp, I immediately went down to the rig to see how things were progressing. I was greeted by a glum-looking Thousand.

"Hey, Thousand! What's the problem? What happened?" "I'm sorry, my Baas. We pulled about half the rods out and the spanner that holds them slipped and everything went back down the hole." His eyes were looking everywhere except at me. He knew I would be pissed off. This could be a big problem. "How the hell did you do that? I go away for a short while to get meat for all of us and now you tell me the rods are down the hole!"

We would have to go down and fish them out of the hole. My best chance of success would be with a tapered fishing tap to screw into the open drill rod. But not only did we not have a proper rod clamp to prevent this happening in the first place, there was no tap either. The only option I had was go down with open rods in the hope of joining up again. Checking the thread on the first rod going into the hole, I carefully lowered the rods, one by one, making sure as they went down, that every joint was tight. I needed to know the exact depth of the top of the fallen rod string. Going in too fast could damage the threads, which would then not join up without the use of a tap.

Using a hacksaw blade I marked the quill rod precisely at the depth required. Due to the hole being drilled at a 45° angle meant the rods would be lying on the bottom on the foot wall side of the drilled hole. I ran the quill rod through the quill shaft and tightened the chuck just above the point of contact of the fish. This allowed me with the use of hydraulic control to go down delicately into the open female side of the rod that had dropped.

The rods screwed together beautifully and after making sure they were tight, we started pulling, taking extra care each time a rod was held with the wrench. Eventually all the rods were out and we removed the 10' of core. Due to the water in the hole the rods' decent had been cushioned and there was no damage to the core barrel, the core or the drill rods. Had it been a dry hole this would have been far more risky.

The client, who was paying, only cared about the rock core samples we were removing from the ground. He was not interested in the problems we had doing that. We were able to solve the problem, and were very careful after that. The hole was completed to a depth of 760 feet with no further problems.

All the core samples from the first hole were delivered to the geologist's base camp some five miles away. There, these would be logged and safely stored. Regrettably little sign of a promising ore zone was evident in the core samples from the current hole waiting to be transported back to camp.

Peter, the project geologist, informed me they would be reassessing their options for this area after considering the results from the laboratories. In the meantime we would be moving a further fifteen miles down the escarpment into the Mozoe River Valley, and then another four miles up into the Ruangwa River Valley, where we would be drilling the remaining six holes.

To enable us to get our equipment to the new site we would have to clear and cut out a track for the remaining four miles. The track we would use down the pass came to an end at the Mozoe River. Peter assured me he would see to this. He had four axes to cut down trees and he would send in extra labour. He warned us that the bush down in the valley was a lot denser, as the river flowed throughout the year, and there was plenty of surface water. It was going to be quite an adventure.

Peter had let our office in Salisbury know that the hole was complete and there would be no more drilling taking place in that area, we would move out and head down into the valley, therefore losing the miraculous spring water find. We would now wait for the results from the laboratory to determine whether we would continue with the project or not. Visually there were certainly no indications of promising intersections, so the prospects for returning to do further drilling were slim.

Chapter 34

The Morris truck would return to the site, to help with the move. There was loads of work to be done to prepare. Peter had my list of requirements, re-drilling spares, together with rations and other supplies as follows.

8 x 100 lb bags of mealie meal (maize meal), Six cases of tinned vegetables, (mainly peas), 50 rounds of ammunition for my rifle to ensure our meat supply while in the valley, as much diesel as we could load onto the truck with all the drilling equipment. 1 x 50 gall drum of petrol for our water pump which was driven by a Briggs & Stratton petrol engine, and of course, my Cokes and cigarettes, and Boxer tobacco for the crew.

I drank no alcohol, but after a long day of drilling I did enjoy my Cokes at night on getting back to camp. Smoking had a calming effect on me. I smoked about twenty a day. When under stress I would light up and take deep draws of nicotine-rich smoke. I only smoked non-filtered Gunston plain. There was a saying that the only good thing about smoking a non-filtered cigarette was that it was guaranteed to kill you before you got lung cancer.

While waiting for the truck to arrive we rigged down. This involved loosening the bolted section on the sheer legs to lengths that would fit onto the truck. As the drill rods were made up into thirty feet lengths for drilling, they had to be loosened and broken down into ten feet lengths. The rig was pulled off the timbers and dragged to our original ramp made for loading and off-loading. To get the back of the truck level with the ground, we had dug an incline hole for the truck to reverse into. This was ready by the time the truck arrived. It was then just a case of running the hoist cable from the winch down through the bottom pulley, attaching it to the ¾" round bar bent into a U shape that was welded onto a channel iron, which in turn was welded inside the twenty foot load body just behind the cab. The machine then simply pulled itself up and onto the truck.

As we still had water flowing down the mountain we cleaned up the drill rig and pump beautifully, and serviced them with a complete change of oils and filters. We would arrive at the new site ready to go with a well maintained rig. When the truck arrived, only half the supplies ordered had been sent, so I decided to stock up from the store on John's farm, before proceeding down the escarpment. I left the guys loading up while I drove to the farm. I didn't know what our water situation would be, so decided to take as much drinking water as possible. I had the 1,000 water tank. Being without food down in the valley would be bad enough, but to be without drinking water would be disastrous.

Clever and Major joined me for the trip to the farm. Taking Major to the farm was always complicated, because John had a pack of eight large Fox Terriers. It was their territory, and they were always in protective mode. When we arrived they were very vocal, and kept jumping up at the passenger door, trying to get to Major. He would bark, but by and large was not particularly concerned about them. But I had to leave him in the truck, so needed to find a shady spot to park in. It also meant stopping before getting to the farm to let him out to run around and do his business. However, in spite of these inconveniences he insisted on coming with me wherever I went. This is something I should have taken heed of later into the contract.

It was good to see John and Sally again and catch up with news. They offered me a bed for the night. It was tempting, but, with the imminent move down the escarpment and with Clever and Major in the truck outside I declined the offer. But I did ask if I could have a shower before heading back.

"You go right ahead. Take as long as you like. There's plenty hot water," laughed Sally. "In the mean time I'll sort out your order. Thank you for the business." When she smiled at me it made my knees go weak. She was an extremely attractive woman in every way, had a great personality and sense of humour, and was a fantastic cook. When John chose his life partner, he chose well.

After the shower I felt like a new man. My tin tub in the open air under the stars was not quite like a full-blown shower with as much hot water as I needed. I found John outside working on one of his tractors.

"Thanks so much for the shower. I feel very good. Can I help you with the tractor?" "No, it's fine thanks, I'm just changing fuel and oil filters. She has been playing up a bit so I'm sure some TLC is all she needs. Take your truck down to the store and see if Sally has sorted out everything you need, so that you can load." He pulled a face straining to loosen the fuel filter.

"Well, if you're sure you're alright with the tractor I'll do that, and then make my way back to site. The truck from Salisbury should be loaded by tonight, so the plan is to leave at first light tomorrow morning," I said. "We have one hell of a trip ahead of us tomorrow, getting all that equipment down the escarpment."

We shook hands as we said goodbye. "You're welcome to come out to my camp and use my tin tub bath in exchange for the shower I've just had." I joked. "I don't offer that luxury to just anyone."

We both laughed. I sauntered off past an old red pick-up rusting under a huge shady tree, climbed into the truck with a fresh bowl of water for Major. Thirsty, he gulped it down. Even in the shade the temperature in the front of the truck was extreme. I fired up the Bedford, waived to John and drove down to the store.

Sally, being her normal efficient, gorgeous self, had all the supplies I had asked for ready at the door of the store. "

Hi, Sally, thanks again for allowing me to use your shower. It has really made a difference… well, from my side anyway. I'm sure from your side I still look just as much a wreck as I did before."

Being polite she said, "You look as good as you always do." I felt my face turning a darker shade of sun burned brown, and I realized just how cute I really thought she was.

Before I could stop myself I said, "To repay you your kindness I offered John an opportunity to come out to my camp anytime and use my tin tub bath. If, for any reason he can't make it, you would be more than welcome." With this she smiled and also changed to a brighter shade of sunburn.

Feeling a touch embarrassed I quickly turned around and started loading the truck. This took my mind off all the other stuff going through my head and in no time we had everything on and ready to go. I went up to Sally standing behind the counter in the store and signed the invoice.

"Thanks again for everything. Send the invoice to the office in Salisbury, and whoever next comes out will bring the cheque to you." I was trying to sound as casual as I could, but we both knew my voice was nowhere near its normal note, and we both knew why.

"You know that you are always welcome. Thanks for the order. But I will have to decline your offer on the tin tub, for obvious reasons." With this we had a good laugh dissipating down the electric atmosphere we had built up. On saying goodbye, she warned me to be careful out there, adding, "It's not the safest area to be working in."

With that I walked out, climbed into the truck and drove off, heading east from the farm.

When I was a few miles away from the farm, with no chance of a problem with John's dogs, I stopped the truck and let Major out to loosen up and have a good run. While Major ran around with his nose to the ground, picking up all the strange, different and wonderful new smells, Clever and I walked over to sit under a large shady tree. We got stuck into the lunch pack Sally had packed for us.

We were hungry and made short work of the chicken sandwiches. They were really good. I opened the other little plastic box and found some cheese and tomato sandwiches, which were also devoured in a few minutes. Our lunch was chased down with a Coke. Major had also gulped down his water and plate of food with the same urgent hunger.

We arrived back at camp to find the Morris Truck fully loaded, needing only to have the tents thrown on in the morning, after spending our last night in them on this side of the escarpment.

We all hit the sack early after checking both sites to ensure there was no equipment or mess left behind. We checked that the sludge sumps were filled in, so no unsuspecting animal could fall into them. As always, the guys had completed all I had asked them. Before going into my tent I thanked them for their commitment, not only for that day, but for the whole time of drilling the two holes here on the top of the escarpment. I cautioned them to eat and sleep well that night as tomorrow would be a long, hard day.

Chapter 35

The next morning, even before the francolins had become vocal, I was up and about. When I staggered from my tent I could see the smoke of the fire and smell the brewing coffee drifting in my direction.

Clever knew me well. When I surfaced in the morning, he always had coffee ready. Was it the caffeine I needed or the nicotine from my first cigarette after coffee, or both? After coffee and those first deep draws on a cigarette, I had the energy and presence of mind to go down and check the trucks.

All the guys were up and about. They were busy breaking down their tents and loading them onto the truck. There was some excitement amongst them and an urgency to get on with the move. We were all tense, which was a good thing. It would keep us all on our toes. I had been down the escarpment with Peter, the geologist, and knew how difficult it was going to be. I had done my best to explain to my crew.

Peter's labourers had been working on the road from the Mazoe River through to the drill site further up the Ruangwa Valley. The bush there was thick, and there were huge trees. Where possible, to avoid cutting down trees that had been there for hundreds of years, the road was cut around the largest of them.

I wasn't happy with the work done on the pass. While the road was good enough for a light vehicle to get through, I was not confident that a fully loaded eight-ton two-wheel-drive Morris truck could make it. I couldn't take a chance on the truck toppling over and rolling down the mountainside.

By 7.00am everything was loaded. The loose equipment was tied down securely with rope. This included the rolls of PVC piping I had ordered from head office. I hoped to use these to pump water from the small Ruangwa River to the drill sites. Peter had informed me that we'd be drilling fairly close to the river.

The trucks had been fully checked over: Oil full, water full, fuel in the tanks, battery brackets secure, brake and clutch fluid full and wheel nuts all tightened. At last we were ready to leave. The sooner we got going the better. The sun was above the horizon and was going to be a stinker of a hot day.

I drove in front of the convoy, checking the road conditions. Immediately behind came Pete, my driver, in the Bedford truck, followed by the loaded Morris truck. In case help was needed from behind, to either pull a truck backwards, or to go to the farm for help in the case of a breakdown, Peter followed at the back of the convoy in his Land Rover,.

We had all bases covered. I had the Bedford driving in front of the Morris to test each repaired drift as we got to it. Although heavier than the Land Rover, especially with the full tank of water on the back, the Bedford was much lighter than the fully-loaded Morris. Leading the convoy I would be in a position to check each drift before we passed through.

There was no room for error on either side of the road. We all wanted to get to our destination as soon as possible, but we needed to be slow and cautious, if our little cavalcade was to arrive safely.

We rolled out of camp, and bade farewell to our miracle spring. For years to come, this would continue as a life-saving water hole for the large numbers of game in the area. We passed the place of the rhino chase and on to the top of the escarpment where, only days before, the rhino had veered off the road and spun around to face our vehicle. The memory gave me a cold shiver. Clever and I had been fortunate to escape. This area already carried many memories. It was not the most worker friendly area in the world, but it had been an amazing, once-in-a-life-time place to have worked in.

I pulled up, climbed out and walked back to the trucks. "Guys," I started, as confidently as I could, "I want to tell you all once more to be careful and wide-awake as we go down here. I'm sure all will be fine, but if I don't feel happy I will stop you. We will then sort out the problem and move on." I was trying to encourage myself as much as them. "If any of you drivers have any concerns, now is the time to tell me. Once we start to roll, we'll have to keep going as there will be no turning back."

I was worried about James, the driver of the Morris truck. He seemed uncertain and concerned, but said nothing. "James, you don't look too happy. Is there something you want to tell me?"

"Sorry, my Baas. You are right. I'm not happy about driving this loaded truck down that pass." He hated having to confess, but could not keep quiet once I had asked.

"I have been driving for a long time, but from what I have heard and what I see, I'm too scared to take the responsibility of driving down there." That was a complication I had not anticipated, but I could see his fear and admired his honesty. I realised that being that scared could cause him to make mistakes, with dreadful consequences. I made an instant decision.

"Okay, James. This is not what I had planned, but I think there's only one thing to do." I paused, wondering if I was doing the right thing. "I'll drive your truck, and you can drive up front in my vehicle. You have the experience to know what is safe for a load like this. and what isn't. Any sections you feel you wouldn't want to drive through in the fully loaded truck, or could be dangerous in any way, you must stop us so we can repair the road. Do you understand?" "Yes, my Baas. Thank you. I understand." He was hugely relieved.

Peter, the geologist, had climbed out of his Land Rover and come over to find out what the delay was about. "Is there a problem with one of the trucks?" he asked. "No, everything's fine. James is going to drive my vehicle and I will drive his truck. He's concerned about driving down the pass. It would be better if I take over that responsibility." I was trying to sound confident. "Well," retorted Peter, "if you think it's the right way to go, then let's get on with the show. The heat is already building up fast. " He too was worried and agitated. He well knew what lay ahead. "I just need to get Major out of my vehicle and into the truck. He wouldn't want to travel with a strange driver."

I walked off to my vehicle, opened the door and called for Major to come with me. Always keen to go hunting or even just for a walk, he jumped out immediately. But it took some convincing to persuade him to jump up into a strange truck. He stood looking at me as if to say there was no ways he could be tricked into jumping into someone else's truck. James was already in my vehicle and was ready to go.

"Come on, Major, get into the truck. Now!" I shouted at him, but the only reaction I had was a cocked leg against the front wheel as he relieved himself. I realized he needed to know I'd be in the front of the truck with him. I climbed up and closed the door, then leaned over and opened the passenger door, calling for him to come around to that side. Once he saw me sitting in the driver's seat he leaped up and sat on the passenger side as though he had been there many times, and couldn't understand what all the commotion was about.

I gave a couple of toots on the hooter to let James, the new leader of our convoy know he should slowly move off, and head down the pass. He obliged and we were all on our way. The first section was steep. I traversed this part in low gear to ensure full engine braking. There were some tight turns, but we were able to negotiate them. The road flattened off for about 500 yards and we relaxed a little. We had successfully negotiated the first section without any problems. We had confidence to face what lay ahead. A bad section was coming up. A patch of road had become a deep trough. Over years, rain water running through what had started out as a small cleft on the flattened area of the road had widened it. Although it had been repaired, after driving over it, James had stopped to let us know he wasn't happy for us to take the chance of driving over it. Piet and I stopped and got out. James was right. It did look unstable.

Although it was able to take the weight of a Land Rover which, with its aluminium bodywork, was lighter than most 4x4 vehicles, would it be stable enough for the trucks? Peter came over. He was impatient.

"Come on guys. We have repaired this section. There won't be a problem." "If these were your trucks, with all this expensive drilling equipment loaded onto them, would you be this confident?" I asked. I was not prepared to just go forward on his word alone. "Yes. We have thrown in a lot of backfill and it should hold up just fine."

From where we were standing it did look safe. Reluctantly we agreed to continue, but with extreme caution. We could only have one go at it. If it collapsed, we would be in serious trouble. The repair crew had backfilled the road section only, leaving a precarious and deep wash-away to the left of the road which dropped down into the valley.

Peter could see what I was looking at. "Come on, Trevor. It should be fine. Have you any idea how much backfill it would take to fill that area? If you expected us to do that amount of road work we would have had to bring in heavy earth-moving machinery from Salisbury." Peter was losing patience. This surprised me, as he was constantly having a go at us about safety procedures. A few more of these stops would put him in a hell of a state.

I understood his position, but needed him to understand my concern, and that I had to take full responsibility for any decision I made. "I'm going to let the Bedford through and see how it holds up. With a bit of luck it will be fine and I can then drive my truck over. But

I would have been happier if we had some tree trunks dug in on the left hand side for extra support." I said this more as a comment than a request.

"Piet, I need you to come through with your Bedford, but you must do it confidently. Once your front wheels have crossed into the bad section you must keep going regardless of what happens. Do you understand?" I said, looking him in the eye.

"Hey, my Baas. If you were prepared to help James by driving his truck all the way, please help me too. I'm also scared. You would make me happy if you drove the Bedford through here. " he said, hopefully.

"Come on, Piet. You managed to get through all those bad areas on the way to the first site. This is no more difficult. With luck on our side, there will be no problems." I said.

Piet was trying to look as down hearted as he could as he slowly walked back to his truck. He was hoping that if he took his time I would change my mind and drive it through for him. When I didn't oblige, he climbed up into the old truck and fired it up.

I walked over the bad section and called for Piet to come on through. As his wheels entered, there was slight give in the back fill. I waved my hand frantically for him to keep coming, and the engine RPM increased and on he came. There was no question that, with the weight of the 5 tons of water on the back of the truck, there was a noticeable sinking movement and shift in the loose semi-compacted ground under the tyres. Fortunately, Piet, being a good driver and one who listens and follows instructions, continued through with his foot pressed firmly down on the throttle.

Although leaving deep tracks through the problem area, he got over safely. He was pleased with himself.

"There we go Piet," I congratulated him, "Well done. Don't you feel better now, having driven through there yourself?" "Ah, Baas. I wasn't really scared, I was just saying so for fun." he said, trying to save face.

"Well, Piet, that's fine. In future when you tell me you are scared I will know it's just for fun. You are now committed to driving up or down, or through anything that comes your way. " I was trying to look serious, but was not being successful. Piet wasn't sure if he should laugh or cry.

It was crunch time. Would there be any more movement in the back fill? How much damage had the Bedford truck caused to the supporting rocks? Could there be a total collapse?

While I had been up on top calling for the Bedford to come through, and taking note of any change or movement in the surface, Peter had gone down the bank a little way to see if there was any movement in the rocks or back fill on the left side leading down to the open wash away. He had assured me that all was fine on that front. With both of us confident that the repair work was in fact compacted enough for the equipment to pass, the decision was made to go ahead.

Chapter 36

Climbing into the driver's seat of the big truck I called for Major, who now happily jumped up into the cab. I started the engine. Due to an air leak in the air lines I had to run the motor for some time to build up the air pressure again to disable the safety automatic lock on the rear brakes. It works well unless the truck has a flat battery. Then a tow bar or chain can't be fixed to the front to pull-start it because the brakes would be locked. In a situation like that, it would be a real mission to manually loosen the brakes. Today, at least, we didn't have that problem.

Eventually the safety blow-off valve went off with a loud hiss, letting me know that the air pressure had built up to the correct pressure. As I approached the questionable area, I felt an imaginary something on my left shoulder telling me to go for it, and another imaginary something on my right shoulder warning me it was not a good idea. However, having already committed myself I went with the prompt from my left shoulder and accelerated into the back fill.

Peter was standing on the other side where I had been when the Bedford came over, urging me to keep pushing through. My heart sank as I felt an obvious drop on entering the back fill. But I was at the point of no return and I stood on the throttle. It was, after all, a short section that would just take a few seconds to get through.

I instinctively knew I was in trouble, but kept my foot down, with the engine screaming. Just a few more seconds and I would be safely through to the other side. The sudden jolting stop and inconceivable listing over to the left blew this possibility out of the window.

Knowing what was awaiting the truck and equipment if it toppled to the left, I immediately took my foot off the throttle and slammed the clutch in with my left foot. My thinking being stopping the wheel spin and shuddering of the truck it would be more stable and hopefully keep standing with wheels on the ground as opposed to rolling down the mountain.

Major stood up on the seat to see what the sudden stop was about. Thoughts flashed through my mind at the speed of light. I was shocked by how far over the truck was listing. What was holding it up? For how long could it hold? If I were to get out would my weight leaving the right side of the truck be enough to make it topple over down the mountainside? What was the right thing to do? Was there a right thing to do?

My stomach was hollow. I had made the decision to go for it and I had driven the truck into this disastrous situation. Are Major and I going to get out of this alive? If we do, will I be looking for a new career?

Once this story got around the drilling industry, about how I wrote off the truck and all the drilling equipment, and also tipped it down the side of a mountain into a ravine where it was impossible to retrieve, there wouldn't be a drilling company anywhere in the world that would hire me. This would not look good on my CV – not only in the drilling world, but probably in any other career. With my mind going into this ballistic mode, I figured that going down with the truck might be the best way to go. You know... like the captain going down with his ship. Then I would be a hero.

Peter, whose fault this was for not fixing the road properly in the first place, was running around like a headless chicken. He was calling for me to jump out before the truck went over the side. He had no heroic visions of me going down with the truck. As gently as possible I opened my door and eased my way out of the truck, closely followed by Major, who made his normal boisterous exit and ran around the front.

I went the opposite way and was shocked to see that the back left wheel was almost over the edge. Fortunately it had settled into a hole left by a large boulder that had dislodged and slid out to the left, wedging itself against another large bolder which had in turn jammed itself against a thin tree. The complete weight of the truck was being held up by a spindly tree. Thank goodness it was there, but how much longer could it resist the force pushing against it? How long before it uprooted, and sent the truck over the edge?

The first thing to be done was to secure the truck to a larger tree on the other side of the road. Then we could lighten the truck by offloading as much as possible. If we were going to get out of here at all, it was not going to be fully loaded. "Peter, have you got a long length chain in your Land Rover?" I shouted urgently. "No, sorry, only the standard tow rope," he shouted back. "Would you like me to bring it?" He was already running to his vehicle. "Yes, please. And attach it to the front of this truck and the tow hitch on the Bedford truck - as fast as you can." My mind was racing over what to do next. "Piet, help him get the tow rope secured in place quickly. We don't have much time."

Things were now desperate. The truck had given a little creek and had moved another inch closer to the drop off. "Once the rope is in place I need you to drive forward gently in your truck to take up the slack on the rope. When it's taught, stop and keep your foot on the brake. Then get someone to put rocks behind the wheels to prevent any movement backwards."

The little tree held firm, as the list of the truck to the left put tremendous pressure against the two supporting rocks and the tree. The hole in which the back left wheel had settled was quite deep, making the situation for the top-heavy truck worse.

"Aaron, get two umgwalas[6] from the back of the Bedford truck and the 14lb hammer, quickly! You are the strongest guy here. I need you to hammer them into the ground firmly next to the rock by the back wheel to help support the weight of the truck and keep the small tree from collapsing." The sweat was pouring off me, and it wasn't caused only by the heat. Aaron came running with the tools and we both went around the truck to implant the umgwalas.

This was a dangerous task. Firstly it was difficult to get a solid footing. We were standing on a steep and slippery embankment. Secondly, once we started hammering in the umgwalas the disturbance could send the whole truck crashing down on top of us. But there was no time to stop and think about the negatives. Our only option was to concentrate on the positives.

Steadying ourselves in place, I held the cut off drill rod next to the rock and on my nod Aaron sent the 14lb hammer crashing down on top of it. It sank in about 2 inches and I kept nodding. Fortunately Aaron kept swinging down the hammer with all his immense strength. Within ten hefty smacks, it was in far enough to hold, while we did the same with the other umgwalas, about 5 inches away from the first one, right up against the same rock. In no time both were well set and secure. It was a huge relief. This eased the situation, but we were still in trouble, however I was confident that we could manage the trouble.

---

[6] Umgwalas. - Old drill rod cut into +- three feet pieces sharpened on one end

"Right, I need all of you to come and off-load the truck. It will not get through fully loaded," I shouted to everyone. We will need to take everything off, except the machine." The machine was too heavy to begin with. If we could not pull the truck out, there had to be a way we could use the winch by attaching the cable to a tree, to pull it up with the hoist.

The labourers began to off-load. The truck stood firm. All the ropes holding the rolls of PVC piping had to be untied and taken around to the front before we could painstakingly unload everything else until there was just the machine left on the back. We even offloaded the water pump by sliding it down two 10ft rods placed against the side of the truck, with the side-door opened.

In spite of the intense increase in heat from the burning sun, I was not sweating nearly as much. I called for the jack to be brought around to the problem wheel so that we could jack it up high enough to slide a rock into the hole underneath the wheel. It would not be possible to drive the truck out, with the wheel tightly jammed into the hole.

The resistance could also cause other problems. The clutch could burn out. The half-shafts could break. That kind of problem would cause long delays. We would have to leave the equipment spread all over the narrow track leading down the escarpment until such time as spares to repair the truck arrived.

"Come, James. This is your truck. Bring the jack and help me sort out this problem." We had a difficult task, because of the angle of the axle.

"Okay, my Baas. What must I do?" he asked, sliding himself and the jack under the truck, where I was. The thought crossed my mind that we were at least lying in the shade. We were in an extremely dangerous position, with one small benefit.

"We need to make sure we have a solid base for the jack. It must not slip. We'll jack the wheel as high as we can and hope that the truck doesn't slip any further sideways."

While we secured the base and started to pump the jack handle, Aaron scrambled around the danger side of the truck. He had found another large rock to place under the wheel, assuming we could jack it up high enough. Sometimes hydraulic jacks can give endless problems, but this one worked like a dream. With creeks and groans, the wheel began to lift out of the hole.

"Piet, I hope your truck has the rope pulled tight. We are so close to getting out of this mess. We don't want to take any chances." "Yes," Peter answered, "it's tight and it's a strong rope."

"Yeah, sure." I scoffed. "You said something similar about this little crossing. It almost cost us our equipment and has certainly lost us two hours, plus the reloading time. That's assuming we get the truck out of here."

I was smiling, knowing I was just as responsible for the mess we were in. I had agreed that we should go for it.

"We can't make it to the new site before dark, so I suggest we plan on camping at the river tonight and continue through tomorrow morning. We've had enough fun for one day." I was trying to be realistic, not negative.

"Yes. You're right. It will give us a chance to have a good clean up in the rapids. I have bathed in them a few times and am still around. It's safe." He smiled broadly, looking forward to a cool swim. The idea appealed to me too. It would be a pleasant break from my tin tub. A constant flow of clean, cold water over my hot, sweaty body sounded like heaven as I lay under the truck on the hot earth trying to jack up the wheel.

Slowly the wheel rose higher and higher until the jack had fully extended itself. It looked somewhat precarious in its fully extended state and I was concerned that it might fall over before Aaron had the rock safely in place under the wheel. But Aaron, being Aaron, had the rock in place in no time at all. Slowly I loosened the release valve to lower the jack. Once the full weight of the truck had been taken by Aaron's rock, I pulled the jack out to allow a bigger rock to be inserted under it. Then we would do the same for the other wheel.

Soon we had the truck standing level. Even with the jack fully removed there was no ground movement at either of the back wheels. The ungwalas had held firm.

"Piet, I'm going to get into my truck and start the engine. Give me a minute or so to build up the air pressure then when I hoot I want you to drive forward and pull me over and out of this mess. I don't want to use the power of the truck unless I have to, as the drive in the rear wheels could de-stabilize the rocks."

"Hey, my Baas. That's a big truck to pull. Are you sure it's a good idea?" he asked in consternation.

"Yes, Piet, it will be fine. With that full load of water you have plenty of traction on your back wheels." Once again, I was trying to convince myself. I was doing a good job of it. "If I see you're struggling then I'll help out this side."

Once the air pressure was right, I signalled and Piet drove off. I followed after like a tame lamb. It was a huge relief. I began planning my new CV to replace the one I had written in my mind three hours ago. It was almost an anti-climax.

All the guys were jumping up and down and shouting with joy, including Peter, the Geo. Once fully back on solid ground, I stopped Piet by applying my brakes. Then I jumped out of the truck and joined the celebrations.

"If we are going to get to the river tonight let's start loading and on our way as soon as possible. We still have a way to go and who knows what lies ahead of us before we get there." We were in high spirits. Everyone got stuck in and in record time everything was back on again and tightly secured. At last we were able to continue our adventure down the pass.

Chapter 37

As we wound our way down deeper into the valley I was in awe of the beauty of the pass. There were deep gorges on one side, with huge granite boulders performing balancing acts to put any circus to shame. They appeared ready to fall, but had been standing that way for millions of years.

Being the end of the dry season, there were few leaves on the trees. Through the heat haze, we could see all the way down into the depths of the valleys. Already we had passed three herds of kudu. One herd had a magnificent bull with abnormally large horns. He proudly showed these off by standing still and looking directly at us. His harem of three females were satisfied with their stud and had no interest in us.

Although the road was steep in places, with sharp bends, we eventually arrived at the Mazoe River late that afternoon. There were no more mishaps. If it hadn't been for our close to disastrous problem earlier, we would have easily made it all the way through to the site. However, we were relieved to have made it down this far and we knew that the worst part of the trip was over.

The next day we had a new challenge to face. We would have to negotiate a tricky section of steep gradient road going up and over the mountain between where we were now and our new drilling site. Going up on this side was going to be bad enough, but going down the other side was seriously steep.

Two questions bothered me. After unloading at our new site, would the empty truck make it up and over the pass on its way back to Salisbury. And even more important, once we had completed the contract, would we be able to drive the fully loaded truck back up and over the pass?

But all we had to do now was to put up out tents and settle down for the night. We may have managed well without tents for one night. But with all the wild animals in the area, it would not have been wise to sleep in the open. Being taken by a leopard, stood on by an elephant, trampled by a hippo or having a snake join us on our stretcher were not experiences we would relish. It was wiser to spend some time putting up our tents. Without exception, we were all excited to arrive at our destination, but we were also desperately in need of a bath.

"Well done to all of you," I said. "It's great to have arrived here safely and if we hadn't had that problem earlier, the trip would have been boring." This got everyone laughing, as we set about putting our tents up before going for a swim in the river.

I had given the instruction that nobody was to go into the river until Peter and I had checked it out for crocodiles.

"Trust me," I emphasised, "It hurts like hell when they bite you." This produced more laughter. It was good to see the guys in high spirits.

It wasn't long and all the tents were offloaded and erected. I pitched my tent under a beautiful big tree close to the water where there was a little green grass. I was thinking irrationally. We were spending just one night there. So shade wasn't a consideration. What I should have asked myself was: Who eats grass at night?

The tents were up, wood for the fire had been collected and we all set off down to the river. It was a stunning area with a long section of rapids from bank to bank with water frothing and foaming as it rushed through the rocks, instantly calming as it ran into a large, deep pool. Even though the water flowed fairly quickly through the pool there was little sign of movement. Straight after the pool the river made a sharp right turn with a high sheer cliff on the outside of the turn, having been slowly cut away over the years of constant flow.

On our side the vegetation was thick with large trees and far greener than the top of the pass where we had just come from. The opposite side of the river was quite a contrast with a white sand bank running at least 100m back from the river and sweeping all the way around the bend. This had been caused by the water moving far slower on the inside of the bend and slowly silting up with sand over the years. The river joined the mighty Zambezi River, some fifty five miles away just below Tete in Mozambique, and then on down to the sea.

There was no sign of crocodiles on the sand bank or anywhere else for that matter. I was not sure if this was good or bad as far as bathing in the river was concerned, because, if they were not on the sand bank where were they? We knew there were many there as we had seen them on my site visit with Peter earlier. I was slightly concerned and would not have been persuaded to go into the main pool for any amount of money, but I felt the rapids would be safe.

"Okay, guys, let's go and have a bath. You must all stay in the rapids though and although I'm sure it's safe, you must stay alert."

I stripped off naked and taking my soap and shampoo with me I waded out into the water, followed closely by Major. I started soaping myself all over and washing my hair. When nothing came out to attack either Major or me, everyone followed my example and came rushing into the water. There was boisterous singing and shouting, basically to make as much noise as possible, more to frighten away the crocodiles than anything else. The problem was, however, that, if anything, it would more likely alert the crocs to a possible food source.

It felt so good to not only cool off, but also to thoroughly clean myself from head to toe. All the guys were doing the same including Peter and by the time we came out of the river we were all squeaky clean. When you say 'good and clean and fresh', believe me it had nothing on how we all felt. All that was needed now was a large venison steak and sudza, followed by a good night's sleep. Once we had all eaten I called to the guys, telling them to sleep well as we had another long day ahead of us.

So much for sleeping well, just after 4.00am I woke up with something brushing up against my tent and making ominous crunching sounds. Due to the heat I had left the front and back flaps open. Major lay in the opening looking alert and growling softly.

I moved up next to him and stroked him on the head to keep him calm. It amazed me how he seemed to know that whatever it was out there, it would not be a good idea to go charging out after them. Peering out around the corner of the tent in the direction of the crunching sounds all I could see was an enormous black shape moving slowly. It then struck me how stupid I was to select this grassy patch for my tent. Looking around, my eyes grew accustomed to the dark, and I realised my tent was surrounded by hippos munching my grass. I knew stats that hippos are responsible for more human deaths that all other animals put together. This was not a good fact to pop into my head right then.

What to do was the question on my mind? Do I shout for help, or would this alert the hippo to think they were in danger and cause them to attack the tent where the shouting came from? As I watched I sensed they were not actually at all interested in my tent, so I decided that if Major and I kept calm and quiet and left them alone they would move off to a new patch of grass once they had finished cutting my lawn. Normally I would have wanted Major running out and chasing off whatever animal was out there, but, now I held him, stroking him and talking quietly to him. He seemed to understand that bravery, or, more accurately, stupidity was not the way to go here. Instead he gave my face a sloppy kiss with his tongue.

It was starting to get light, the hippo became easier to see as I watched, and, as I hoped, moved along, interested only in eating the grass. Eventually they were well away from my tent and heading back towards the river. Once there was movement from the other tents with the guys coming out to start a new day, the hippo walked a bit faster towards the river.

It had been a scary experience, but in some way also a special one. Now that they were almost into the river, Major ran out and barked loudly at them as if to say: You guys are bloody lucky I let you go. He then came back wagging his tail: Gee, Dad did you see how I chased those fat slobs away?

Chapter 38

By 6.30am we were packed up and on the final four mile leg of our journey. The track we followed was new and only recently cut by hand so it had many twists and turns as it wound around large trees, so much so, in fact, that I jokingly asked Peter if his guys had been drunk when cutting the road. Along the route we had to stop every now and then to clear more space through the bush to get the trucks through.

Approaching the short steep pass, to avoid possible problems I decided to connect Peter's tow rope between his Land Rover and the Morris truck and have James help pull me up the slope.

It sounds silly having a small Land Rover pulling this fully loaded 8 ton truck up the mountain, but in effect I would be using my power for 90% of the climb and James pulling in 4 wheel drive up front would just give me that extra help to ensure I had enough power to get over the top.

Once the rope was connected we headed on up the mountain and, although he was obviously pulling all the time to keep the rope tight up front, I felt I could have managed without his help. Fortunately the Morris had amazing pulling power.

On safely reaching the summit we stopped and removed the rope. It was steep down the other side. Once again I selected low gear and using engine and exhaust braking where necessary managed to get safely down the other side. One mile away from the pass, Peter, at the rear of the convoy, flashed his lights for us to stop. We had arrived at the site we had all talked about for the last few months. We were in the Ruangwa Valley at last.

"Well!" exclaimed Peter as we climbed out of our vehicles and looked around, "This is it. This is where the notorious Ruangwa Drilling Project will take place. What do you think?"

Strangely, it felt like an anti climax. The terrain was similar to the bushveld in most other places I had worked. It didn't feel wild, remote and uncharted - as we had conjured up in our excited conversations. It felt familiar, like I had been here before, like I knew it. I experienced a strange feeling of having waited for this place my whole life. Everything I had ever done or been, or ever thought or looked for, led up to and ended here in this moment - here, in this patch of bushveld in the Ruangwa Valley.

Shaking myself out of this pensive musing, I said, "Come on, Peter, show us around. Show us the camp site, the drill sites and the water source. We're ready to get going."

Firstly, we looked for a good camp site, as close to water as possible. There was an area with three medium to large trees supplying a fair amount of shade to an area of about ten square yards and only about fifty metres from the river. This, I decided, would be my camp site.

Two hundred yards downstream and also close to the water was another area with more trees giving a much larger area of shade which would be ideal for all the staff tents. Shade was important. We would need relief from the furnace-like heat. The heat in the area from which we had just come was indescribable, and I could already feel that it was a lot hotter here.

Being the dry season, the water in the river was hardly flowing at all, and had not been for some time. However, close to where we had camped the night before, there was water trickling steadily from one large pool into another on its way down to join the Mazoe River. This indicated clean water that, once boiled, would be fine for human consumption. As far as we could see, all the way down the river were clumps of trees, thriving and green, flourishing close to a water source. The clumps of trees we had chosen for our camp was ideal. They were at the centre of the already marked out drill sites. There was easy access from both campsites.

Having decided on where we were going to live, the next thing was to see the sites of the holes to be drilled. "Depending on the results we get," explained Peter, "some of these site positions could change," "That's no problem," I said. "All I ask is, if they change, try to keep them as close to the water as possible. It would save a lot of time, and avoid breakdowns, if we could pump water to the sites rather than carting it in by truck."

Luckily, all the sites were close to the water source and the piping we had brought with us would easily reach most of them. Everything was falling into place and I looked forward to an interesting and successful project.

Now it was offloading time and the first thing we needed to do was set up camp. After that was done, we would get to setting up the rig and begin drilling.

The guys were in good spirits and worked fast and efficiently. In a few hours the campsite was ready. Clever, the cook, was left to clear my site and the camp lady named Mudiwa translated meaning '*Loved one*' set about clearing the team's camp site of dry grass, branches, sticks and stones.

She was a boon to the team. She did all the cooking, cleaning and other "household" chores. This made it possible for the crew to give their full attention to the job. She was one of the reasons I was happy to be away from their campsite. I bathed out in the open in my little tin tub and needed privacy. However, being isolated could make me more vulnerable to the wild animals in the area. But, of course, I had Major to protect me. I was safe.

Close to the first drill site there was a wash away that could, without too much extra work, be made into a useful ramp for off-loading all the drilling equipment. Peter had his team digging the ramp while my team offloaded the drill rods, shear legs and other lighter equipment. The excitement was apparent. We soon had everything off loaded. The truck driver was anxious to return to head office, but, it being late afternoon, I told him to rest and leave early the next morning, and that we would accompany him until he was safely up and over the top of the pass.

Once everything had been off-loaded we headed off to sort out our individual tents. Clever had cleared my area of grass, dry sticks and small stones. It looked spick and span. There was no chance I would have the problem of a rock or stick under the ground sheet. He had also cleared the area where he would do the cooking. By 5.30pm we had roughly finished sorting out our campsites and all had a place to sleep that night.

Chapter 39

Picking up my .22 rifle and beaming from ear to ear with excitement, I called to Peter.

"I'm going to show you how to go rifle fishing. I saw bream in the river. It will give us a change of diet from the meat we eat seven days a week." With a look of surprise on his face Peter said "I didn't see fish in the pools and how do you shoot fish?"

"Come, look and learn. It takes a good driller to teach a geologist a thing or two about life." I thought that was amusing, and laughed. Peter, on the other hand, didn't smile, but followed me down to the pools without saying a word. I imagined him thinking "You smart-arse young drillers think you know everything."

As we came close to the pools I signalled for Peter to walk slowly and be quiet so as not to chase the fish away. I hoped they were still swimming near the surface. I spotted the slow movement of their dorsal fins gliding through the water. It was a fairly big shoal of large bream. I stood still and motioned for Peter to do the same. Smoothly lifting the rifle to my shoulder I fired off four quick shots operating the pump action on the rifle as fast as I could. Having used the rifle hundreds of times, I knew it well and could shoot accurately. The concussion of the bullets hitting the water caused the fish to panic. They raced in different directions, sending off waves of ripples in ever-enlarging circles.

Once the ripples settled, we were amazed to see three dead bream. Like two little kids who just caught their first fish, we retrieved them with a long stick found close by. To be honest, they were the first fish I had ever shot, so there was reason to be excited.

"Next time you go into Salisbury, please remember to bring back all my fishing tackle. There will also be large barbel in the pools. The guys will like that. It will help cut back on the hunting I have to do for meat." I was excited about this new-found source of food.

In a short time I had filleted the three fish, giving us six thick fish fillets cleaned and ready to cook. Clever, in the mean time cut potatoes into thin strips to make chips. He had the fire going with the oiled frying pan over it and was soon battering the fillets with flour. They sizzled and spat as he placed them in the hot cooking oil and within a few moments there was the delicious smell of frying fish. The chips were fried in a separate pan.

We hadn't eaten all day, and were famished. Bream is one of the nicest tasting fresh water fish, but out there in the bush it tasted better than any fish I had ever eaten. When we were done, Peter had a satisfied expression on his face. "That was good! I will not forget to bring your fishing equipment. You have never been keen on hunting, and I know nothing about fishing. I'll make a deal with you. When possible, how about I supply you with meat from game I shoot, and in return you supply me with fish?"

Readily I agreed. "Who said life was going to be tough out here?" I laughed, and felt completely relaxed. By this time dusk was falling. The orange glow of the setting sun had almost faded. For that night, Peter would use my tent and camp bed, and I would sleep in the truck.

"Hey, us drillers need to look after you geo's." We both laughed. "Right, we have another long day tomorrow. I think we should hit the sack."

Swallowing the last few mouthfuls of my Coke I went off to clean my teeth and wash my face. Having arrived so late we were going to have to go to bed as we were. In the morning I would sort out bathing facilities. I was too tired to be concerned about it then.

Chapter 40

I was up early, before sunrise. First thing I got the fire going for coffee. I had not slept at all well in the truck and desperately needed a caffeine boost. I could hear gentle snoring from the tent. Peter had obviously had a good night. Clever, having seen me making the fire was over to my site in a flash. He had water in the kettle and was stoking the fire for more heat. In no time the water had boiled.

Once I had a cup of coffee, I decided to leave Peter sleeping and walked over to where we had off-loaded. The guys were already there, sorting out the hoist cable to pull the machine to the site.

With a reliable team like this, regardless of conditions and hardships, we would go the whole way on this contract, efficiently. It felt good to be young, fit, enthusiastic, confident and cocky.

"Morning guys, I hope you all slept well and are ready to get going?" I was happy, and smiled from ear to ear. The excitement of at last being here in the valley had set in.

"Yes, my Baas. We were fine after we got used to the new sounds of animals in the bush around the campsite. We were all scared. " said Aaron. I could not deny that there had been new night sounds breaking the quiet of the African bush.

I sent the driver off in the Morris truck, explaining to him that the geologist would also be leaving later. If there were any problems he was to sit tight until Peter arrived. He was happy to get going on his way back to civilization.

While Thousand saw to pulling the machine, the pump and timbers across to the new site, Aaron and I carried the rolls of PVC down to the river where we would lay the piping to supply water to both the camps and to the drill site, using tee-pieces where necessary. Once that was complete and the piping connected to the pump, we tested the system. It worked. This was going to be a lot easier than carting water by truck.

I joined Thousand, who had made good progress with pulling the equipment to the site. Within an hour everything was ready to start the process of rigging, and digging the water sumps. Peter had, in the mean time, surfaced from my tent and made coffee. He sauntered over to see how things were going.

"Afternoon, Peter. Did you sleep well?" He ignored my sarcasm. By 2.30pm, the water sump had been completed and splash cemented. By 5.00pm it would be dry enough to take water.

Once again, as specified, we rigged the drill up at 45°. We were ready to go. Aaron started the water pump which filled the sump. Before it filled I was excited and surprised to see Gus's Land Rover arrive on site. It was really good to see him climb out and walk over to us. We get on extremely well and it's always good to have him come to site. I walked over to meet him. "Hi Gus what a nice surprise."

"Thought I should come down and see if you guys are doing any work down here" he said with a smile. "It's one hell of a road down that pass, how on earth did you manage to get the trucks to site?"

"Well to say the least, it wasn't easy, but hey, we made it safely and are looking forward to get going." I replied.

Peter and his guys left to get back to their camp before dark. Going up the pass in the day was bad enough. At night it was not a good idea. We looked forward to seeing him again in a week or so.

"Yes I was happy to see the driver had managed to climb the pass with no real problems on his way back but he tells me there were a few anxious moments fully loaded on the way down?" he said with a concerned look on his face.

"Oh, nothing serious just came to within a whisker of rolling your truck down the side of the mountain together with all the equipment." I replied with a wry smile.

"Well thank heavens you are here safe and sound, you can tell me the story over a steak tonight, looks like you are ready to go?" Produce and then talk was always his motto and I felt the same way.

Sarcastically I replied "Well if not for your arrival I would have drilled down a couple of feet by now." He jokingly slapped me on the back and said "Well in that case let's go and get the chuck spinning."

The sump was full by this stage and I was able to drill down to ten feet and install the stand pipe. This time, unlike the problem encountered on the previous drill site that took three days due to the sand and boulders, this overburden was cased off and complete by 6.30pm. The surface overburden had been made safe. We were ready to drill in the NX casing first thing in the morning. Satisfied with the day's progress we shut down for the night.

"You guys have done well getting everything down here and rigged up in so short a time. I was expecting problems and delays. But here we are, rigged up with the stand pipe in place."

Fortunately he had brought a tent and stretcher for himself to sleep on and in a short time Clever and the guys had it up and ready for occupation. I was pleased to know there would be no need for me to spend a night in my Land Rover which would have been even more uncomfortable than the truck I slept in last night.

From the next day we would begin our sixteen to eighteen hour daily shifts that would become the norm until the contract was completed.

Chapter 41

That night, in our new camp, was rather daunting. At around 11.00pm I was woken by a strange sound. I cleared my head from a deep sleep. Major was sitting bolt upright at the front opening of the tent. I was never quite sure why he always slept there. Was it because it was cooler there, or did he want to stop any danger that might threaten to come in? He was emitting a low growl. For a few seconds I lay listening hard. The night was silent. What had woken me? Then it came again - a soft coughing sound. What was that? Then it came again. Major was tense and alert. My nerve-ends were tingling.

I was not sure whether to go for the gun or the torch. I chose the torch, thinking that unless I could see what was out there, I would not know whether to shoot. Silently I slithered out of bed and, armed with a torch in one hand and holding Major with the other, I sat at the open tent door, listening.

All I heard were the normal sounds of the night. A cricket was grinding away with his loud chirruping sound that was enough to keep anyone awake. Here and there a night-bird chirped or called. I was listening for the other sound. It had not been a vicious, dangerous sound. But it was a chilling-the-spine kind of sound.

Suddenly there was a distinct scratching noise. In a flash the torch was on, and the ray of light caught the animal climbing up a tree no more than fifty paces from the tent. Yellow eyes flashed back at me, and I saw the yellow body and black spots of a fully grown leopard. What could I do? I could not shoot. Having just been through the tragic experience with Peter, I was not prepared to even consider shooting. But we could also be in real danger.

Major, for all his brute strength and bravery seemed to know he should stay with me, and not go bounding out after the animal. He stood up, looking straight out at the leopard with all his muscles taught and his body shivering in anticipation.

The hair on his back stood upright in a stripe, all the way down to his tail. All he needed was a nudge, and he would be at the tree in a flash. I spoke softly, trying to calm him down. If he went out there, he would be killed. Fortunately, his protective instincts for me were more powerful than the urge to chase. He relaxed and sat down, letting me know he wasn't going anywhere.

The thought flashed through my mind that a vicious attack from Major could surprise and panic the leopard. It might leap from the tree and escape from the danger presented by Major, and disappear into the bush. But it was a chance I couldn't take.

Was there just the one leopard? Was he here with his mate? If there were two of them, were they on the prowl for food? My head was in a whirl. I didn't know what to do next.

Calling to Gus, or shouting to my guys for help was not a good idea. Firstly, the guys were two hundred yards away and had they known of the leopard, coming unarmed to my aid would not be helpful. Gus's tent was behind mine. He was asleep and would wake with a start.

If there were to be any sudden action, the animal could attack me, Gus, or one of my guys?. As I sat there, my brain was on a mission for a solution, and no answers were being found.

I decided that if I left it alone, let it check us out and see that we were of no threat, it might return the favour. As convincingly as I could, I told myself that human flesh would not be its first choice. In this remote area it would not have encountered humans before. This was his territory. We were invading his space temporarily. There was no reason to fear him, or for him to fear us.

I turned the torch off and climbed back into bed. Major came and lay beside me. I had peace of mind, knowing he could and would protect me. I scratched and stroked his head until I eventually fell asleep.

At 5.00am I was up and immediately went over to the leopard's tree. There, clearly, were its footprints. The night visit wasn't a dream. I returned to my tent to find Gus climbing out of his.

"Morning Gus, how was your night, I hope you slept well?" "I had a good night, but woke once to a strange sound." He was trying to flatten his hair which was standing up in all directions. "Hope you also had a good night?"

"Well yes, but also a bit unnerving." I told him what had happened. "Wow I wouldn't have thought a leopard would come in that close. Are you sure you weren't dreaming?" "I wondered about that too. When I woke, I went to check the area and found leopard footprints."

After drinking our morning coffee, we set off to the machine. As normal I never wore a shirt – just boots, socks and shorts. It was too hot to wear a shirt. My skin tanned dark, and my hair bleached by the sun. Nor did I wear or even own a hard hat. Personnel Protection Equipment (PPE) was non-existent back then. In that heat, the other workers wore full overalls. Considering the amount of time we spent in the area, and the absence of PPE, it's quite remarkable that there was not a single injury. We all knew how to handle the equipment, and worked with efficiency and attention to safety.

When we arrived at the drill site, the guys were busy going through the machine and pump prestart procedure checks. I wondered whether to tell them of the night visitor. They were already nervous. They could put their tools down and demand that Gus take them back to civilization and away from the wild animals.

I asked if they had a good night. They were all happy and unaware of the leopard's visit. I was relieved to know that. I decided to say nothing of the leopard. But, as always I warned them to take care, and to keep their eyes open for any possible dangers like snakes, scorpions or anything else. I also told them that if they needed to go out to relieve themselves during the night, they should take a torch.

Aaron, however, was not only big, strong and, I would imagine, brave if the need arose. He was also smart. He came over and quietly asked, "Hey, Baas, did something happen last night? You seem to be a bit on edge. You are not normally like this." "Yes, Aaron, something did happen. But I don't want the others to know about it. I will tell you about it later when we are alone." I knew I should tell him as at least one responsible person should know of the possible dangers of a leopard in the campsites at night. But right then, we needed to get on with the job of drilling holes.

By that evening, Gus was happy with how we were getting on with drilling, and early the next morning he left for Mavurodona.

Chapter 42

I could only drill the BX casing to forty feet, as I had already drilled into solid granite. I had securely tightened a casing shoe to the bottom of the casing before inserting it just in case we might need to ream[7] at a later stage. I lowered the BX core barrel which would be used to drill a 2 ½" core sample to drill hole completion. We had full water return. This saved us from having to continually pump from the river. It reduced the need for rod grease as water, to some extent, acts as a lubricant. This also allowed for the use of soluble oil to be mixed with the water which works effectively as cutting oil. It helps both in penetration rates and bit life when drilling into hard formations, as we had here.

Granites and gneisses are hard and we had to drill through it to get to the target depth. The expected host rock for the ore would be amphibolites. Expected formations, including any fault zones, are determined through the initial geological trench soil sampling. Extensive geological mapping included detailing hanging and footwall formations situated above and below the anticipated ore zone.

As long as there were no major fault zones at depth, the general dip angle of the formation can be fairly accurately planned. This involves the angle of the drilling. The ideal intersection angle for the drill bit to penetrate the strata is 90°. So, for example, if the surface trenching showed a dip angle of 45°, the drill would be collared at a similar angle from the opposite side.

Peter was a good geologist and had performed extensive geological work in the valley so, within reason, his estimate of the target depth should be accurate. He had told me to expect 'pay dirt', as he called it, at around the six hundred and fifty foot mark.

We had already filled the core barrel twice and had completed twenty feet. I set about drilling the third run into the solid gneiss. My

---

[7] Ream: To drill the hole bigger to insert casing

happy mood was suddenly snapped by a commotion behind the machine, close to the back shear leg. I turned to see Major spinning in circles with what I thought was a young crocodile hanging onto his throat. I pulled in the clutch to stop the rods spinning in the hole and ran over to where this extraordinary scene was taking place.

The seeming monster had managed to leap up and bite into Major's throat just below his jaw line. More out of frustration than pain, Major was making a loud snarling sound, somewhere between a growl and a squeal. As hard as he tried he could not get a grip on this monster that had attacked him. Had he stopped spinning he could have got a grip on the back end of the body, but he was bent on trying to spin it off his neck. On closer inspection I was surprised to see it was not a crocodile, but a large monitor lizard. It was by far the biggest one I had ever seen. It was also the last one Major wanted to see.

It was difficult to intervene. He kept spinning with the gruesome looking thing hanging on. The other guys were of no help, as they were superstitiously terrified of any creature like this one. They have many such superstitions and are even afraid of the harmless chameleon. Also, they were fully aware of Major's incredible strength. If he was unable to get rid of this vicious thing, how could they help?

My concern grew. I had no idea how much damage the gruesome creature's mouth could cause to Major's throat. I remembered being told that a monitor lizard had the filthiest of mouths, which could cause terrible infection. I shouted to Clever to come quickly with my rifle.

Without thinking about the consequences of my actions, I rushed in and grabbed the lizard by the tail as he swung in an arch through the air past me. It had a terrible scaly feel to it which made me want to let go immediately, but, being desperate to help Major, I clung on as tightly as I could.

This not only stopped Major spinning, but panicked the lizard. He let go and spun around to bite me. I, in turn, went into panic mode and I heaved with all the power I could muster. Using his weight and the spinning action of a discus thrower, I spun and sent him flying through the air.

To my astonishment, before he had even hit the ground, Major, enraged to the point of hysteria, caught him in a flash, in mid air, and had him firmly held in his powerful jaws. He held his formidable opponent firmly just behind the head. The monitor thrashed violently from side to side with powerful swishes of his long tail, trying desperately to free itself from his steely grip.

The weight of the lizard was about 50 lb and yet Major was shaking it from side to side like a rag doll. The lizard was extremely resilient. When Major stopped shaking him for a second, he continued writhing, shaking and hissing with his long tongue flashing and spittle frothing from his mouth.

It was quite a shock to think that just five minutes ago all was quiet and orderly, with everything going along just fine, when - out of nowhere - we suddenly found ourselves in the middle of this pandemonium. Major continued thrashing his head from side to side over and over again, not for a second losing his grip on the back of the lizard's head. He gave the impression that his locked jaw would never come open again.

The strength of the lizard was also impressive. I had come across them many times, but hadn't realised how powerful and aggressive they could become. They usually scurried away, doing no more than flashing their forked tongue. None of us had any idea what happened to cause the amazing performance we were witnessing. Most probably, Major being his inquisitive self, had annoyed the lizard to the extent that he attacked. However, right now, the cause was immaterial. What was important was how was I going to change the situation?

In the mean time, Clever came running up to the rig with my rifle. I took it from him, but didn't know what to do. There was so much energy and jerking movement from the fighters, I couldn't shoot and be sure of not hitting Major. If they would just settle down for a few seconds it would give me a chance to aim and fire.

I was no longer concerned about further injury to Major. He had things under control. But I was concerned about the injury already inflicted to his throat. I walked right up to him and when he saw me so close he gave one more violent shake of his head. This seemed to do the trick as when he stopped, the lizard was at last motionless. Sensing that the end was near, Major put in one last effort, shaking his quarry with a purpose seemingly to separate the vile thing's head from its body.

The monitor lay motionless. Major seemed satisfied the fight was over and released his grip on its neck and took a step back. He stood looking at it as if to say, "Come on. Try your luck again and see what happens when I really get angry." I immediately took the opportunity and shot it clean through the head. The only movement was from the impact of the bullet striking the hard skull. I was sure he was dead even before I pulled the trigger.

Normality returned. I asked Aaron to take the lizard into the bush and leave the body there for the carnivores to eat. It would make a good meal for a leopard, a black backed jackal or even for vultures.

I called Major, who responded immediately, coming up to show off his injuries. It was worse than I had imagined. He had lost a chunk of skin below his jaw. It looked raw and painful. I realised immediately that he would be unable to lick it and keep it clean during the healing period. With Major in tow I went to my tent to fetch the bottle of Detol Sally had kindly given to me the last time I was at the farm. She had also given me a bottle of Mercurochrome which I now dug out of our pathetic first aid kit.

As I washed the wound with the Detol in my bid to stave off infection I was surprised at how docile and submissive my wounded friend was. Once the Detol had dried off I applied a liberal amount of the red Mercurochrome. I repeated this treatment every day for the next few days. Being as fit and healthy as he was, within a week Major was completely on the mend and safe from the dreaded infection. My relief was immense.

Chapter 43

By now it was mid morning. The heat threatened to melt our bodies. It hung like a weight on the shoulders and came rising up from the scorched ground. Throughout the day, we all drank gallons of boiled water. The water from the stream was good, with the side effect of keeping us regular which was better than being constipated.

We were all losing weight, but we were fit and healthy. We were in a great place, away from the temptation of fast foods. Our diet consisted of sudza, tinned peas, beans and venison. This diet, which may sound dull to adventurous eaters, was obviously not doing any of us any harm.

Working eighteen hour days, we completed our first hole within three weeks. Eighteen hour work days were easier to achieve than one might imagine. The heat built up in the tents to almost oven temperatures during the day lasted well into the night, making sleeping before midnight impossible. Also, being out in the bush with no distractions or temptations, there was nothing else to do anyway. Hard work was the only bridge between boredom and sanity.

The leopard continued his nightly visits. At the beginning I had been concerned, but he didn't bother any of us. I began to take his visits for granted and on the few occasions that he didn't arrive, I actually felt disappointed. His demeanour was never threatening. He seemed to be curious about these humans who had arrived in his territory. We didn't disturb him, and he returned the favour.

I never saw him in daylight. By the time I came out of my tent, before sunrise each day, he had gone. Where he went, what he did - who knows? We had a night-time bonding and I didn't have to worry about feeding him. How many people get to enjoy such a pet?

To add to the excitement of the leopard's appearances, on many occasions when I came out of my tent early in the morning, the cleared swept area around my tent was covered in elephant foot prints. I never heard them. Nor did Major even bark. Even if he didn't hear them, surely he could smell them? Yet he left them alone to go about their business. It's astonishing that such animals can move soundlessly in the dark, without even bumping my tent, or stepping on a guy rope. I began to take the elephant visits for granted as well. I was not concerned for my safety. They felt like part of my group of unusual pets.

Nature is magnificent. Being a long-standing visitor in wild, unspoiled Africa I got to appreciate how special it was. It was a rare privilege to be part of this world, and to be treated with respect by its inhabitants.

Our basic wages were not great, but our final cheque was dependent on our production. The production bonus was based on the total feet drilled each month. It was well geared to be an incentive to put in as much drilling time as possible. It progressively increased at each 180' drilled beyond 400'. Each time we exceeded the progressive targets, the new bonus value would revert back to 0'. It was therefore definitely to our advantage to put in the time to achieve as much production as possible. This also applied to all of my crew, and we were all happy to put in the hours. Overtime was never an issue as we were paid for the extra hours via the bonus scheme. At the end of the day, we were not just working under hard conditions to get the drilling done, but also to make as much money as we could.

In turn the company we worked for was not in the exploration business because it was a good idea. Ultimately they also wanted to make money. The equation was simple. The higher our rate of production, the higher the profit margins each month. It was really a win-win situation for everyone. Or, should I say for those who were prepared to work.

For this month we had a week to move the rig to the new site and drill the hole down to one hundred and fifty feet to make the magic number of one thousand feet for the month, which was the next bonus increase. Needless to say, we worked hard and had the machine moved in record time.

Whilst drilling the first hole, instead of allowing my crew to sit in the shade of a tree whilst I operated the rig. I had them digging the new water sump at our next site. I only needed their help once the core barrel was full and we had to pull all the rods out of the hole. This gave them time to prepare the new site saving at least one day during our move. By the end of the month we had the new hole down to one hundred and eighty feet. We were all excited about our achievement, so much so that I stopped the rig, had the crew clean it quickly, and told them I was going to give us all a treat.

I rushed back to my camp to get my soap and towel and got them to do the same. I was confident that the supply of Cokes, cigarettes and bullets I had ordered through Peter, the geologist, would arrive the next day as promised.

I loaded up the last half case of Cokes and the two packets of cigarettes together with the few rounds I had left in the breach of my rifle. I was elated. This was the first time I had ever been on a machine that had drilled 1,000 feet in a month and we were going to have a party down at the Mozoe River to celebrate.

There was real excitement in the camp. Everyone was rushing and bustling, getting organised to leave. Like a bunch of kids setting off for the beach, we climbed onto the Land Rover and headed for the river, with Major sitting in the front between Aaron and me. Even he had an excited look on his face. After working as hard as we had, seven days a week, we were going to make the most of this break. It would be a one-day de-stress therapy.

Our trip down to the river was uneventful, apart from the section of road that had been closed off by elephants. They were not happy with our movement through the area and on a number of occasions they pushed trees over the road. This time, however, I had helpers to clear the road. The guys were a bit nervous about the possibility of the elephants still being close by. They wouldn't be happy about us moving their trees around. But, with much encouragement, we cleared enough space to get through. From there it was one more mile to the river. We arrived safely without interference from the elephants.

We set about making a big fire, ensuring it was well away from any brush that could catch alight. "Aaron," I said, "Major and I are going off to look for our lunch. Please come with us." Taking my rifle out from behind the seat, making sure the safety catch was on, I asked Aaron to hold it for me and the three of us headed off in the vehicle. We had only travelled about half a mile when Aaron spotted a duiker standing in the shade of a tree. It was only one hundred and fifty feet off the road so I quickly took the rifle from him and, pointing through the open window on Aaron's side, shot it through the head.

We leapt out of the car and ran over, with Major being much faster than either of us, getting there first. He gave the animal a good shake by the throat to make sure it would not run away. Aaron, with no effort at all, lifted the animal and swung it over his powerful shoulders and carried it back to the vehicle, where he carefully laid it in the back.

We were away for only about 15 minutes. The guys were impressed and had a good fire going in anticipation of our celebration. Wood to make the fire was readily available as dry logs and dead branches lay scattered around all over the place.

In no time at all, two of my labourers, Thousand and James, had the duiker's back feet tied together and hanging from a tree. From this position they cut the throat first to bleed the animal. Next they sliced the stomach open with all the entrails squishing and plopping out onto a piece of plastic brought for this purpose. The liver and kidneys were delicacies and these were carefully laid to one side to be cooked over the coals. The remaining part of the stomach would be left for scavengers. The skinning process always impressed me. It was quick and efficient. While all this was going on the rest of us went down to the rapids.

What a life! It felt good to get into the cool water and sit submerged up to my neck. Knowing the only humans for miles around were my guys, made me feel immensely peaceful. The rapids led into a large pool some twenty yards from where I was sitting in the rapids. In this pool there were many hippos who, at regular intervals, popped their heads out of the water in a shower of spray and made that weirdly beautiful grunting, popping sound that only a hippo can make. On the right hand side was a sand bank with two massive crocodiles sunning themselves, one with his mouth wide open, getting the full warmth of the sun.

The possibility of there being another crocodile stalking us somewhere in the rapids didn't cross my mind. Major had always been interested in hippos and jumped up to face them whenever they came up for air. I wondered if he knew that the mass that came out of the water was just the head. Did he know that the body was still hidden under the water? In the not too distant future he would find out just how big they are, at close range, and quite dramatically.

Eventually, having sat in the water for long enough, I splashed my way out onto the bank and went to see how the guys were getting on with lunch preparations. Seeing a few good and well cut steaks set aside for all of us to enjoy today really had my mouth watering. The eyes most certainly enhance the hunger pains. The remaining meat was then cut into thin long strips for ease of hanging at the camp. This method for preserving meat worked well. Although it didn't look great after a day or two of hanging, once cooked up it was delicious.

The fire was ready. Having burned down sufficiently to produce beautiful glowing coals to cook on, Clever, being the official chef, was given the responsibility of preparing and cooking the steaks for us. Once he had finished doing the steaks he opened up the large pot of sudza, and a smaller pot of tasty gravy. We all got stuck in, eating out of the same pot with our hands, in typical African tradition. We took a chunk of sudza from the pot, rolled it into a ball, dipped it into the gravy and popped it into our mouths, together with a chunk of meat.

It was as good a meal as I have ever had. Our eating in this rough and remote area with such guests made the food even more delicious. The bond we had established in our time down here was special. In "civilization" back then, the colour issue between black and white was a serious issue. But out here in the wilderness it didn't exist.

Dessert consisted of a Coke for each of us together with a new open box of cigarettes for whoever needed one. At that moment in time we were all as healthy, happy and satisfied as was possible for humans to be.

Chapter 44

Aaron surprised me asking if I could teach him to shoot. I only had five rounds of ammunition left, but, knowing that supplies were going to arrive the next day I was confident this would not pose a problem. Everyone was having fun so why not let them have a shot or two? There was an empty tin in the back of my Land Rover. I placed it on a rock about twenty yards away and came back to teach Aaron the art.

After going through the safety aspects with him, and showing him how he should hold the rifle, I explained how important it was for him to take a slow deep breath and hold it once he was satisfied he had his sights set on the target. Then I explained the difference between squeezing and pulling the trigger. He was ready to take his first shot.

I checked that he squeezed both hands inward while levelling the rifle onto the target to keep it as steady as possible. Once he appeared to have everything under control I whispered for him to hold his breath and I quietly told him to shoot the tin. With this he yanked on the trigger and the bullet ricocheted off a rock wide off the target.

"Hey, come on, Aaron!" I laughed, "You won't even scare an animal with that one." There were shouts of laughter and whoops by the others who found that first-shot failure hugely entertaining. Humans sometimes find the failures of other humans amusing, when they don't have the balls to try anything new themselves - for fear of failure. Aaron was not impressed with their reaction.

"Thank you, Baas. I have tried and failed, so will just leave it like that." He was embarrassed. Being my right-hand man, I couldn't leave him in that shamed state. "No! I will not let you stop until you prove yourself by shooting and hitting the tin," I declared. "None of the other guys are brave enough to even try, so come and show them how good you can be."

This was a challenge he couldn't refuse. But it was risky. Even though, under the circumstances, out there in the bush, the guys looked to him as their leader, failure with this could change their attitude completely. On the other hand, if he succeeded in shooting the tin, it would strengthen his dominance over them. Out there, in the remote wilderness with its many dangers, to maintain morale a leader was necessary. To get through our work load, I needed compliance from everyone. For that to happen there had to be a leader.

Once again I set everything up and went through the whole process of how to shoot accurately, with emphasis on steady, hold your breath and squeeze, not to *pull* the trigger but *squeeze* it. There was an atmosphere of anticipation amongst the guys. Could he do it? Or was it going to be hilariously funny a second time?

"If you miss, don't even think of the reaction from the other guys," I said quietly into his ear. "Don't let them distract your concentration. Trust that what I have taught you is right, concentrate on my words only, doing exactly what I said, and you will hit the target. "

With that, he set himself up, held the rifle as steady as a rock, squeezed the trigger and fired a round. The tin went flying through the air with a hole clean through the middle. Aaron was as surprised as the others were, but he was proud of himself and that his leadership was secured.

What I wanted now was for him to shoot his first animal. But that would have to wait till later. With today's shoot, we had enough meat for the next few days.

There's always one guy in a crowd who thinks he's smarter than the rest, and tries to challenge the leader. This time it was Kenneth. He asked for a chance at shooting the tin. We all knew he was trying to upstage Aaron. I had to give him the opportunity, as denial would create an issue between him and Aaron. Methodically, I went through everything again so there were no excuses for failure.

The atmosphere was more electric than before. Would Kenneth do better than Aaron and hit the tin with his first shot?

He carefully took aim and he not only pulled - as opposed to squeeze - the trigger, at the same time he closed his eyes. The shot fired flew wide of the target. Once again there were whoops and shouts of derision from the onlookers. But none of the onlookers had the guts to at least try.

Three rounds later the tin went flying through the air, landing five yards away. Although eventually successful, Kenneth had failed to out-shoot Aaron. Instead of dethroning him, he had elevated Aaron's dominance over the crew and secured his place as leader of the pack. I was pleased with how it turned out. Two guys vying for leadership would not work well in this job.

By going through our little shooting exercise, together with our celebratory party of smoking and drinking Cokes, we had used up all our supplies. There would be no more until new supplies arrived, which should be in the next day or two. We had so much fun that day, I hadn't even given it a thought. We had some meat for the next day so would be fine. I still had a half-pack of cigarettes.

With the remainder of the meat neatly packed into a cardboard box, we eventually cleared up, made sure the fire was completely extinguished, and set off back to camp, our home for the remainder of the contract.

The return trip to camp was uneventful. As soon as we returned, Aaron asked Kenneth to hang the meat. He didn't hesitate, and the meat was hung in no time. Aaron's authority was established.

Chapter 45

Our one-day break was as good as a month's holiday. We had worked long, hard hours in the baking sun, every day without a break, for a whole month. The next morning we were up before light fresh and ready to get going.

As we settled into a new month of drilling, the enthusiasm and drive of the team was good to see. There was no evidence of animosity between Aaron and Kenneth, so there was every reason we would reach our target production again this month - over one thousand feet. We would not be hampered by rain. Although the heat sapped our energy, heavy rains would make our lives and work impossible.

But we did have one big problem. We were out of supplies. If our order for new supplies didn't arrive in the next few days, we would be without essentials and luxuries - no drinks after work or during the day, other than water from the Ruangwa River, no cigarettes, no meat or fish as my fishing gear had not arrived, and there were no bullets left for hunting.

To get the guys to continue working at the pace they had achieved the previous month, they had to have enough food. We had loads of mealie meal and boxes of tinned peas. That was all. While this would certainly fill the belly, it would not provide the nourishment needed to work the hours required. But, the supplies were on order, and should arrive any day.

A few days turned into a week, and then two weeks. There were still no supplies. I was getting really bored with my nightly drink of water mixed with Eno Fruit Salts. With a stretch of the imagination the fizz of the Eno was the closest thing to a Coke. Everything on the rig was going well, but the guys were starting to complain about being hungry. Aaron came to me.

"Please, Baas, when will the food and cigarettes arrive? The guys are not happy and are complaining. They can't carry on without meat or smokes. " I tried to reassure him.

"Yes, Aaron, I know. I'm in the same boat. I know that all we have eaten these last two weeks is dry Sudza and peas. I've even tried ground elephant dung rolled in newspaper for smoking. It doesn't work. Don't try it." That got Aaron laughing. "All I can tell you is that the last time the geologist was here, some weeks back, he told me that the supplies were on their way."

In response to Aaron's doleful look, I said, "Listen, Aaron, there is nothing I can do about it. To make things worse, we only have a few days diesel left, so I can't even drive to the farm." Our situation was serious

"I'm just as sick of the sudza and peas as you are, but at least it keeps us going. The supplies will be here soon. There has obviously been a problem, but they will sort it out and get our supplies to us. We haven't been forgotten." I was trying to convince myself, too. There was no means of contact with the outside world. The guys were not as confident as I was.

"Let's get down to work. We have something to look forward to. When food and cigarettes arrive, we'll enjoy them all the more."

I had no sooner said this when we heard the sound of a vehicle grinding its way towards our site. But our hopes were dashed. It was Peter's field assistant. He was not bringing supplies. He had only come to collect the core.

"How is it possible you have not brought our supplies? More than three weeks ago, I asked Mr. Peter to order and arrange to deliver our supplies. We have not heard or seen anyone since." I was really angry, pulled open his door, and hauled him out to give us an explanation.

"I'm sorry. Mr. Peter was called away to meetings in Salisbury. I think he must have forgotten about your order." He looked surprised at the way I had man-handled him. It was not his fault.

"Hey, I'm sorry. For two weeks we've had little to eat. We have no bullets. We've had nothing to drink apart from the water from the river. None of us has had a cigarette for well over a week." I was immensely disappointed. "Once you get back to your camp, is it possible for you to radio through to your head office and tell them of our predicament?"

"Yes Sir. I will be able to do that. We have good radio reception at the moment. I will get the message through on my 4.00pm radio schedule. At worst I will get it through at 7.00am tomorrow morning." He looked genuinely concerned.

With that we all helped him to load the core samples and sent him on his way with a new list of requirements, which including a repeat request for fishing gear. If we ever ran out of bullets in the future I would at least be in a position to feed us on fish from the river.

The reassurance that supplies would soon be on their way made us all feel better. We had nothing new to eat, drink or smoke but our mood had changed, and we all put our shoulders to the wheel and worked hard. The drilling was going well on the new hole with no problems. We had gone down six hundred and seventy feet.

Another five days went by, and there was no sign of relief supplies. At mid-morning I was forced to shut down the rig at a depth of seven hundred and twenty feet. We were out of diesel. I was annoyed with myself for not driving to the farm when I had the chance, with the little fuel we had left at that time. I could have replenished our diesel and food supplies there, but was certain our supplies were on their way. Now here we were, not only hungry, but also without diesel. The rig was silent, and all we could do was sit and wait. How could this have happened? Everyone knew we were down here, yet nothing was being done to help us.

It was hard to believe that, since our celebration party at the Mazoe River, some sixteen days ago, we had been without supplies or communication with anyone, other than the field assistant. We had put so much hope in him sorting things out for us. Had the radio message gone through? What were we going to do? I had no fuel to drive anywhere to get help. We were all looking lean, mean and famished. I would be happy to never see a plate of sudza again. I didn't have the heart to ask the guys to wash the rig. They were too hungry, angry and ready to walk off the job. If it wasn't for the dangers of the wild, we probably would have all walked away. But all we could do was sit tight and wait.

Late one afternoon I thought I heard the faint sound of a vehicle. Then there was silence. Was it just a figment of my imagination? Or did the wind change direction and blow the sound away? I was terribly down-hearted, not only for myself, but for all of us. We had gone through three of the toughest weeks of our lives.

I waited, listening expectantly. Nothing, I told myself the sound must have been a hippo in one of the distant pools, and my ears played tricks on me. Then Major perked his ears and stared alertly down the road. Could it be he heard the same sound?

Then it came again - the unmistakable sound of a vehicle. It wasn't my imagination. It must be our supplies. I didn't care who was bringing them, just so long as they arrived. To my astonishment and disappointment, it was a police vehicle with a white policeman driver and a black policeman passenger. Surely they would not have known we needed supplies? I walked over to the vehicle and introduced myself. "Hi, this is one hell of a surprise to see you guys. For you to be down here, you must be lost. No one in their right mind would drive down into this valley for no good reason. I'm Trevor. It's good to see some new faces."

"Good afternoon. I'm Sergeant Nigel Williams and this is Sergeant Ndlovo." He sounded very official. "I don't mean to make you panic, but we have information that there have been terrorists crossing from Mozambique into this area. We were informed by the District Commissioner in Shamva that you were down here with your crew. We don't believe there's any real danger, but we do need to warn you. We would also like to know whether you have seen or heard anything strange or any movement of people at all?"

How could anyone be this seriously official after such a long and crazy drive? He must be pushing for promotion to Captain. "No, we have not seen anyone, nor have we had contact with anyone other than the geologist and his staff." I thought he must have a good reason to come all the way out here to these desolate parts.

"Well, may we ask you to keep a look-out for anything unusual and report to us immediately." he said in all earnestness.

"Yes, sure," I answered. "But — serious question - just how do you propose we report it? We have no phone, radio or, for that matter, any diesel to drive out of here." I went on to explain our situation to him, then adding, "Taking notice of unwanted guests right now is of little concern to us when all we can think about is food."

"I'm sorry. We had no idea of your problem. Is there anything we can do to help you?" He looked genuinely concerned and so he should have been. We were in trouble.

"Well, I'm not sure what you can do about cigarettes and drink, but, hey, you could go and shoot us a buck. None of us has seen meat for the past two-and-a-half weeks. We've lived on Sudza, peas and water. "

"What you need to understand," he said, "is that this rifle is Government Issue. I'm only allowed to use it for self-protection." Was he serious? He then went on to say, "If I were to shoot something for you and it got back to head office there would be serious consequences."

"Listen to me," I said, trying to bring him down to planet earth. "I'm Trevor. You are Nigel. We are miles from any civilization. There is no rank to pull here. Rules are made to suit conditions. None of us would say anything to anybody - apart from thanking you. I'm sure Sergeant Ndlovo here will not be inclined to say anything after enjoying the meal my cook, Clever, will serve you guys." Sergeant Ndlovo smiled and nodded his head in agreement.

"If the worst comes to worst, you could honestly say it was for the self-protection of others, the others being us guys down here, slowly starving to death." With that, our genuine desperation for food got through to him.

Chapter 46

"Well, I guess we could shoot something. That meal you're offering sure sounds great. A meal for a bunch of hungry men is protection," he said, looking more relaxed. "I was sent to come down and help you, so let's go and get some food." With that he headed off to his vehicle, beckoning, Clever and I followed obediently.

Nigel's Land Rover was a far later model than mine and ran noticeably more smoothly. On those bad roads, the suspension was a lot softer.

"You know," I said, "I would be quite happy to help you out by swopping my vehicle with yours. I wouldn't even ask you to pay in any extra for the deal."

"I'm sorry," he began, in all seriousness, "but this is not my vehicle…" but stopped as I burst out laughing.

"Hey, man. I'm pulling your leg. You need to relax and enjoy life a little. The world isn't such a serious, straight up and down place. You would be amazed at the fun you could have if you let you hair down sometimes." His rigidity was robbing him of the simple enjoyment of life.

I was the opposite. I believed in spontaneity and going ahead with whatever seemed like a good idea. Consequences could be dealt with as they arose. There had been times when this attitude backfired, but generally I enjoyed my life to the fullest.

"To be honest," he confessed, "I have lived a sheltered life. I grew up with a demanding mother who still likes to control what everyone does and says. I envy someone like you with a 'who-gives-a-shit' attitude." I felt sorry for him and realised this was not the first time he was confronted by this issue.

Rhodesians, on the whole, have a live-for-today-and-enjoy-life attitude so this policeman was a little unusual.

"I'm sorry if I'm being personal. Just tell me to shut up if I overstep the boundaries. But, at the end of the day, life is what you make it. Now let's drop the subject and find some food. "

"Yes, let's do that," he said. "And I don't give a shit what you think, I'm going to shoot whatever we find." We both burst out laughing. It was good to see him starting to enjoy himself.

Within two miles we came across a fully grown bush buck. He was standing some one hundred yards off the road under one of the few bushes in the area offering any shade. Nigel slowed down and stopped in the middle of the road fully aware there wouldn't be another vehicle coming - why worry about pulling over?

My heart sank a little, personally I left bushbuck alone. They are one of my favourite animals. Usually, I would drive on and find something else to shoot. "There!" he exclaimed, with excitement in his voice, "That should give us enough meat to have one hell of a feast. I have always wanted to shoot a bushbuck."

Clearing my throat, I said, "Nigel, if you don't mind, I'm not happy shooting bushbuck. I know they are good eating, but it's a personal thing. I always leave them alone." In spite of really looking forward to a good meal of meat, I was adamant it shouldn't be a bushbuck. "There is so much game down here that within the next mile we should find a duiker, impala or klipspringer. Let's leave this beautiful animal to live out his life."

"What the hell!" He burst out, "I don't understand you. First you talk me into doing something I wouldn't ever think of doing, and now that I want to do it you're talking me out of it." He looked puzzled and cheesed off.

"Look, Nigel, it's your call, your rifle," I said, "and if you're happy to shoot it then go for it. Believe me, I will still enjoy eating it, as I was not the one to shoot it. However there is another problem. The shot might scare the three elephant to the right of where the bushbuck is standing."

The elephants were in the limited shade of some large trees along the river bank, well camouflaged. To an untrained eye, even as big as they are, they manage to blend in with their surroundings. To cool off they roll in the mud along the river and the layer of mud that sticks to their skin helps to protect them from the burning sun. It also gives them the same colour as the surrounding soil. We could have easily driven straight past them without seeing them.

"Good grief! I hadn't seen them at all. Aren't they a little close to your camp for comfort?" he asked concerned.

"Not at all." I assured him. "I have often found them walking through the camp at night, within yards of my tent. Many times I've climbed out of my tent in the early morning to find elephant foot prints, even though I had heard nothing. I even have a pet leopard that visits at night. The animals have never bothered me. If they are left alone, they do the same for you. "When you think about it, elephants don't eat people and although leopards would, why should they when there is so much game around? If I were a leopard I would find wild game far tastier than humans. "

"Are you serious?" he spluttered. "I couldn't be as comfortable as you, with the guests you get."

"Beggars can't be choosers. We don't get many visitors out here, and so we welcome almost any guest that comes along. Even the police, under exceptional circumstances. You have no idea how lonely it can get." I laughed."Now, getting back to the bushbuck, are you telling me that, as hungry as you guys are, you would leave him to look for something else?" he asked.

"Yes, without doubt. In all the time we have been down here I have never shot one. Why do you think Clever, who is standing at the back as spotter, didn't call our attention to it? It certainly isn't because he didn't see it. He misses nothing. But he knows my rules." I looked him straight in the eye.

"Well," sighed Nigel, "if you feel that strongly, let's drive on. As you say, there are loads of buck down here and I'm having fun looking for them. It's a long time since I went hunting." He looked pleased with himself for making the decision.

"Thanks, Nigel. I and the bushbuck really appreciate your understanding." Hey, I thought, who knows? I could start to like this guy. As he revved the engine to pull away, the bushbuck looked straight at us and even from a distance I thought I could see gratitude in his beautiful soft eyes. He then lowered his head to continue grazing. He was relaxed and not at all concerned about us. The elephant also took no notice of us.

We travelled another couple of hundred yards when, out of nowhere, around the corner came another Land Rover. It stopped abruptly right in front of us - in a cloud of dust. What a shock we both had. A herd of buffalo would have been less of a surprise.

This time, Nigel pulled over to the side of the road, and stopped. We climbed out of the vehicle and I was even more surprised to see that it was Mr. Longstaff himself, driving a fully loaded vehicle. I was not only pleased to see him, but even more pleased with what seeing him meant. Our supplies had arrived. We were out of trouble. He pulled over to his side of the road, climbed out of his vehicle and walked across to us.

"Hi, Mr. Longstaff," I said as I walked up to him and received his strong, firm hand shake. "You have no idea how good it is to see you." Indicating the policeman, I said, "This is Nigel, who will explain later why he is here." Hell, it was so good to see him!

Shaking hands he said "Pleased to meet you, Nigel, and, yes, I'm most certainly interested to know what you could possibly be doing way out here. Hope Trevor has not been getting up to any mischief?" He fixed me with a fierce and penetrating look.

Nigel laughed and said, "Hell no. I'm not even sure what mischief he could get up to down here in this valley. We are down here on a precautionary visit as we believe there could be terrorists coming over from Mozambique into this area. It's good to meet you too. I hope you have brought the supplies Trevor and his crew so desperately need."

"Well, yes. I have come with all I was asked to bring, via garbled messages through our client. There seems to have been a misunderstanding and for some reason we were not informed of the problem until yesterday when we phoned the client to find out if there was anything we could bring down for them." He paused for a second. "I was asked if we had received the list you had sent through weeks ago with Peter the geologist. It was found lying in their out-basket. We had not received it and immediately realising your predicament we started urgently getting all the supplies together. I'm truly sorry about the delay."

"Right now, nothing matters other than you are here, and we can eat again," I declared, adding, "And we can also start drilling again. We've been out of fuel for a few days now." I continued hastily before Mr. Longstaff could comment, "Please tell me you've brought loads of cigarettes with you. I have even tried smoking dry elephant dung ground up and rolled in a piece of newspaper. Somehow, I don't think it's going to be a top seller." We all laughed and with that he walked back to his vehicle and returned with a packet of cigarettes and matches.

"I have never smoked in my life and strongly suggest it would be a good idea for you to quit now, while you're still young. But it's a choice you need to make for yourself." I knew what he was saying was true, yet all I could think of was opening the box and lighting up.

I couldn't believe how bad the first couple of draws on the cigarette tasted. I knew it was due to not having smoked for a couple of weeks – but I was confident, with practise, smoking would get back to giving me that satisfying and necessary nicotine fix.

"Thank you, Mr. Longstaff. I might start to work on that sometime in the future. Right now, after the two and a half weeks we've endured, to hell with my lungs as the rest of my body is crying out for a serious nicotine boost. "

"Where were you guys heading for now?" "Nigel kindly offered to shoot a buck for us to eat. We are also out of bullets so we haven't had meat in weeks. We're ready to eat anything that moves." I went on to say, "Although I have a permit to shoot for the pot, we would both appreciate your discretion on this. Please don't say anything to anyone, as there could be repercussions for Nigel."

"Don't worry, I haven't heard a word. But, as I have brought some really good rump steak and 80 lbs of ration meat for the guys, there's no need to shoot anything for a week." I wiped my mouth as I felt sure it had started salivating in the corners as dogs sometimes do when ravenously hungry. Rump steak cooked over hot coals has always been a favourite of mine.

"Thanks, that's wonderful news for all of us, and also for whatever poor animal we were about to shoot. That's worth celebrating by lighting another cigarette," I said with a broad smile on my face.

"I can see I'm not going to win with your smoking. It's your lungs you're damaging. But remember that somewhere down the road I'm going to tell you: I told you so." Little did we realise just how true this prophesy would turn out to be.

Chapter 47

Back at camp we were greeted by an excited team who enthusiastically off-loaded Mr. Longstaff's Land Rover. Just knowing there would be food again gave them all the energy they needed. First, the food supplies were unloaded to both camps. Then the diesel was taken down to the rig so we could fill all the tanks and get back to drilling.

I siphoned five-gallons out of the drum of petrol for the water pump. This would be stored in a container kept on site for this purpose. The remaining fuel, with the drum, was offloaded at my camp.

Along with the food, Mr. Longstaff had brought four full boxes of ammunition for my rifle.

In spite of his lecturing about smoking, he had also brought four cartons of cigarettes for me. For the guys there were two large bulk packets of boxer tobacco. They liked to roll their own cigarettes and that was enough tobacco to keep them all going for a long time. It was a further delight to know I could say goodbye to the evening water and Eno drink. I now had three full crates of Coke and I was going to savour every single one.

It was all more exciting than Christmas. There was an irony to this euphoric explosion. To feel this good, we had to endure two-and-a-half weeks of hardship. Hardship helps us appreciate the things we so easily take for granted.

"Thank you, so much, Mr. Longstaff. Now we'll have full bellies, full fuel tanks and heaps of enthusiasm. There'll be no excuse for slow production. You're going to be amazed at what we're going to produce for you."

"Hell, Trevor. I'm sorry you guys had such a hard time these last few weeks. It shouldn't have happened. As for your production, I see with the hole depth, had you not been forced to shut down, you would have easily made your target of 1,000 again." He paused, thought, and continued, "Let's see how deep you go, and I'll decide whether to give you an extra bonus this month." With that, he turned and walked back to his truck. From the floor on the passenger side he produced a cardboard box containing new spare drilling bits, reaming shells and core springs. "This should and had better last you for the next few holes to be drilled. This is an expensive box. Please take care of it. I need full reports on the feet drilled by each bit."

"Yes Sir. I have all the bit reports, together with the daily drill log reports, ready to go back with you. Copies of all the daily reports are fully signed up to three weeks ago by the geologist, which is the last time we saw him." "Good. I'll take the up-to-date signed copies with me, for invoicing purposes. Please remember to get the other copies signed when he gets here." Then after a short pause. "Now, seeing that you have been standing for a few days now, let's get down to some drilling." Yes, we were back to normal.

"I have been told," Mr. Longstaff continued, "that you have been working the guys between 14 and 18 hour shifts? I'm not happy with that. What do the guys feel about working those hours?"

"Yes. Depending on how the day's production goes, we do work those hours. We need to have this contract completed before the rains arrive. Working long hours is the only way to do it. We all know that, so we get on with the job. Besides, no one complained about their bonuses last month. In fact, they were pretty excited about them. Also, I work along with them. They see my commitment. It's natural for them to give the same commitment in return." I looked at him for a response.

"Well, you're the buggers on site. If everyone is happy, then I guess you must get on with it."

Being accustomed to long hours of work, the forced days off, waiting for supplies seemed like weeks. I told Clever that once the food was ready he was to bring it to the rig because we were going to start drilling again. We were all eager to 'get the chuck spinning' as we drillers would say.

I methodically went through all the start up procedures to ensure all was well, and in half-an-hour I had the rig and pump running, ready to start advancing the drill bit further into the hard granites some seven hundred and twenty feet down the hole. Power is produced through a Perkins 4 cylinder diesel engine and transmitted through a gear box, into the drill housing via a short prop shaft, up through idler gears to the pinion gear for drill rod rotation speeds of up to 400rpm. The engine had proved itself as far as reliability is concerned and ran like a dream from day one.

Clever arrived with the food and everyone got stuck into it like there was no tomorrow. I kept the rig running while the guys ate, and then I left them to it while Mr. Longstaff, Nigel and I sat in the shade of the biggest tree to avoid the merciless sun, while we tucked into our rump steak, sudza, spinach and gravy, washed down by a cool Coke.

It was a banquet. There were some sighs of satisfaction, but otherwise not a word was spoken by any of us as we ate.

Once our hunger had been satisfied we were ready to start serious work. "I was told by head office in Salisbury," said Mr. Longstaff, "that there could be another four holes to complete down here."

"Yes, that is the impression I had, hence the panic when we ran out of diesel. As it is, we're going to be pushed for time. We'll have to keep up the long working hours."

"Well, at the end of the day, all we can do is our best, which is what you guys are doing. Have there been any intersections of interest?" he asked, hopefully.

"There have been some areas of interest, but we have not had any feedback on lab results yet. Having not really seen anyone for a few weeks I'm not too sure what is going on. Have you had any news from Peter, the geologist? Is he back in camp or still in Salisbury?" I was a bit concerned that there could be a problem with him since he has been away for this length of time."I'm told he will be back on site this week, however, I'm not sure if he will have any results with him," he replied.

"He was an excellent supplier of game meat. About six weeks ago he arrived with a fully loaded vehicle of a kudu, bush pig and duiker." I said, with a feeling of disgust. "I know our only means of obtaining meat is by shooting something, but there's a limit." I paused for breath. "I prefer having him do the shooting as I have never liked it, but he does it more for enjoyment than for sustenance. He does have more guys than we do to feed, but he went overboard."

"Ah, then," said Mr. Longstaff, "I have something that might please you. I have brought you some fishing gear, on the understanding that tomorrow night we will eat fish. I was told that there were a few large bream swimming around in the river." he said, with a smile on his face.

"Thank you. That's good news. The fishing gear would have made a difference for us if I'd had it here over the last few weeks. We could have had fish to eat every day. There are loads of them in the river, but there was no way to catch them."

I took back the controls of the rig and we drilled for the rest of the day through to around 9.30pm when Mr. Longstaff said," Hey, guys, enough is enough. I have had a really long drive. It's time for all of us to hit the sack."

"Okay, Sir. I'll just complete this ten foot run and then head to the camp. You could go over and see that Clever is preparing food for us and have a bath. I'm sure he's heated up water for your bath by now."

"Yes, thanks. I'll do that, and see you in a little while. Make sure you come on over as soon as this drill run is finished. We can get back to full production tomorrow."

I continued drilling. Within the hour I had completed the full ten foot drill run. I pulled a few lengths of the thirty feet stands out of the hole to ensure there was no chance of being stuck in the morning. The drill string was ninety feet off the bottom of the hole, so I shut all the motors down and we all set off to our camps. On arriving at my tent Mr. Longstaff had already bathed and the fire was ready with red hot coals.

"Well, Clever has your water good and hot in the five-gallon tin, ready to go into your bath. You need to go and get yourself cleaned up. Clever and I will sort dinner out, he is making some sudza to go with our rump steaks. Nigel has had a clean up, so the bath tub is all yours," said Mr. Longstaff, rubbing his hands, as he often did, as he walked across to the fire.

I felt so good after the bath. The three of us sat down with our plates of food, Nigel and Mr. Longstaff with beers, and I with my usual Coke. I had missed Cokes as much as I missed cigarettes.

After eating one of the best meals possible, it was time to go to bed. Nigel's guy had put up his tent for him some sixty feet away from mine and after saying good night, he disappeared into it and pulled the zip tightly closed.

"Gee, he's going to get really hot in there." I said. "You sleep in my tent, Mr. Longstaff, but keep the flaps open. It doesn't cool down much here." "Don't be silly. It's your tent. I have a stretcher and will sleep under the front awning. I love sleeping in the open, so long as there's a cover over the top of me for the dew," he said with total finality in his voice.

"Mr. Longstaff, please, I don't want to be funny, but there is a leopard that visits on a regular basis up in that tree and the elephants often come wandering through the camp at night. I'm so used to them that I will be happy out here." I paused. "My last camp, up on the top of the escarpment, where you slept outside, was tame compared to what we have here. So please, I'm serious." I could see from the look on his face I was not winning.

"You bloody youngsters think you're so tough and that we old buggers can't rough it a bit. I'm not asking you if I can sleep outside. I'm telling you." And that was that. "Well, that's fine, Mr. Longstaff, but I'm sure I will get to hear from you before the sun comes up." I helped put his stretcher together and we both settled down for much needed sleep.

Around 2am I was violently shaken awake to the extent I was sure I would have a heart attack. "Trevor, there're elephant all around the tent, what are we going to do?" he panicked.

"Well Sir, I did try to tell you that would most likely be the case," I said wearily. "The first thing we need to do is be as quiet as possible. If we don't spook them they shouldn't bother about us at all." I climbed off my bed slowly and stuck my head around the corner of the tent opening.

There was a half moon up in the sky making just enough light to see all these big black masses slowly wondering around out there. Once again I was in awe of just how silent they were. I asked him as quietly as possible what had woken him as they were making no noise at all.

"It was the rumble in the one's stomach. It was so close to me, as you will see in the morning from the spoor. Fortunately I had such a fright waking up to see a full grown elephant standing next to me that I just froze until he moved on a few paces. " He paused to take a look outside the tent." "That was when I came in here, I really thought you were pulling my leg about the elephants," he said.

"Well, there is no harm done and if we swop places we can both get some sleep," I said quietly and moved slowly out to his stretcher, before he could even put up any argument.

The last thing I remembered before falling asleep was him telling me to be careful out here. I was up before 5am and had the kettle boiled ready for coffee by the time Mr. Longstaff came out of the tent.

"Morning Sir, how did you sleep?" "After my adrenaline rush, I slept well. Gee whiz, just look at all the foot prints. Thinking about it, it's amazing how they left us alone. " he said with an astonished look on his face.

"Yes, I don't worry about them anymore, but I must be honest, I felt terribly vulnerable the first few nights down here. I'm serious about the visits from the leopard as well, and, I must say, after my other experiences up on the top of the escarpment with the leopards, he worried me even more than the elephant in the beginning and yet he has also not bothered me at all." By this stage Nigel had joined us and had been shocked on seeing the fresh spoor around his tent when he stumbled out.

"Hell, I came down here to warn you that there was maybe a 5% chance of your encountering some terrorists. Well, had I known things were this wild around here, far more dangerous than my reason for coming down, I probably wouldn't have bothered you. I must say you need to have balls to stay down here on your own like this. "

"I always say, only the good die young, so I should be fine for a few more years yet," I said and we all laughed.

Chapter 48

The morning went well on the drill rig and by 11.30am both Mr. Longstaff and Nigel were set to leave together in convoy.

"I'm happy we're going out together, Nigel, as I have another surprise for Trevor." Mr. Longstaff looked across at his vehicle. "I have had everything done on my Land Rover including having the insides completely upholstered. It's like a new vehicle."

I looked accommodatingly at him, because I already knew all that. "The surprise is," he continued, "I will be leaving it here with you and taking yours back to Harare to have it fully refurbished.

I was speechless. I couldn't believe what I had just heard. "Hey," he joked, "If you're not happy with that, I can leave you here with your old rattle-trap. That thing is a disaster looking for a place to happen. I can return in my vehicle. It will save me all the money I'm about to spend on yours."

"No, no, sorry Sir," I stammered, "I just had a problem believing my ears. Thank you so much. I will look after it like my life depends on it. " I said, still trying to get my head around the good news.

"I urge you to do that. If anything happens to it, it might just come to that. " Thankfully, he had a smile on his face when he said it.

By midday, the two of them left, waving as they disappeared over the first rise. Their dust settled and suddenly things felt really empty. The last few days had been special, with them around. Feeling that way made me realize just how lonely I had become.

Well, I had a drilling contract to complete and the harder we all worked the sooner we would get out of this valley.

The following few days went well on the drill site. The hole was progressing successfully. The elephants had not come through the camp again. The leopard was obviously off hunting elsewhere. We had food, bullets, fishing gear, cigarettes, and Cokes. Life couldn't get much better out here.

Why it is that life doesn't stay that way I'll never know. I was close to getting another ten feet of drilling under my belt which would have made thirty feet of advance for the day. Out of the corner of my eye I saw sudden movement by the water pump. It was Kenneth, leaping backwards and throwing the petrol container he held in his hand spinning off with a trail of fire behind it. Not only was the container on fire, but far more serious, the petrol engine on the pump was also alight!

He had, in spite of my repeated instructions to never, *never* try and fill the engine with petrol while it was still running, had done just that. It was a miracle that there wasn't a petrol spill, or that he didn't get burned when he threw the can. I still go cold contemplating the possible serious injuries he could have sustained. Our medical aid equipment included nothing for burns.

I immediately pulled the clutch in to stop the rotation on the drill bit and pulled back two feet on the hydraulics to ensure the bit was free from the bottom of the hole.

We all ran to try and put out the fire. Needless to say there were no fire extinguishers within forty five miles, never mind having one on site. All I could think of was shovelling sand on the engine to try to extinguish the flames. Two of the guys were doing the same where the fuel container was merrily burning away.

Thankfully and due mainly to our clearing of the site before moving in the equipment, there was little dry grass around and none where this had taken place.

Major, in the mean time was running around us in circles barking frantically, not really sure what all the fuss was about or how he could help.

In a short while the fire was out. We were left with a burned-out Briggs and Stratton engine and no spare one on site. I was ready to kill and bury Kenneth for what he had done.

He walked sheepishly over to me, I assumed to apologize. I didn't even have time to think about it. I was enraged. I punched him really hard a couple of times and threw him into the drilling sump. This had rod grease floating on the top of the water and sloppy, sticky mud at the bottom from the drill cuttings. Not the ideal place to go for a swim. He stood up, bumping his head on the ten foot drill rod that supported the suction pipe, with slime dripping from his body from the head down.

"Have you any idea what an idiot you are? Not only have you burned out the pump, but you could have killed yourself. Or, had you thrown the container the other way, we all could have been badly burned."

"I'm sorry, my Baas." he said, looking terribly sorry for himself, with greasy muck running down his face.

"Well, Kenneth, right now sorry isn't going to cut it for me, nor will it fix the pump. For the next few months you'll not be receiving any bonus. You'll have to pay for what you have done."

With that I turned and walked off to have a good look at how much damage the fire had caused.

"Aaron, go and help him out of the sump and get him cleaned up." I was now feeling guilty for the action I had taken. I have always been known to have a short fuse. Right then, I had no fuse at all.

It was obvious that the engine on the pump was destroyed, with no possibility of repair. Just as we were really getting our act together, here we sat with a disaster caused by carelessness. Kenneth was one of my top guys and was always efficient. Yet for some reason this human failing of carelessness that we all have from time to time, popped its ugly head up out of nowhere.

I was not sure what to do. Would I have to drive all the way to Salisbury to collect another pump? I couldn't think of any other plan. A few days of standing time was unavoidable. This we could ill afford.

Chapter 49

I walked back to my camp and returned in the Land Rover so that the pump could be loaded. There was no point in leaving it here. It would need to have a new engine fitted. Once loaded and tied down tightly to stop it crashing from side to side in my nice new Land Rover, I drove back to my tent. Not being sure how long I would be away I threw some clothes into my little canvas bag.

In a short while I was set and ready to go. I would head first for John's farm, and phone the office in Salisbury from there. I decided to leave Major at the camp with Clever as he could be a nuisance, especially at the farm. This turned out to be a terrible mistake.

"Clever, I want to leave Major with you. Give him a big plate of food, then hold him with his lead until you can't hear my vehicle at all. Hopefully that way he will settle down with you until I get back," I said to him.

"Well, my Baas, I will try. But he is strong. He won't be happy staying here without you." It was good advice. I should have taken it seriously. All I had in my mind right then was how to get another pump, as quickly as possible, so that we could start drilling again.

"If you hold him for long enough, I'm sure he'll be fine. Go and tell Aaron to pack some things. I want him to come with me." I closed up the flaps on my tent and called for one of the guys to come and help me fill the vehicle with diesel.

Within thirty minutes we were off. I gave Major a hug to say goodbye, and told him to look after everyone in the camp while I was away. He looked terribly confused. I hated leaving him behind, but felt I had no option.

Reluctantly I climbed into the Land Rover, drove off and kept looking in the rear view mirror until Major and the camp disappeared behind the rise. I had a hollow feeling in my stomach and wasn't sure if it was due to the pump, or to leaving my faithful friend behind.

I was impressed with my new vehicle. Compared to what I had been driving, it was a Rolls Royce. I was careful to drive clear of any overhanging branches. I didn't want any scratches on it. Although a major problem was the reason for driving out of the valley, it felt good to know I'd be back in civilization for a day or two. I hadn't been up to the farm for quite some time and was looking forward to seeing my good friends John and Sally again.

With Aaron, we ground our way up the pass above the Mazoe River. Even if I travelled that road every day I would always be impressed by its raw and rough beauty.

On arrival at the original water point I stopped to go and see what had become of it. It was pleasing to see it full of water with fresh and diversified spoor all around. There were now many different animals drinking from the water point.

I was born with a gift for bonding with animals. Through all my life animals of different kinds singled me out of a crowd. I have often admitted to preferring animals to people. Dogs, in particular, are more faithful than humans. Your dog will love you no matter what. You can go on a man's night out, arrive home smashed out of your bracket, at three in the morning, your dog will welcome you home. If you give your animal the tender loving care he needs he will look after you, and protect you with his life.

Four hours after leaving the valley we arrived at John's farm. It was good to see them again. They were glad to see me and yet shocked at the weight I had lost.

They were impatient to hear all my news, but I asked if I could first use their phone to call my head office in Salisbury. Of course, they told me to go ahead. "I assume it still works the same way - or have you guys gone hi-tech and moved up a notch from the party line?"

"Goodness, no! We wouldn't know how to use one of those hi-tech jobs. When you call, just give the handle on the side a really good spin and with luck the exchange will answer you and you can book your call."

It didn't take long to be connected to head office. When I heard the clear voice of Mr. Longstaff, my heart sank. It would have been easier if he had not been there, so that I would not have to give him first-hand information of our disaster.

"Hello Sir, how are you?" I asked, with my heart pumping a lot faster than normal. "Hello Trevor. I'm fine, I think. Why do I get the feeling you have something to say that I don't really want to hear?" he asked tersely.

"Well, Sir, I'm not really sure how to tell you - except to come straight to the point. We have had an accident on the site. The good news is that nobody has been injured." Before I could go on he shouted down the phone.

"What the hell have you done with the new Land Rover. I knew I was taking a chance leaving it down there with you." He shouted so loudly I was sure my hosts must have heard him. "Well, Sir, if that's what you thought, I have more good news. It's not the Land Rover," I stupidly gushed.

"For goodness sake, boy, are you going to tell me what has happened or not?" He was getting frustrated by my beating around the bush. "One of the guys filled the Briggs & Stratton engine with petrol while it was running." Before I could go on he bellowed even louder.

"How the hell could you let him do such a thing? How many times have I warned you about the consequences? We have you on site to drill and make sure these things don't happen." "Well, Sir, I'm sorry but..." I tried to complete my sentence, but Mr. Longstaff was really angry.

"Don't you butt in while I'm talking. I can tell you right now you're going to pay for this out of your wages, even if it takes a full year. Assuming you don't get fired before that." I had never heard him so angry.

"I assume the engine has been burned out?" I don't know why, but, at that moment the thought shot through my mind, "I wonder how his day has been before my call."

"Yes Sir. I'm at John's farm and have it on the back of your Land Rover, which is being washed this minute by Aaron. It looks brand new!" Why did I need to tell him that? "You've only had it a couple of days, so it should look good!" His voice carried clearly down the party line. I wondered if anyone was listening in on our conversation.

"Sir, I need your advice as to what I should do next. If I have to drive through the night to come and collect another one I will leave right away." I must have sounded desperate. "I'll do whatever it takes to get the rig drilling again."

There was no point in trying to tell him I was busy on the drill rig with my back to the pump when the accident happened. It was not my fault. But he was right. I was responsible for everything that happened on site. Maybe, some other time, down the road, I would have a chance to tell him the whole story. Right now wasn't the time.

"Well, luckily for you," he said, "I took a complete spare pump through to Dave at Mavurodona. It's about forty five minutes from John's farm. He can give you directions, as he came through with me the last time I was up there."

"You will have to leave the old one at John's farm and whoever goes up there next from this side can pick it up and bring it in for repairs."

"Thank you, Sir. I will organize that immediately. Once again I'm really sorry for what happened."

"Well," he growled, beginning to calm down, "at the end of the day, the main thing is nobody was injured." He seemed to have accepted the news and composed himself.

"Yes Sir. We were lucky Kenneth didn't catch alight. We all had a big fright. We have learned a good lesson, even thought it was an expensive one. I promise you, it will never happen again on my rig." I was pleased I could at least talk to him again.

"Right, you'd better get going, so you can sort things out. In a few days, I'll send Gus from the office down to you. He'll bring you a few supplies I made a note of on my visit. Please have the rig up and running again by then." He wasn't asking me. He was telling me.

"I will do that, Sir. And thank you once again." I replaced the phone on its cradle and gave the handle a quick short turn to let all the other farmers on the same line know I was finished with my call.

Chapter 50

With enormous relief I went out to John to tell him what I needed to do. He immediately said "I'll come with you. I know where to go and we can be back here in a few hours. You spend the night here on the farm with us, enjoy one of Sally's meals, and leave early in the morning."

"Trevor, I don't see Major?" John said with concern. "I wasn't sure where I would be going to sort the pump out so, reluctantly I decided to leave him back at the camp." I felt a lump in my throat. "It's the first time I've ever left him!" John thought I had taken quite a risk leaving him behind, but he understood my thinking, and within fifteen minutes we were on our way to collect the spare pump.

On arrival Dave was not happy about his spare pump being taken away. But I told him it was an order from the top and he had no option. "If you're unhappy about it, you'll need to take it up with Mr. Longstaff. Could one of your guys help us load it onto the vehicle?" I had never gelled with Dave and wasn't going to waste my time discussing the problem with him. In no time we had the pump loaded and ready to go.

"How has production been on your site?" Dave asked me. "Considering the formations and conditions, it has gone well. We're averaging around thirty feet per shift but, we're running sixteen to eighteen hour shifts to achieve those figures," I proudly told him.

"Well, I'm getting far more than that. On the one really good day I drilled just on sixty feet," he boasted, and then added sarcastically, "I have a driller's handbook here. You can borrow it if you like. It will help you improve your production."

In the mood I was in it took enormous restraint to not dramatically adjusting his front teeth with my fist. Fortunately, and surprisingly for me, I held back. I was in enough trouble with the boss already without adding to my troubles by beating up one of his blue eyed drillers.

"I suggest you stick that book wherever it fits best. You can't drill from a book, and I'm surprised you don't know that. Besides, in this beautiful soft formation you're drilling here, you'd double your production if you were working the same hours we do." It was obvious his comment had not gone down well with me. "The day will come when you'll be drilling in hard formation as we are, and when that happens I want to be there so I can ask you to go and get your book out."

"Sorry Trevor, I shouldn't have said that. Mr. Longstaff has told me how hard your formation is," he said, sheepishly, and rightly feeling a real jerk. "No problem," I relented. "Thanks for the pump. It's going to help me a lot." With that we bade farewell to Dave and his crew and drove off, back to John's farm. We had a special evening together. As always, Sally was a vision of beauty to my deprived eyes, and she served us a wonderful meal.

We sat and talked for hours. We had a lot to catch up on before we eventually got into bed at around midnight. It felt good to sleep on a real bed in a real house. I had set my alarm and it was hard to wake up at 4.00am. I was really tired and was not looking forward to the drive back down into the valley. But by 4.30am we were on our way, having said goodbye to my hosts the previous night. As always Aaron was on time, and standing next to the vehicle ready to go.

We set off into the darkness on the god-forsaken route back to the site. In the end, we were not going to lose a lot of time as a result of the disaster. But in the back of my mind I had an uneasy feeling that back at camp, something was wrong. In the past I had experienced premonitions like this, and they were usually reliable. So I was concerned. When you're impatient to get somewhere, the journey seems to take longer. We wound our way down the escarpment, and arrived at the confluence of the Mazoe and Ruangwa rivers. I needed a pit stop.

While I stood there relieving myself, I watched in awe at hippo grazing on whatever green patches they could find. Soon they'd return into the river, as the eastern sky brightened, and before the sun came blazing down. We climbed back into the vehicle and set off on the last section of our journey back to the campsite and to drilling. Apart from the bumps, ruts and rocks on our road back to site, the journey was uneventful. Yet the closer we got to camp, the deeper became my apprehension.

On our arrival I drove straight to the rig to offload the pump. The guys, having heard our approach, were waiting for us. My first thought was: "Where is Major?" He would have heard the vehicle long before anyone else did and come running up to meet us. I reversed the vehicle as close as possible to where the pump was needed and climbed out.

"Come on, guys, let's get this offloaded chop-chop. We need to get drilling and catch up on production loss of the last two days. Where is Major?"

Chapter 51

Clever had arrived, and was looking terribly nervous. "Hello Clever, I can see by your face something is wrong. Where the hell is Major?"

"I'm sorry, Baas. I held him for an hour after we couldn't hear your vehicle, before letting him off his lead. The minute I let him go, he took off at full speed in the direction you had left. And we haven't seen him since." He knew serious trouble was coming.

"How the hell could you let that happen?" I exploded. "You let him go too soon, you bloody fool. We haven't seen him anywhere on our trip back, so tell me, where the hell is he?" My outburst was more a concerned reaction than an angry one. I knew Clever would have held him long after the sound of our vehicle had died down.

I didn't know where to even start looking for Major. We hadn't seen him on the way. I was at my wits end. This was what my premonition was about. Even if he was tired and lying on the side of the road resting he would have run up to the vehicle. All we could do was give him some time. I looked directly at my faithful cook and said, "Clever, I'm sorry I shouted at you, it's my fault. I should not have left him here in the first place."

Major's disappearance was far worse than the pump catching fire. It made me resent even more what Kenneth had done, as that had indirectly caused his disappearance. How could I have been so stupid as to leave him here? It should have been obvious to me that he would follow after me, regardless of how long Clever held him in the camp.

With that we set about commissioning the pump so that we could start drilling. Fortunately the pipe fittings were all the same size, however even if they had not been I had thought ahead and removed the old ones off the burned out pump, so it would have been fine anyway. I then checked the oil, which needed topping up.

Before filling the engine with petrol I grabbed Kenneth's chest by his overalls and yanked him down with his nose just above the fuel tank. "Pleeeeze take note, look carefully. The engine isn't running while I fill it with fuel. Not only did you burn out the pump, but even worse, through your carelessness, Major is now missing." I continued, "You had better pray Major finds his was home safely. If we don't find him, I'll make sure you'll regret it for the rest of your life." In my emotional state I needed to make him suffer.

"Hey, my Baas. I will never make that mistake again. If I do you can leave me here when the contract is complete for the leopards to eat me."

"Well, I tell you, Kenneth, if Major doesn't come back I'm going to leave you down here anyway. I hope you suffer as much as you have caused Major to suffer." I really felt like punching him, but that would not bring back my dog. And I was also to blame. I had chosen to leave Major behind.

By 9.30am I was drilling again, so we had only lost two days. We would drill a few hours extra every day and soon catch up. When setting completion dates for a contract we generally take into account possible standing time due to breakdowns. But right now, Major was far more of a concern than lost time.

The next day, production ran well, but there was no sign of Major. Where on earth could he be? Was he still alive? Was he lying out there, somewhere in the bush, sick or injured? Would I ever see him again? There were many leopards out there. Would he suffer a slow and terrible death?

These thoughts ran around and around in my head. It was hard to concentrate on the job. But in spite of my distracted mind, we continued drilling and made good progress.

Three days after Major's disappearance we were surprised by a vehicle arriving at camp without any of us hearing it approach. It was Gus. Mr. Longstaff had told me he would be coming, but with Major's disappearance I had forgotten. He climbed out and walked over to the rig, saying hello to the guys on the way. "Hi, Trevor, I thought I'd surprise you by coming down to see how the new pump was going," he said with a concerned look on his face.

"Hi, Gus. It's really good to see you, and yes, as you can see, the pump is running like a dream. However, as you can also see, Major is not here and I'm extremely concerned. He has been missing for three days." I felt a lump rise in my throat. Major had become part of me, and was now missing. "Well, he has been seen. But it's not good news." The concern furrows on his brow deepened.

"Please don't keep me in suspense. You have no idea what I have been through since he left, trying to follow me when I went to fetch the new pump from Dave. I should not have left him behind."

"Well, two nights ago he arrived at John's farm, where he was attacked by John's pack of dogs. Once the dust settled two of John's best dogs were dead, and Major, with injuries of his own, left the farm when he realised you weren't there. John is not happy about it at all. But he knows the bond between you and that dog, and that Major came looking for you. It's unfortunate that his dogs attacked him.

"But he hasn't been seen since. Knowing he could be out there somewhere, I kept a good look out for him on my way through from the farm, but there was no sign of him. I don't want to sound negative, but I doubt that even a dog like Major, with what he has been through, could survive much longer out there in the wild."

Tears blurred my vision. This couldn't be happening. My dog could not die. The bond we had was as strong as any human and dog could have. He could not die. I turned away from Gus to gain control, at the same time lighting a cigarette.

"How long are you going to be staying down here with us?" I asked. "I'll be heading back first thing in the morning. I have some supplies for you and then I'll move on to Mavurodona to see Dave. I hear he has managed to get his rods stuck in the hole. With that beautiful formation he's drilling in, that should not have happened." I couldn't resist responding. "Well, please give him a message from me. Tell him to get out his drilling handbook and do some reading. He'll know exactly what I mean. It's a private joke between us, and I'll let him tell you about it, if he wants to."

This brought a small smile to my face, in spite of Major's disappearance.

I asked Gus to take over the rig for an hour and went down to the river and caught four bream for dinner. He was impressed with the fish and chips Clever served up.

We ate beside the rig, while we pushed deep into the night for production. It felt like a five star restaurant.

After a productive shift, at 10.00pm we finally shut the machine and went back to camp. As always, Clever had hot water ready for our baths. After a couple of drinks we went to bed and slept soundly through to 5am.

After the last visit from Mr. Longstaff, which had coincided with a visit from the elephants, I had organised for Clever to build a temporary room out of reeds and thin poles. It lead off from my tent and Gus was happy to sleep in there. If it happened to rain, he would have got wetter in the room than standing outside. The roof of reeds was at best makeshift and gave some shade. As long as there was no rain, it worked well.

Chapter 52

After our early morning coffee, I lit my first cigarette and bade farewell to Gus. He needed to get going early, to try and sort things out at Mavurodona. In the stillness of the early morning the dust from his vehicle hung in a thick cloud long after he was gone.

I set about all the prestart procedures on the drill rig and had everything up and running by 6.00am. Around 8.00am, to my complete surprise, Gus arrived back on site. I immediately thought of Major. Had he found him? If so, was he alive?

I ran over to meet him and there, lying on his front seat was Major. I cannot explain the joy I felt at seeing him or the amount of gratitude I owed Gus for taking the trouble to bring him all the way back to me.

"Thank you Gus, thank you so much," I said running around to the passenger side of the vehicle. I was shocked to see the state Major was in. In that short time he had become skin and bone. He tried to get up, also happy to see me, but he couldn't manage.

His feet were badly swollen and he had deep scratches on his chest and hind quarters. These could not have been caused by the dog fight he had been in on John's farm. It must have been a leopard. But how could he have survived a leopard attack? I leaned into the car, hugging him, and asking "What on earth did you think you were doing going off like that looking for me? You have no idea what you have put me through, let alone what you have put yourself through." He gave me a sad look and I could see he was in pain.

With some difficulty, but with great care, I lifted him out of the car and carried him across to my tent. I laid him down on his blanket. For my trouble I received a sloppy kiss with his huge tongue licking my face as I lowered him. Hell, he was so special to me, and once again tears rolled down my face. This time they were happy tears.

Clever had a bowl of water heating up on the fire. As soon as it was warm enough I set about cleaning his wounds, once again using liberal amounts of Detol and mercurochrome. I was concerned about infection, which could give him a slow and painful death. Out here, there were no other people, let alone any vets.

I considered asking Gus to take him back to Salisbury where he could be treated by a vet. But remembering he was first going to the other site where he could possibly spend a few days, that was not a practical option.

Major was strong, with a will to live. I felt sure that his strong resolve and my tender loving care would get him through. Besides that, I didn't want him out of my sight again.

Fortunately Gus had a first aid kit in his vehicle with a full bottle of Savlon which he left with me to help wash the wounds. I thanked him again for everything. Although Major was in a bad way, he would surely have died had it not been for Gus. For the rest of my life I will be grateful for his help.

On his way out, Gus had stopped at the Mazoe River to have a look at four hippos in the water. As he walked towards the river he noticed there was something lying in the shade of one of the trees. He admitted to feeling rather apprehensive about going up to see what it was, but he wondered if it was Major. He then heard a feeble bark and ran over to him. He was shocked at the state he was in. He tried to get him up so that he could walk to the vehicle, but Major was too weak to walk. He drove his Land Rover as close as he could and lifted Major up onto the front seat. Although it must have been very painful for him, there was hardly a whimper from Major.

I thanked Gus, over and over. Knowing how urgently he needed to get to the other site I apologised for all the time he had taken to rescue Major.

"You would have done the same for me, had it been the other way around," he said, "and good luck. I know you'll have him up and about in no time." As he disappeared in another cloud of dust, I stood and watched in awe. I immediately continued cleaning up Major's wounds. Clever made him a large plate of food and brought a bowl of water. I had to get back to the rig, so left him with Clever, with instructions that if there was any change to let me know immediately.

An hour later I came over to the tent to check on him and Major was asleep, having devoured his food and slurped up a load of water. What a relief. That would get strength surging back through his frail, painful body.

Within a couple of days, with my regular care of his wounds, and good food, Major was strong enough to get up and walk slowly down to the rig. He wanted to be as close to me as he could.

The swelling on his feet had gone down substantially. Thanks to the Savlon, his wounds, although not looking great, were not infected. He had already put on some weight. At last we were over the hill. Soon this nightmare would be behind us. I still had to face John and Sally, following the death of their dogs. I felt terrible about what had happened, but I also knew that Major had to fight in self defence, and was driven by his desperation to find me. But I felt responsible for John's loss.

Major guarding the entrance to my tent

Chapter 53

In a few weeks Major was almost as good as new. He was not as good looking as he used to be because of the scarring. But he was back to running around and leaping up into the vehicle whenever we went off anywhere.

He was ready to come with me one day when going to shoot something for the pot. Clever was busy doing washing so I decided not to take him with me to spot game as usual. My only concern was that if I needed to go into the bush to shoot, Major would be alone in the front of the vehicle. I figured it would not matter this one time. This was a mistake.

About two miles further down the road I spotted an impala about three hundred feet off the road close to a granite kopje. Impala meat is good to eat and the ram was a big one.

Gently I pulled up and stopped the vehicle. I would need to go into the bush and stalk the animal, so decided to leave Major in the passenger seat. Normally this would not be a problem, as Clever would hold him until I called. Ensuring the two small side windows were fully open to give him air, I began to stalk the prey.

There was a reason the ram was as big as he was. He was smart, with sharp senses. He quickly realised there was something going on. As soon as I got close enough to get a shot, he cantered off behind some bushes. This went on for some time. His evasive tactics took us on a route that doubled back towards the road some distance in front of the vehicle. I was determined to get him. We were down to the dregs of our meat supply, and, without food there was little commitment to work.

While staying concealed behind the dry bushes scattered around, in a crouched position, I inched my way closer to him. I was concentrating solely on the impala. I gave no heed to where I was walking or what I might step on. Suddenly there was a loud hiss, the type of hiss that sent tingles down my spine and raised the hairs on the nape of my neck. I stopped dead in my tracks and looked down. There, coiled in front of me, ready to strike and only one step away was a puff adder. I carefully took one step back and remained still. Slowly he relaxed and lowered his head back onto the ground.

Puff adders are the leading cause of snake bite deaths in Africa. Their venom is potent and causes swelling, huge blood blisters, gangarene and disfigurement, and death, anywhere from thirty minutes to three days later. But they are lethargic, and rely on their effective camouflage for protection. They don't move out of the way as most other snakes do, and so are easily stood on. They would rather be left alone than bite a human. If a puff adder feels threatened it assumes a striking position with head down, and nose pointed toward the ground, inflates its body, and emits a deep, scary hiss to warn intruders away. If its warning is heeded it will slowly back away, hissing. But if not, it can strike from any position and in all directions, with speed and force. As I backed further away I could see that he had no further interest in me and was moving off in another direction.

With the adrenalin rush, there was more sweat on my body than from heat alone. I turned my attention back to the impala. He had moved further away up onto a small ridge next to the road. Now that Major was no longer barking in the car, the impala had settled down. This gave me the chance to get in close enough to fire off a shot straight into his head. He leaped into the air, stumbled for a few yards and dropped like a stone.

I ran the three hundred yards or so back to collect my vehicle, to drive it closer to the impala. The impala was large and even once backed right up to it, it would take a mighty effort to get it loaded.

On opening the door of the Land Rover my heart dropped like a stone into my boots. In his frustration on having been left alone to watch me stalking in the scrub, Major had managed to destroy the insides of the cab! Not only were the seats ripped to shreds, but so were the side panels of the door. I stood there dumbstruck, hardly comprehending what I was looking at. Could this just be a bad dream? As much as I loved Major, the thought of shooting him there and then flashed through my mind.

This was the vehicle Mr. Longstaff had just spent thousands on including reupholstering the seats. This was the vehicle I had given my word to looking after with my life! What I saw before my eyes could not be real. It was some kind of nightmare. This could not be happening. Major, by this time, had jumped out the open door and rushed down the road to carry out his usual part of the hunt, ensuring the impala was dead by shaking it by the throat.

In slow motion I pulled all the shreds out of the disaster area and threw them into the back. On doing this I saw the state the seats were in with the springs sticking out. I lifted the floor mats and placed them over the seat so that I would be able to sit on it.

It was great to have shot the impala and not to have been bitten by the puffy, but if I could have waved a magic wand and gone back an hour in my life, and exchanged a new seat for no meat and let the puff adder bite me, I would have done just that.

Why was I forever getting into situations that made me wonder how I would go about telling Mr. Longstaff? This time, more than before, it was going to take some explaining. I knew that once I had finished explaining, I would be given my marching orders. This, coming so soon after the pump burning out, was the end of the road for me.

In a trance I climbed into the vehicle and sat uncomfortably on the floor mats, started the engine and drove down to where the impala was, with Major busy ensuring it would not escape. On reaching them, Major slunk around to the other side of the vehicle, knowing his shares were not good. He knew he had done wrong and when I climbed out and called him around to my side, much like the puffy, he slithered around the back wheels on his tummy, with an 'I'm-so-sorry-Dad-please-forgive-me' look on his face.

As incredibly angry as I was, I could see no point in giving him a hiding. Firstly, being so tough he really wouldn't feel it and secondly, he already knew he had done wrong. And after all, I had only myself to blame for leaving him in there unattended. "Maybe," I said to myself, "one day when I get big I will stop being so stupid."

I turned the Land Rover around and reversed up to the little ridge where the impala was lying. He was far too heavy for me to lift on my own. I would need to drag him on board. Luckily the ridge was just the right height and once the back door was opened and lowered down it was almost level with the ridge. Holding tightly onto his front legs I managed to pull and heave his limp body into the vehicle.

"Well, Major, after all the shit you have caused for the day you could have at least helped me get him onto the truck." With that he gave a quick sharp bark and leaped onto the back and stood over the Impala as if to say, 'Don't worry, Dad, I will make sure he doesn't jump off.' I shook my head, managed a little chuckle and climbed back onto my latest fashion floor mat seat covers and headed back to camp.

On our arrival at the camp Kenneth and Aaron came over to help off load the impala to be skinned and carved up. "Hey, my Baas, what's all this stuff in the back?" Aaron asked on seeing what remained of the upholstery scattered around.

"Just have a look inside the front and you will see." I retorted. He was shocked and called all the others over to have a look. We are so interested in disasters and love to share news of them.

"What is Mr. Longstaff going to say now?" asked Aaron. Through the years, on several occasions, he had been on the receiving end of Mr. Longstaff's wrath, so had a good idea of what was coming my way.

"Well, I don't think I'll tell him. It will be less painful if I just shoot myself!" I could see by the look on his face he wasn't sure if I was joking or not. At that moment I wasn't sure myself.

"Seriously though I'm sure that this time I will be fired. I promised to look after this vehicle and look what I allowed to happen." I was expecting the worst and anything less than the worst would be a bonus.

"Well, we can't all stand around looking at this mess. We have work to do. Sort out the meat, and the rest of you get back to the machine so we can get some drilling done."

With that Aaron and Kenneth offloaded the animal and we set about getting on with the job. While I'd been away, Thousand had done an excellent job operating the controls. It was good to have him there to rely on.

Once the hole was completed, it was time to head off to Salisbury for supplies and diesel, and to face the music regarding the Land Rover seats. While I was away the guys would set up the new site. Taking Major with me, I left at 1.30pm.

On the way, I stopped off at the farm to attempt to apologise to John and Sally for what had happened to their dogs. While they were both still emotional over the tragic incident, they were understanding and didn't blame me for it. They were not happy with Major, but they understood that what he did was in self defence.

Major was always excited to see them and was barking impatiently as John went over to open the door and give him a hug. Naturally he saw the mess of the seats and I related to them the sad story - to their huge amusement. It was some sort of comic-relief pay-back for their disaster.

I offered to pay for replacement dogs of their choice. They refused my offer, and said I should just forget about the whole sad affair. Nothing we did or said would bring back their beloved dogs. They were going out of their way to be kind. After a short stop with them, I said that I needed to be on my way to Salisbury before dark.

They wouldn't hear of me leaving at that time of the afternoon, and insisted I stay over for the night. "I even have some good dog food we can feed Major," said John. "If we keep him full, he just might not try to eat your car again." We all laughed loudly and Major, seeming to know what the joke was, gave off another loud bark.

After a hot shower and a good night in a real bed I thanked them for their hospitality and left early the next morning.

On arriving at the office in Salisbury, I went straight to Mr. Longstaff's office with Major at my heels, to report the incident of the seats. Although we were desperate for supplies, I was not convinced that after telling my story, I would be taking them back.

"Hi, Trevor, I heard you were on your way here, and all the supplies you need are ready for your return trip." He stood up and shook my hand with his normal friendly, firm hand shake.

"Hello, Mr. Longstaff, how are you?" I said, trying to keep my voice as calm as I could.

"Well, thank you, I'm fine. How have you been keeping? You are looking fit, but have lost a bit more weight. It's good to see Major looking so well after his ordeal." He bent down to pat Major who gave a sharp bark in reply. "I'm fine thanks," I answered. "There's a lack of decent restaurants down there, so it's no surprise that I have lost weight." We both laughed.

"I'm really pleased you're in a good mood as there is a serious problem I have to tell you about. I'm not too sure how to go about it." "Well, the truth is normally the best way to go about it." He was still smiling.

"Well, Sir, the last time I said I had some sort of accident you immediately thought it was the Land Rover," I began. It was amazing how quickly the smile disappeared. This was not going to be fun.

There was no change to Mr. Longstaff's stern face as I began relating the story of leaving Major in the vehicle while I went off stalking an impala for the pot. On hearing about the shredded seats in the Land Rover he sat silently with a stunned expression. I would have preferred him to have blown his top. This stunned silence was worse than his anger could ever be.

"It was entirely my fault," I said to fill the ominous silence, " I take full responsibility and will pay in full to have the seats reupholstered once again." What more could I say? It was exactly what had happened and now I needed to face the music and the music eventually came.

"You bloody little whippersnappers never can look after anything. You know well how much money and time had been spent on that vehicle and yet you just don't give a damn and are quite happy to let this happen?"

His good humour was now a thing of the past. "Well, no Sir, I wasn't happy at all." "Don't you butt in while I'm talking to you!" he bellowed, "I should fire you on the spot. I can clearly remember you telling me when I left the vehicle with you that you would look after it with your life. Well, now I need to ask you, how much value do you put on your life?"

He sat there glaring at me, looking so angry I began to wonder what my life expectancy was going to be. "Yes Sir, I know what I said and really meant it. Apart from this episode the vehicle hasn't got a single scratch on it. You know yourself what the roads conditions are like down there. It never entered my mind, not even for one second that Major would do such a thing. To be honest, Sir, he wasn't there when we made the deal, so hopefully you will spare his life." I tried to smile at what I thought was a little joke.

"You never cease to amaze me. Now you are making jokes about this serious situation." Although his face was still stern, I detected the slightest change in the corners of his mouth which I took for a muffled smile. At that moment, Gus, the MD, burst through the door.

"What the hell have you done to the seats of the Land Rover?" He looked even angrier than Mr. Longstaff, which I would not have thought possible. "It's okay Gus. I have already had this out with Trevor. I must give him his due. The minute he arrived he came straight in to tell me what had happened," He looked over at me and said, "Trevor, could you please go out and load the vehicle while I discuss this with Gus?"

I was out of there in a flash having no idea what the future held in store for me. It was only about ten minutes later that Gus came out and told me to go back in to Mr. Longstaff's office as he wanted to talk to me. I looked at him for a clue and he just shrugged his shoulders and walked off towards the workshops.

"Sorry Mr. Longstaff, but Gus said you wanted to see me," I said as I entered his office. "Trevor, I'm really disappointed about the vehicle, and yes, extremely angry as well. My first thought was to fire you." He became more serious."But you have done really well down in the valley and I would like you to complete the contract." I was just about to thank him when he held his hand up to stop me.

"However, as we now need to repair that vehicle *AGAIN*, you will have to leave it here and go down in the other Land Rover. The one that already has old and buggered seats." This time there was a smile on his face. "The total cost of repairs will be taken off you salary until such time as the full amount has been recovered."

"Yes Sir. I hear you loud and clear, and thank you, I'll make it up to you and Major also said to apologise for his actions," I said with a sigh of relief.

"Okay, so get out of here and reload the supplies into the other Landy and get on your way as soon as possible. Don't ever allow anything as stupid as this to happen again. What worries me is these occurrences normally happen in threes, so I dread to think what the next one might be."

"I understand, Sir. And thank you. I promise you won't be sorry." With that I turned and walked out to reload the vehicle and get on my way before he changed his mind.

Chapter 54

I phoned Mike Mitchell a good friend who had said he would like to spend some time with me in the valley. He was between jobs and immediately accepted my invitation. I had met Mike through his gorgeous blond sister Trish. We had gone steady for a few months before I met Les.

Within an hour I was fully loaded. After saying goodbye, I left the office and headed off to collect Mike. On my way I stopped off at Crystal Candy to see Les, my fiancé, who had been working there for some time. She was really surprised to see me as I had not told her I was in town.

It was wonderful to see her after all this time. Our only contact was via letters delivered whenever someone came down to see me. She told me I was getting too thin and so I asked her to come and live with me down there so that she would be able to fatten me up a little.

But I knew this could not happen. We were both saving up to get married at the end of the year. She needed to keep her job, and in any case, I couldn't expose her to our rough conditions. But it felt good to dream.

We spent a happy hour together in her office catching up on all that had happened since we had last seen each other. She was shocked to hear of the incident with Major and the seats, but was soon laughing about it. I suppose, looking at it from the other side, it was rather funny. Her Boss had no complaints about the time I spent with her at work as he knew how little time we were able to spend together.

Sadly the time came to say goodbye. I had to fetch Mike and get through the last dangerous section of the valley before dark. It was hard to leave her. I assured her that we were getting to the end of the contract and that it would not be too long before we would be together again. I kissed her goodbye, fired up the old Landy and waved as I drove off, sitting on worn out seats with a hollow feeling in my stomach.

When I arrived at his house, Mike was ready and raring to go. We hurriedly loaded his few belongings and set off. The back was fully loaded and in the front Major was squashed in between us. In no time we were on our way, talking nonstop of news and events that had happened over the last few months.

I stopped in at John's farm to say hi and to introduce Mike. It was mid-afternoon, so it had to be a short visit. They invited us to spend the night. As tempting as that was, we decided to head for the site. We bade farewell and set off into the wilderness that lay beyond their farm. Once again civilisation would become a thing of the past.

We made slow progress. The road was dangerous, and our load was heavy. Mike was impressed with the huge granite kopjes and all the animals we saw. There were two large kudu cows standing not too far from the road. I pulled up, and for a few minutes we sat and watched them. They looked straight at us with their ears flared wide, listening for any sound that might alarm them. When I eventually pulled away they both went bounding into the bush, seeming to float effortlessly over the small bushes with their fluffy tails erect. I was always impressed by how such large animals could be so agile and graceful.

I pointed out to Mike where we had drilled the first two holes and then stopped to show him the spring of water I had found when we first moved in. We were amazed by how many footprints there were around the pool. Mike asked to climb to the top to see what I had done to join the two streams. The little wall we had built was still intact. I was sure it would be for years to come. He was awed by the beautiful view looking way down into the valley. We had seen some large cumulous clouds building up on our way in. It was as though they had waited for us to get to the top before beginning their spectacular show.

Chapter 55

Suddenly, down in the valley, there was a flash of forked lightning followed by a loud crack and the echoing rumble of thunder. Almost instantly there was another flash. This time it seemed to latch onto something and hold onto it for a few seconds, remaining bright. Once again the loud crack of thunder followed, but this time from where the lighting had struck there was a puff of smoke. This happened another three or four times. We were spellbound. Neither of us had ever witnessed anything like it. The roll of thunder was continuous, and rumbled through the granite valleys.

Abruptly, we came to our senses and hurried, slipping and sliding down the rock face to get to the vehicle before we were a target of the lethal, dazzlingly bright lightning. Once safely in the front of the Land Rover I was surprised to see even big, brave, strong Major, was shivering with fright.

We were in awe of the beauty and power of the thunderstorm. I convinced Mike that we were safe in the Land Rover with its body of aluminium standing on four rubber tyres. We would not be a conductor for the lightning. I didn't believe myself any more than he believed me.

Then the heavens opened and rain came pouring down. Large drops hit the dry, hot and dusty soil. The smell of new rain on dry ground is one of the most intoxicating smells on earth.

The rain was going to make it difficult to get down the escarpment which was not easy even when it was dry. Now there was slippery mud everywhere. The arrival of the rain eased the thunder claps which became less frequent. We needed to get going, before there was a wash-away keeping us from ever arriving at the site.

"Hey, Trevor! I didn't come down here with you to go hurtling off a cliff or being struck by lightning before we even arrive. I'm too young to die, and I wouldn't want to die here." He was nervous. On our way into the valley we had already traversed a few small passes. I told him he had not seen anything yet. The escarpment we were heading for was much steeper, with tight turns and sheer drops. There was no room for error.

"Mike, we have been good mates for years. Do you honestly think I would do anything dangerous? You know me, always careful." I said it with tongue in cheek and he responded by laughing.

"Shit, Trevor, if anyone else told me that bullshit I might listen. But coming from you, the one who never holds back, is always full of shit and who doesn't ever get nervous about anything, I just know you're joking."

I shook my head and said, "Well, we're a couple of miles from the top of the escarpment and we could be lucky and find there's no rain there. These thunderstorms can be localised."

We drove off into the rain, hoping that all the supplies were dry. The windscreen wipers, although in working order, were ineffective. Vision was restricted to a few yards. Even someone as stupid as me would not think of attempting to go down the pass in these conditions.

I was about to turn around when, as suddenly as it had started, the rain eased off and stopped. Although there were large heavy clouds still hovering, when we reached the top of the escarpment, it was dry and we could see no sign of rain down in the valley.

"There you go, Mike. What did I tell you? This will be a walk in the park." "Well, it looks fine here. But what happens if the rain starts again further down. We could be stuck half way without being able to go up or down." "Hell, Mike, I didn't know you could be so pessimistic. Just believe that it won't rain and, trust me, it will be dry all the way." With that I set off down the steep road leading down into the valley. I pointed out to him the place that the Rhino had spun around and scared the hell out of us. Having been through so much since then, that incident seemed to come from another life time.

Mike was agitated. "If this all goes really wrong, don't ever tell me I didn't warn you. You always bloody well think you know everything and that you're indestructible. But we're not indestructible. The end will happen in its own time. Why the shit are we going out of our way to look for it?" His eyes widened as we started our descent.

"Mike, I would never put your life in danger. I know I do things that are out of the ordinary, but I can promise you, I would never let any harm come to you," I said confidently.

"Well, to be honest, if I have to get to the bottom of this pass, I'm really glad it's you in control." He had resigned himself to a rough trip down.

Slowly, but surely we wound our way down. Apart from the odd lightning strike it was dry. As we arrived at the last one hundred yards of the pass, as dusk was falling, a huge black beast appeared in front of the Land Rover and ran thundering down the road. It was a fully grown hippo. It had travelled far in its search for food.

We followed it all the way down the steep decent, as it headed for water. The road was very steep, and it would not be possible for him to stop. His huge, top-heavy body threatened to overtake his short legs which were going at full speed. Surely any minute now he would go somersaulting down the slope. That didn't happen. Eventually, with spray flying, he crashed through the reeds into the safety of the water of the Mozoe River. There was a loud splash, and the ripples moving outwards were the only sign he had been there. In my mind, I could see him running along the river bed almost as fast as he ran on land.

By now all three of us needed a pit stop. I let Major out of his squashed seat in the front and he raced off in the direction the hippo had gone. He stood on the river bank barking, letting the hippo know how lucky he was to have got away. The arrogance of the dog never ceased to amaze me. He was sure he could tackle the hippo, and ran up and down the river bank barking furiously for some time. Eventually he admitted defeat, squatted down, and did what he needed to do. Then he ran back to the Land Rover and leapt up into his seat, ready to go again.

Chapter 56

We arrived safely at the camp just after dark, to find Clever with water on the fire in anticipation of my arrival. On seeing I had a guest with me he set about organising another five-gallon container of water for Mike's bath. He informed me that all was well, the machine had been moved to the new site, the dead men bolts had been installed and cemented in and by morning we should be able to pull the shear legs up and start drilling again.

We had brought some steaks with us along with ration meat for the guys. Shovelling coals from the fire, we soon had two steaks cooking on the braai grid, and we ate them with the Sudza and tomato and onion gravy Clever prepared for us in a large pot. He had also prepared a large plate of food for Major, who was as hungry as we were. He wolfed it down noisily slapping around his hideously long tongue, shovelling food into his mouth.

I told Mike about our nightly visitors, and said that he would sleep inside the tent while I slept in the little reed room next to it. He was more what we would call a '*townie*' and not a '*bush baby*'. He had spent little, if any, time in the bush with wild animals. So, quite happy with the arrangement, he transferred the few things he had brought with him into the tent. He was sure I was exaggerating regarding the visitors, but was not willing to take a chance.

We were tired and by 11.30pm were bathed, teeth brushed, and asleep in bed. Major, as always slept at the bottom of my bed. At 2.15am he nudged me awake. Was it the change in the weather and the rain that brought such a large herd to visit us that night? The tent and little reed room were completely surrounded by elephant. It was the largest heard I had seen, and even I felt vulnerable. I slipped through from my little room into the tent to wake Mike, putting my hand over his mouth. I didn't want him to wake with a fright and panic. He jerked up from a deep sleep and sat bolt upright with eyes wide open, trying to fathom where on earth he was. He saw me with my finger to my lips, letting him know to be silent. Fortunately he took heed. I whispered to him to be quiet, and told him we were surrounded by elephant. He looked out through the opening of the tent and slowly walking past, within touching distance was an elephant. I felt him stiffen and squeezed his arm to reassure him. He was terrified. I quietly suggested that he relax and enjoy the experience.

We sat together looking out through the tent until about 3.00am. It was awesome, watching such a crowd of huge beasts, capable of killing us in seconds, peacefully wandering around outside. Mike asked if he could try and take a photo with his cheap little camera. It was not a good idea, as the flash could give them a fright. As they filed past the tent I was again astounded that a heard of such large animals, each one weighing tons, could move so silently. What was noisy was the stomach rumbles they emitted. This was done deliberately, as a form of communication in the herd. They also emit a sound in a frequency not audible to human ears, but which can be heard up to four miles away by other elephants.

Elephants are family orientated animals. They protect their young in the herd at all costs, who stay close to their mother like a shadow until around four years old. By that age, even though smaller than full grown elephants, they're old enough to fend for themselves. They move away from their mothers but continue to enjoy the protection of the herd.

Elephant are renowned for their intelligence, their complex matriarchal social structures, and their communication methods. They spend on average sixteen hours a day eating grass, twigs, bark, seed pods and fruit, of which 60% becomes waste and is deposited in huge heaps of dung. During these hours they also wallow and roll in deep mud, throw sand over their bodies and drink around forty-gallons of water. They suck water up through the trunk and then squirt it back into the mouth. The males are well-endowed, which is plain to see when following their tracks down a sandy road. The male often leaves a drag mark between his footprints. When sexual organs were handed out, they were at the front of the queue.

By the time the herd left, Mike had calmed down. He realised that as long as we didn't react, our survival was sure.

"Why is it that Major doesn't chase them, or at least bark?" he asked. "Good question. He seems to know to stay calm. Could it be that he's as shit scared as we are?" I said, smiling. "Okay, Mike, I have work to do tomorrow and need sleep. It won't do you any harm to do the same." With that I returned to my reed hut and fell asleep immediately.

By the time the early morning light crept onto the horizon I was up and about. Mike had an interesting night with our visitors, and had a long day ahead, so left him to sleep.

There were foot prints and large dung piles around the tent, spreading off into the bushveld. The attraction was the huge tree under which I had pitched my tent. They eat the seeds from this tree. Now it seemed they had eaten every last seed. The area was now barren, and there were no more of their favourite groceries left. I was sure they would move on to another eating spot.

I brushed my teeth, drank a cup of coffee, and set off to the machine with a lit cigarette in my hand. The guys were already on site and I marvelled once again just how hard they worked without complaint. Thousand had completed all the checks to make sure the umgwalas were solidly embedded in front of the two front legs of the shear legs, ready to be pulled up.

"Kenneth, I assume you have checked that there's enough petrol for the pump engine once we're ready to start drilling?" I asked, smiling. The guys laughed and Aaron slapped him on the back saying, "Eh, Kenneth, you are going to be stuck with this for a long time." We had everything rigged and ready to go by 8.00am. I knew I had found my niche in exploration drilling and would make a career from it. There was nothing else I would rather do for a living.

Around 8.30am, Mike arrived at the rig, looking bright and chirpy. "Morning Mike, how did you sleep after the visitors left?" I asked. "Surprisingly well, what an experience. You certainly have a different life out here. It will be great for a few days. But…" he hesitated as he looked out at nothing but trees and bushveld for as far as the eye could see, "on a long-term basis I wouldn't do very well. I don't think I like my own company well enough." "I felt the same way," I said. "Yet now I enjoy every day I live here – even the days with drama. There aren't many people in the world who have the experiences I have, almost every day." "Well, to be honest, I don't think there are many people who would want to have those experiences badly enough to live under these conditions." he said. "Look, Mike, since you are only here for a few days why don't you go and have a bit of fun and catch us a few fish for breakfast. We'll need about eight fish. Clever will give you my rod and show you where to get worms," I said.

With my imagination running wild, I could already smell the fish cooking. Suddenly I was hungry and also excited to have my good friend Mike with me for a few days.

"Trevor, you know me. I know where all the discos and nightclubs are in the city, but haven't a clue how to go about catching a fish," he exclaimed. "Well, Mike. There's no time like the present." Unfortunately, I'm too busy to come down with you, but Clever will help you. After catching your first fish you won't want to stop. It's a great feeling when a bream is pulling the line off your reel. It's almost better than sex." I laughed. "Hope you don't mind mud on your hands, or threading worms onto the hook, or taking the fish off the hook." "I think you're pushing it a bit," he said dubiously, "but it sounds like it could be fun. Hey, will I be safe down there with elephants and leopards all over the place?" He was out of his depth here in the bush and had to be coaxed into enjoying himself.

We had all been living under these conditions for months, and felt perfectly at home. I had to remind myself how vulnerable we felt when we first arrived. Yes, we could understand Mike's apprehension.

"Mike, trust me. You will be fine. Clever and Major will look after you. Major loves going down there. When you catch something, be careful, as he tries to grab the fish off the line as it comes out of the water." So, off went Mike with Major and Clever, to catch some breakfast for us. When he discovered how much fun it was, he would want to go fishing every day. Fishing is a relaxing sport. The only thing on your mind is wondering what the fish are doing and what they are feeding on today. Down here in the valley it was easy to catch them, as there is not much for them to feed on in the river.

I usually used as light tackle as possible because it was good fun landing the Three Spot Bream which thrived in the rivers. This bream has a broad tail and it's one of the best fighters there is. It never gives up. To best appreciate this, you need to have the experience with light tackle, and not just hear stories about it. Then of course, there is the barbel which, although much slower through the water, is also a strong fighter. It is lined in at a slower pace. They take a lot of line off the reel before they are eventually tired out. It's strong and steady, unlike the bream that really makes the reel sing.

Barbel are not as popular for eating, because they are ugly and have whiskers and a slimy body. But they are very tasty. Once the skin and head have been removed, they could be mistaken for kingklip. It's been said that restaurants sometimes sell barbel advertised on the menu as kingklip. They grow into large fish, up to 35 lbs. Their sister fish, the Vundu, is similar in appearance, but has a double dorsal fin rather than a single one. The Vundu can grow to an excess of 110 lbs. Hooking one of these in a fast flowing river is impossible to land as they turn and run with the flow and in no time strip all the line from your reel.

By 10.30am Mike was back at the rig and as excited as I have ever seen him. "We just had so much fun. Those fish are amazing to catch." He was like a kid with a new toy and I told him so. "Well," he exploded, "if you had been with us you would have understood. Boy oh boy! They were really hungry and I had no problem catching enough for all of us once Clever had shown me how to set my reel. I lost the first few due to the drag being too tight," he said enthusiastically.

"I can't believe how much of my life I have wasted not going fishing!" "Well," I reminded him, "I have asked you many times to come fishing with me, but there was always a reason why you couldn't make it. All you could see were discos and what chicks would be there!" He burst out laughing, nodding his head in agreement.

Within half an hour Clever arrived at the rig with our beautifully cooked fish. Frozen fish has its place, but, there is just nothing to compare with fresh fish straight from the river, filleted and fried in the pan. Not only had Mike never before caught fish, but he had hardly ever eaten any. Having enjoyed fishing from a young age, I found this hard to believe. If he learned nothing else on his visit down here, he had been converted into being a keen fisherman.

With breakfast over, the core barrel was full and ready for the drill rods to be removed from the hole and the core taken out of it and placed in the core box. Mike was interested to know what was going on. I explained the process of how to pull the rods, how the brake and clutch leavers worked, and how to control the speed of the pull through the accelerator lever. He then learned how we lowered the rod gently using a 24" wrench spanner as a rod clamp onto the log of wood securely placed for this purpose.

I demonstrated once each rod loosened to pull up gently on the winch to ensure the treads were loose from those held in the wrench. Once the rods parted I taught him to lower it down gently onto the rod stand. Within a few days, I had him pulling and lowering rods, slowly and carefully. I suggested he could take up drilling as a career, but he declined saying he would not be able to take the bush and loneliness.

Chapter 57

Mike's week in the bush was coming to an end. He had lots of fun, and caught loads of fish. I told him he could catch as many fish as he liked, but to only keep enough bigger ones for us to eat, releasing the rest for us to enjoy on another day.

It was wonderful having Mike avidly fishing every day. It negated the need for me to shoot for the pot. For the whole week, we lived on fresh fish, which is a healthier diet than all the red meat we had been eating. The other advantage to his daily fishing was that it allowed me to get on with the job, knowing he was having fun on his own with Major. It was also good to see how attached Major had become to Mike during their fishing jaunts together. He was leaving on Monday with Peter, the geologist, who suggested that Mike should stay permanently. We gave him a large bag of fish fillets that Mike had caught, and they had really enjoyed them.

I had promised Mike we would have a braai down at the river before he left. While down there, we could catch some Barbel. With great excitement, on Sunday we all took a well-earned day off the rig. While I sorted out some stronger fishing tackle for both of us, the guys closed up their tents and sorted out the pots for cooking the Sudza. Even Major knew something exciting was going on, and he ran around barking constantly, believing he was supervising.

I knew that, after a full week away from civilisation, Mike was homesick and ready to go. But I also knew he had been introduced to another way of life, and would miss that too.

Once everything was on board we set off with Mike, Major and me in the front with the rifle, and all the guys and the equipment on the back. If we were going to have a braai, I needed to shoot something along the way.

We left early, with the sun just up. Mike had been uncomfortable in the heat, not only during the day, but also through the hot nights which were almost always windless. He had also changed colour from the white city boy to a well-tanned red/brown. His chick back in Salisbury would be impressed.

On the way to the river, when we reached the top of the first pass, there was a tap on the roof. Looking quickly from side to side I saw the klipspringer no more that forty yards off the road. I stopped the vehicle, pulled the hand break on and slowly climbed out of the car. Slowly, but deliberately I took a fine bead through the 'v' sights on the luckless animal, and fired. He took one leap into the air, stumbled, and fell over dead. In no time, amid shouts of glee from the guys, Clever and Aaron had the buck on board and we were ready to go. After eating fish for a week we were looking forward to red meat.

After finding our meat for the day, we continued on down to the main river. When we arrived, Mike and I sorted out our fishing tackle while Aaron took control of skinning and cutting the buck into steaks. Some say that venison should hang for a while before eating, but we skinned the animal, cut it up, and dropped some of the steaks onto the braai grid right there and then. It had an ultra fresh wild meaty taste.

When the fishing rods and the tackle boxes had been sorted out, and the earth worms safely housed in a small wooden box with a string handle, Mike, Major and I waded through the rapids to fish from the white sand bank on the other side. Once on the bank we baited our small hooks with worms and cast into the slow flowing river. Within minutes we had both pulled in a couple of small bream. These we cut into fillets, removed the bream trace and replaced it with a barbel trace. This is a steel trace and swivel, a much larger hook and a lead weight firmly tied with a fisherman's knot to the line. After attaching the bream fillet to the large hook we cast way out into the middle of the river.

While standing with rod in hand waiting for a strike, we watched a hippo that kept exposing his head above the water, giving it a good shake and making that characteristic snorting, grunting, plopping sound. Major, having always shown an interest in hippo, was no different this time. Each time the hippo surfaced he ran to the edge of the water and barked.

Suddenly there was a strike on my rod. Just a gentle pull to begin with, but once the fish felt pressure on the line he took off downstream rapidly stripping line off the reel. This was a big fish and would take some time to land. My rod bowed over almost to the point of breaking. I had struck and set the hook and continued to give short, sharp, jerky pulls on the rod to try and end his mission to go downstream. The trick was to turn his head and get him to swim towards me. Eventually he obliged and ever so slowly I managed to pull and reel him in. The only way I could tell if I was winning the battle was by checking the amount of line on my reel. It was slowly filling up again, so I knew if I continued with what I was doing I would at some stage land this beauty. Mike watched me fighting my fish, when suddenly his reel also starting singing that wonderful song when the line is being stripped off the spool. He gave a squeal of delight and shouted across to me, "If you think your fish is big, just wait till you see this one!"

This was the first big fish he had ever hooked. I shouted instructions and warned him that our lines could become tangled as both fish had headed off downstream.

"Well," boasted he, "I'm not going to let mine swim away down river. I'm going to tighten the drag a little more." "Don't do that," I yelled back. "He will snap your line and you'll lose the fish." I had hardly completed my sentence when there was a loud snap, almost like a gunshot, as his line parted.

"Shit, Mike. Why the hell don't you listen to me for once in your life? You have just lost a beautiful fish and the chance of another one that size taking your bait is slim." I called for him to come over and take my rod, and the battle I was having with my fish. He was leaving the next day. I would hook many more in the future, and I wanted him to have the experience of landing this beauty.

Nervously and somewhat reluctantly he took the rod from me. "Sorry for losing all that tackle and the fish. Tell me what I need to do. I'll listen!" He had laid the rod with the broken line against a dead log to keep the reel off the sand. I lifted his rod and running it though my fingers to maintain tension for tight spooling started reeling in what was left of the line.

"Right! Don't touch the drag, regardless of what happens. He'll make another run. Let him go. Be patient. He'll tire himself out and you will eventually land him." "They are very strong fish!" he exclaimed. "I can't believe how hard he pulls on the line." He was laughing. It was good to see him so excited. He loved every minute of the struggle.

Just then the hippo popped up again, shaking his ears and sending water flying everywhere in a silver spray. Before I knew what was happening, Major left my side and ran headlong into the river. He swam straight for the hippo who had by this time gone back under water.

I shouted and screamed for him to come back, but he was on a mission and could not or would not hear me. He swam headlong in the direction of the hippo's last appearance. I got into a terrible state, and was convinced this would be the end of one of the best friends I had ever had. Major was no match for a hippo, but also the river was crawling with crocodiles. He had no chance, and had gone past the point of no return. I ran to the edge of the river and started to wade in.

"Don't be so bloody stupid, Trevor! What do you think you can do by going after him? You'll just turn yourself into crocodile food." Mike was shouting, while still holding onto the bent rod with the line peeling off the reel. He was not going to let this one get away. "Also, if you go in there and get eaten by a croc or the hippo, who is going to drive us back to the camp? I leave tomorrow and I need to get back there to pack" He was laughing at his own joke. He was right. Going into the river would have been suicide. Even under the circumstances I smiled at his sense of humour.

"Sure Mike, but with you leaving, Major is the only real companion I have down here. I can't just leave him to die this way." I was beside myself, feeling dreadfully inadequate and helpless, having no idea how to save him or to help him in any way.

Major was now out in the middle of the river, close to where the hippo had last come up. Suddenly and violently the smooth ripples running along on the surface of the river exploded with the hippo's head rising dangerously close to where he was.

What happened next would have made a priceless video. I'm not sure who had the biggest fright - the hippo seeing Major swimming as fast as he could towards him, or Major coming to the realization that if what he saw was only the head, just how large was the rest of him?

The hippo immediately disappeared below the surface and Major, spinning and rising up out of the water to his waist with his front legs pumping frantically at air until he sank down again and could swim for the shore like a speed boat with a distinct wake coming off his shoulders.

There was just no way he could out-swim the hippo, even with the hippo running along the bottom. Instinctively I picked up a large piece of drift wood that had been washed onto the sand bank. With all the strength I could muster I hurled it high into air in Major's direction. It landed some metres behind him. I hoped it would be a diversion.

As it hit the surface with a huge splash, almost immediately there was another large swirl right next to the branch that could only be a crocodile. As to whether this was a distraction or just a coincidence I will never know, but would like to believe that it did help to give Major some extra seconds.

In a panicked stupor he came stumbling and running towards me, coming to an abrupt halt right in front of me. He shook himself violently from head to tail. The water flew in a spray from his saturated fur in a large arc. *"What the hell did you think you were doing allowing me into the river like that with all these monsters around?"* his panicked eyes seemed to ask.

I dropped onto my knees feeling that I had managed to be there just this once to repay all the times he had been there for me. I gave him a hug and he returned the favour with a sloppy kiss with his tongue slapping across my face. Pulling away he tore off to Mike barking his head off telling him of the terrifying ordeal he had just endured.

With all the excitement of having Major back safe and sound on the sand bank I had forgotten all about Mike and his fish.

"How are you doing there, Mike? Shit, you townies are such wimps that it takes you forever to land a fish?" In my overwhelming relief I pulled his leg.

"Well, it was you that said I should be patient, so for once I'm just trying to do as I'm told. He can't be far out now as the reel is pretty full of line. I will have him in soon. My arms are getting really tired."

The strain on his face was starting to show, with sweat running like a waterfall from every pour in his body. He was excited, and the temperature well into the 40 deg C. Then there it was. With a swish and swirl of its tail the fish came into the shallows near the sand bank. The water was crystal clear and the huge barbel could be seen moving through the water looking tired and lethargic from a momentous struggle with Mike. To my surprise, especially after the ordeal he had just been through, Major once again shot into the water and grabbed the fish just behind the head and shook it so violently that it looked like he was taking out his frustration at missing the hippo on the poor fish. He then half carried and half dragged it from the river and dumped it onto the sand bank in front of Mike as if to say: *'Now there, that's the way to land a fish."*

The Barbel was huge and when Mike eventually managed to lift the slippery fish and hold the head level with his shoulder the tail was still resting on the ground. His first big one was a really big fish.

"Well done Mike, that was one hell of a fight and something tells me you'll relate this story for quite some time to come!" I said, smiling. "Trevor, please don't tell anyone you actually hooked the fish. I won't tell anyone I caught a bigger fish than you did," he said, laughing loudly.

I replied. "All I can say is if you could sell all the shit you speak you would be a millionaire."

Now we were both laughing and I felt so privileged to be so happy out here in the middle of nowhere and to share it with a really close friend. "Normally I would have released a fish like this one, but after the injuries Major has inflicted on the poor thing it will die anyway. We'll give it to the guys to cut into strips and hang for eating later," I said, looking at the huge fish. "There's a lot of good food there."

Aaron, having watched the whole episode, was wading through the river by the rapids to come and collect the catfish that would keep us in food for the next few days. He wasn't going to let this monster be put back into the river.

"Hey, Baas, that is a big fish that Mr. Mike has caught, bigger than any you have caught before." That was all Mike needed. Now I would never hear the end of it. "Yes, well, I made up the traces and sorted out the fillets for bait and told him where to cast, don't I get some credit?" I asked. "Well, yes, my Baas, but Mr. Mike caught the fish." I could see there was no point in my pushing the issue, Mike was the hero and rightly so. He had fought the fish for a long time. It was a great way for him to complete his visit. He was a good friend and it was satisfying to have shared my life style with someone from back home.

Chapter 58

By this time the coals were almost ready for cooking and the buck had been cut into strips and a few good steaks. I told Mike that we should wander back across the river and get ready for a meal fit for a king – or, at least, a king of the bush.

Mike, being the townie that he was, had never eaten Sudza. On first arriving he had refused to eat it, saying he had never tried it before and would not enjoy it. But with little else to eat, by the second day we got him to try some, together with the gravy Clever made. After that, he was sold on Sudza. It was another good thing he learned on his visit with me. He had also learned to fish, and had become accustomed to elephant coming through the camp. Even the cough of a nearby leopard no longer scared him. In my estimation, he was at last becoming a man.

It was around 2.30pm and we were all good and hungry as we waited for Clever to cook the steaks. Thousand told us he was in charge of both the Sudza and the gravy for the day. Once everything was ready and served up it turned out to be another great meal. As we washed the meal down with a cool Coke, Mike commented that one of the first things he was going to do on getting back to civilisation was to have an ice cold Coke.

On finishing our meal we both lit a smoke and sat in the rapids to enjoy it. We were fairly safe as far as crocodiles were concerned. Should there be one hungry enough to enter the rapids to try us out for a meal, the chances were good we would see it coming and have time to get out.

In the heat of the day, the cold water running over our bodies felt like Nirvana in Africa. Even Major sat there with us, with just his head showing above the water. Mike was in his element, grinning broadly, taking a regular pull on his cigarette and with satisfaction blowing smoke out into the air and allowing it to drift away on the light breeze.

"Hell," he said with a twinkle, "it's tough in Africa. But, hey, someone has to do it, so we may as well volunteer." Much laughter followed and I was so proud of what he had accomplished that day.

After we had all had a good bath in the river we felt like new men and the time had come for us to clear up our mess and head on back to camp. The sun was on its journey down to the horizon. The temperature was still in the high 30's C.

"Mike, as you are leaving in the morning, would you like to drive us all back to camp? This is your last chance," I asked. "There's no way in the world you're going to persuade me to take the responsibility of driving you all back over that pass. Are you trying to shorten your life span?" he laughed. "Right then, let's get going guys. We must get back before dark."

We loaded up the vehicle with the cooking pots, fishing gear, meat, fish and people, with Major once again sitting like Lord Muck on Toast between Mike and me. We headed off in a cloud of dust for the camp.

That night, as if to say farewell to Mike, the elephants down by the pools in the Ruangwa River were having a whale of a time rolling and splashing around in the mud. It was just before dusk. There were some amazing sounds coming from the pools. Mike and I crept up as close as possible to watch the noisy mud bath.

We sat with a Coke in one hand and cigarette in the other, marvelling at the show. One of the elephants was lying on his side in the mud puddle they had created, and was thrashing his head up and down with his trunk flaying all over the place. He was covered in thick sticky mud from head to tail and toe and was blissfully happy about it.

There were young elephants with their mothers in close attendance being ushered around in the shallows of the pool sucking in trunk-full's of water and squirting it into their mouths. I wondered whether they ever accidently sucked up a fish and squirted it into their massive bellies. There were others half in the mud and half in the pool. Instead of sucking clean water into their trunks they sucked a mix of probably 80% mud and 20% water. This they tossed over their heads and sprayed it all down their backs. Had they not been such huge, beautiful and majestic animals, they could have been mistaken for a bunch of naughty children playing in the mud after being told by their mothers to stay away from it.

Mike and I continued our vigil until it was too dark to see them anymore, then headed back to our camp.

Mike was interested by how many of the sounds coming from the pool could be mistaken for a lion's roar. These sounds continued late into the night. Whether there were any lions in the area, well, I had no idea. In all the time I had been there I had not seen or heard them.

There was no reason for them not to be here as we were close to the Zambezi Valley which is well known for its lion population. If there were lions around I would not feel as safe as before. They don't have a problem attacking humans for food.

Peter, the geologist would be arriving early in the morning to load full core boxes and head off to Salisbury with Mike. Having bathed in the river and eaten a late lunch there was nothing we needed to do, after such a big day we decided that an early night would be the way to go.

"Trevor thanks for a great day and for giving me the chance to catch such a huge fish. You have no idea how excited I was about that. It's something I'll never forget and something that I'll probably never be in a position to repeat. " said Mike. "Well, who knows? Somewhere down the road we'll do some more fishing together. Just promise me you'll listen next time," I said with a smile."Yeah, yeah, yeah. I'm never going to hear the end of this. Yes I plead guilty, I set the drag too tight and snapped the line, but I did manage to land the other one. I should get some points for that?" "I promise I will never say another word."

We retired to our respective beds and with the soothing sounds of the crickets calling and the '*woo woo*' of the owl in the background we slept soundly.

Chapter 59

We had reached the completion depth of 615 feet on our third hole. Theoretically, we should only have one more hole to drill. Having Mike visit us for the week highlighted for us just how ready we all were to complete the contract and move back to civilization. By this time we were confident that we would have the contract wrapped up and be ready to pack up and move out of here by the end of October before the rains set in.

Peter arrived at the rig at around 7.30pm. That meant he had been up really early to complete the two-hour drive from his camp. In the back of his pick-up there were two dead impala. "Hi Trevor, thought you could do with some meat. I'll leave one here with you and drop the other one off at our camp on my way through to Salisbury. You can never have too much to eat. You know that better than most, after those two and a half weeks when you were all fasting." He found that funny, and in a weird way it was. "Thanks, Peter, we do have meat. It saves me having to shoot again for a few days. As you know, I'm never happy killing these poor animals. "

"Come on, Trevor. There are so many down here. If anything, you need to look at it as a culling exercise. You are, in the long term, doing them all a favour. Each one you shoot allows another one more grazing. " he said, trying to look serious.

"Well, Peter. I'll believe you. But thousands wouldn't," I said laughing.

He began the process of methodically logging the core that had been laid out neatly in the core boxes. At six hundred and thirteen feet there was a minor intersection of ore zone. I may have been wet behind the ears, but there seemed to be nothing that looked promising. Peter confirmed that the results were nowhere near what the Mining House had hoped for. But he had his red wax crayon and marking pen out, and he went through the motions of marking and taking notes of what was there.

"Trevor, I'm not sure what to do here. This could be a hanging ore zone stringer, forced up from a mineralised section bellow." scratching the core with his pen knife continued, saying "Shortly who knows we could drill into a massive ore-body," he said, with consternation on his face.

"We are only fifty four feet past this section, and the end of hole was originally going to be 600 feet. Do I get you to drill on even though we are already fifteen feet beyond our final estimate of E.O.H. (End of hole)?"

Peter was facing a difficult and expensive dilemma. I, being new at the drilling game, could not be of much constructive help.

"Hey Peter, this has been the only reasonable intersection we have had, what chance is there of drilling into something better?" I wasn't sure what else to say. "If I could make a suggestion," I added more hopefully, "Why don't you take this core box with you and head off back to your head office and let them make the decision?" "Yes," he said. "I was thinking the same thing. I really don't know what to do. I would hate to stop the hole with the possibility of hitting big pay dirt within the next sixty feet. I would always wonder if I had done the right thing. If there was nothing within that time I would feel sure it's not there, but until then, or possibly, a decision by head office, I will always wonder about the possible outcome." "Well," I concluded, "the sooner you get off to Salisbury the better. We can't afford to stand for too long. It will be at least three days before you have an answer for us to go with this hole, or move to the new one. In the meantime, we'll get the new site prepared so there won't be much time wasted."

With that plan in place I followed Peter over to what would be the new and last drill hole. As usual, being the last site, it was furthest from the water and in a difficult area. Fate always ensured that nothing is easy. A lot of excavation would be required to get to the site. Peter offered to leave two of his guys to help with this. I was grateful, as I had no spare labour. I knew somewhere in the contract it was agreed that the Mining House would help out with site preparations where possible. Up to now we had done everything ourselves. Extra help now would be most welcome.

As we walked back I took note of granite boulders we would have to pull out of the way using the Land Rover and the old hoist cable.

Chapter 60

As soon as Peter gave the word, Mike was at the rig ready to go. He had his one and only small clothes bag with sleeping bag and pillow attached to it by a thin length of rope. He looked sad to be leaving and I certainly was. He had been a wonderful companion and I had really enjoyed teaching him a little about drilling, fishing, elephants, hippo and leopards.

When I serviced the rig and pump I taught him how to remove and fill it with new oil, how to fit oil filters, fit and then bleed diesel filters and clean air filters. He had never before bathed in a tin tub or in the rapids with crocs and hippo for company in the nearby pools. His short week down here in this awesome and remote area had been quite an education. I felt honoured to have been the one to give him this opportunity.

Peter and Mike were ready to go. I quickly ran to my tent to get the list of supplies I would need Peter to bring back with him. I was desperate for a couple of drill bits and some other in-hole equipment. If Peter didn't bring them back with him the rig would have to stand until they arrived.

I had kept my orders down to the minimum as we were going to be overloaded on our trip out. We couldn't assume that we'd get everything onto the trucks in the first place. I was not looking forward to the trip out, to climbing the passes with the kind of load we would be carrying. It was going to be one hell of a mission. But that was something to worry about when the time came.

Just before leaving Peter said, "By the way. Just off from the Mazoe River there's a large pool with loads of hippo in it. It's quite something to see. I came across them while looking for a kudu for our meat supplies. If you have a little time to spare, go and see the hippo. It's quite easy to find. Follow the north western side of the river along a rough track, which is hard to see in places. But as you muddle your way along, the track will lead you to the pool. You'll recognise it by seeing a dry stream coming in on the left not too far from the spot you're heading for." He gave me a rough sketch map with approximate distances.

"Thanks. Depending on how we get on with the new site, I might just do that." I bade farewell to Mike and Peter. As I watched them drive away, I felt lost and far from home. Seeing them go made me more determined to complete the contract and get back to civilization. For the next two days we worked hard on the new site, until we were satisfied it was ready for the rig, when the time came.

This contract had been the most challenging and stimulating time of my life. There could be no equal, or even close to equal, regardless of where I might be in the future.

As much as I had enjoyed having Mike's company for the week, his departure left me feeling homesick. I had endured my own company for long enough and it was time to get out of here. I looked forward to getting back into civilization, spending time with Les, going out to a few night clubs and live rock bands playing great music, and dancing till late into the night. Hell, it was so nice to dream. It helped to keep me sane. Choosing to live this kind of life placed me firmly in the minority for men of my age.

I also thought about the close encounters with wild animals when I could have been killed. Yet here I was, alive and well. What would the next encounter bring? I had always wanted to live life to the full. But now it was time to get home for a while and live the life of a normal 21-year-old. The other guys were also ready to get home to their families. Funny how, suddenly, you just know it's time to pack up and leave.

Chapter 61

After spending two days preparing the new site to my satisfaction I called for Aaron. I could do with a break.

"Please make sure my vehicle has at least a half tank of diesel. I want you and Clever to come with me on a little trip." He looked puzzled. "Don't worry," I said, "we will be back today. We're not going far. I want to show you something you have never seen before." He looked more puzzled, but being the loyal, faithful guy he was, he never questioned me and he sprinted off to check the vehicle. I in turn went back to my camp to collect my rifle and make sure it was loaded. We also needed meat.

"Clever," I called, "come, my friend. We're going to look for some meat, and there's a surprise thrown in." Dutifully he closed the front flap on my tent and walked over to where Aaron was siphoning diesel into the Landy. I came over, opened the bonnet and checked the oil. The last thing I needed was to have a problem with the engine on our little private game viewing trip. All looked good and Aaron, Major and I climbed into the front of the vehicle while Clever jumped in the back. The merciless sun unhindered in the deep blue sky beat down on the earth which cried out for rain. Dust billowed up behind the vehicle as we began our ascent over the first mountain pass. We were on our way to what would be a surprise trip for all of us. Little did I know it would turn into a nightmare to haunt me for all time.

Apart from seeing bush buck, duiker and two beautiful water buck with their rear ends clearly marked with the distinctive white circle, all went well on the way down to the Mazoe River. With the main mountain pass ahead, there was little time to spare. We were going into the unknown. Just as Peter had said, within 100 yards, I saw the small track winding off to the right. The road was extremely narrow and there were times when I had to squeeze the vehicle between the mountain slope on the left and the sheer drop into the river on the right. We trundled on slowly around the many boulders. At times I sent Aaron off to the front to check that the track continued. It was one thing tracking game on foot, but here we were tracking a road in a Land Rover.

We stopped on a bend in the road to look down on the river way below. On the inside of the river bend was a large sand bar where two crocodiles sunned themselves. Crocodiles are as close to a prehistoric animal as we will ever get. They have been around for millions of years. They had to have something going for them to have survived for that long. One thing was for sure, it was not their looks.

We continued happily on our way for another thirty minutes and were running parallel with an insignificant dry river bed to our left which must have been the one Peter had told me about. Suddenly Aaron shouted in a panicked voice, "Stop Baas, stop now!"

"What is the problem?" I asked as I put my foot on the brake pedal. He didn't say a word, he was just pointing. To my surprise, as I looked over in the direction he had indicated there was a herd of elephant browsing. It was a huge herd of large, medium and small elephants all pulling at the sparsely spread grass. They were slowly moving in the opposite direction to us and were on the other side of the dry stream. None of them seemed in the least concerned about us. In fact I was not sure if they had even seen us. I noticed with relief that our dust was drifting away from them indicating we were down wind of the herd.

Our Land Rover was the standard grey. They probably thought we were just another animal, or even one of the herd. Their eye sight is not one of their strengths. I told Clever in the back to remain calm and to keep still. Major always seemed to know when to bark and when not to. The only reaction from him was the pricking up of his ears, as he watched these majestic animals with a puzzled look on his face.

I turned the engine off, to ensure they would not feel threatened. For the next thirty minutes we sat in awe, watching them file past one by one, just twenty yards from where we were sitting. There were about thirty animals in the herd. It was an extraordinary experience and sent all of us into a false sense of security. Seeing them this way gave me the feeling of just how easily man and beast could live together. The last one eventually wandered harmlessly past us. All we could hear was the sound of their pulling on branches as they moved on down the stream.

Aaron and Clever were still in a state of shock and I had difficulty convincing them that there were no more elephants. With the road almost impassable at this stage I said we should go the rest of the way on foot as I didn't want to break anything on the vehicle. The two of them thought this was a crazy idea and said we should turn around and head for home. It had taken us hours to get here. I was determined to see the hippo pool regardless of how they felt. Imagine me telling Peter I had been within half a mile of the pool when I turned around to run home without seeing the hippo, due to a herd of non-threatening elephant that moved on without even noticing us.

"Come on guys. You can stay here on your own in the vehicle if you want to, but I'm taking the rifle with me. I will also make sure all the guys back in camp get to hear what cowards the two of you are. " This caused some reaction and so I continued. "Aaron, I'm sure if Kenneth was here he would not hesitate to come with me." That triggered immediate reaction. How could I even suggest that Kenneth would do something he would not do? With that he jumped out the vehicle.

"Come on, my Baas. Let's go and find ourselves some hippo to play with," he said, trying to sound confident. "I was going to stay in the vehicle to look after Clever. But if I go with you, he will follow." Honour was a big thing for these guys, and Aaron was determined to keep his. I smiled and said, "Okay, now that sounds more like the Aaron I know! Come on, it's getting late so we need to hurry."

By this time, Clever had sheepishly climbed out of the vehicle. I set off, leading the way, walking along the bottom of the dry river bed where it was easier, and free of thorn bushes. We walked just a few minutes when once again, Aaron, always first to see danger, shouted loudly, "Run!"

I turned to see in which direction he had been looking. The only thing I had a glimpse of was both of them scrambling up the loose and sandy slope as fast as they could. Turning to look in the opposite direction to see what had scared them I was shocked to see a huge bull elephant charging down on me through the little dry bushes leading down to the river.

As he charged, with ears flapping and trunk pointing to the sky, he was close enough for me to detect in his eyes a hatred for humans. I turned and scrambled my way up the sandy slope, over which my two companions had disappeared a few seconds before. I knew there was no possibility that I would get away from him. In my mind there was no doubt that I was about to die. Would it hurt? Would it be quick? Who would ever find us out here if he killed all three of us? A lot of thinking happens in a second when imminent death is upon us. These, and other thoughts, flew around my crazed little brain. As I crested the embankment I saw that between the top of the sand bank and the Mazoe River there was approximately 50 yards of beautiful white, soft sand. With my head down I ran across this soft divide as fast as I could. But, as in that nightmare we all have had, the more I ran the more I stayed in the same place. The inevitable was bearing down on me.

But this time, there was no dream, no figment of my imagination. This was in real time. I could hear Major barking viciously, but I had no time to look back or even worry about him. All I could see ahead, at the end of the sand patch, was some rocks in the river. I headed for that point knowing that this was the end. I could already feel him trampling me into the soft sand. There was warmth on the back of my neck and I imagined it to be his breath as he screeched in that high pitched crescendo. In reality, it was my nerves taking over my body functions.

It felt like an hour had passed since seeing the elephant and leaping into the river two yards below. But it hadn't been more than ten seconds. As I leapt through the air, I knew I hadn't considered the consequences of such a move. I landed on half-submerged rocks that were covered in green slime, soapy and slippery.

The moment I landed among the rocks my desperation gave me the strength to scramble, slip and stumble my way deeper into the river. I gave no thought to the possibility of being taken by a croc. My only thought was to escape the elephant's outrage.

I managed to wedge myself between two large boulders with all but my head and shoulders submerged. Desperate for breath, I took in a deep lungful of air. There was a loud screeching sound close by. The elephant had also come down the drop and he was slipping and sliding on the slimy rocks. I don't know who was worse off. The elephant was enraged by not being able to get at me. I was close enough for him to pluck me out of my hiding place with his trunk. I had ring-side seats on the view of his frenzy, knowing that he aimed to take it out on me. Every hair on my body stood erect. My pulse raced in my head like machine-gun fire.

I had never heard a more terrifying sound coming from an animal. His screeching was worse than that of the leopard. It's not possible to adequately describe the sight and sounds coming from that furious elephant who was no more than five yards from my hiding place. Even now it sends tingles down my spine and it haunts me still. It's the sight and sound of imminent and violent death.

Unable to keep his footing in his hasty advance over the slippery rocks his front legs gave way. He crashed down onto his knees with his chest splashing spectacularly into the water, sending off a mini tidal wave over the rock protecting me. For a second or two I was submerged. Spluttering and wiping water from my eyes I was horrified to see his head no more than six feet away. The end had come.

I was about to swim further out into the water in a vain attempt to survive. My adversary, however, had become so distressed by his fall that his priorities changed. Frustrated with the slippery rocks and not being able to reach me without falling again, he slipped and stumbled his way back to the river bank he had just come sliding down. He stood there for a while with ears flapping angrily and his tail so erect it reminded me of a warthog's tail.

Only then did I turn my thoughts to what might have happened to Major. Had the elephant killed him? I knew he would have done all in his power to save me, and that could have been fatal. However, in a break in the elephant's trumpeting I heard the most re-assuring sound on earth – furious barking from Major. Immense relief surged through me.

The elephant, slowly, with huge effort, heaved himself up the six foot slope and loped off with trunk swinging from side to side. Irrationally I thought to myself that the only plus from our terrifying ordeal, was the elephant and I had cooled off considerably from the still blazing hot sun, albeit that it was late afternoon. Major was standing his ground on the top of the river bank barking for me to come out of my hiding place.

I felt pain in my arm and on looking down I noticed the water had a red tinge to it. When diving onto the rocks I had taken all the skin off the side of my left arm. On seeing the injury, the pain set in and rapidly increased. As I moved I felt pain in other places. My rib area hurt. Knowing the elephant had, for now, run off, I stood up slowly, carefully, painfully. Then shock set in. I started laughing hysterically. I laughed out loud for the sheer joy of surviving the impossible, for just being alive.

Coming back to my senses, I moved from between the rocks and slipped and stumbled back over the slippery rocks in the water to the sand bank to join Major who was waiting for me. I collapsed next to him with my arms around his neck and he could not stop licking my face for joy of finding me still alive. I eventually recovered enough to climb up the slope and shout for Aaron and Clever. For all I knew they were half-way back to camp, still running for their lives.

Then I thought of the Land Rover. To rejoin the herd, the elephant would have to pass it. Would he take out his pent up rage on the vehicle? If this were to happen, our first problem would be getting back to camp. The sun was already setting. Secondly, and even more serious was how would I explain to Mr. Longstaff how his vehicle managed to be turned into a mangled wreck, miles away from the drill site?

Why on earth did I listen to Peter and come here in the first place? What was I thinking? Why did I do these stupid things? Why did I not remember the warning from the District Commissioner about a previously wounded rogue elephant that travelled behind the herd and was violently dangerous? My confused and mixed up mind flooded with questions and self-reprimands.

I called after Clever and Aaron a second time and was rewarded with an answering call which came from well above me. Astonished, I found the two guys high up in a large tree. The closest branch from the ground was at least nine feet up.

"How the hell did you manage to get up there?" I shouted up to them. "Well, Baas, when that elephant she is charging you, it's amazing what you can do." said Aaron. They always called an animal a "she."

"Okay. Well, now you must come down from there so we can head on home." I was concerned about infection from the wound in my arm and needed to get some disinfectant onto it as soon as possible. "Yes, Baas. You are standing down there on the ground. If you were up here with us you would realize that the elephant has gone and taken with her our climbing powers. We don't know how we are going to get down from here."

"You'll have to climb down as far as you can, and then jump. The sand is soft. You won't be hurt." I was feeling impatient. I was in pain, and wanted to get back to camp "Clever what have you done with my rifle?" I shouted up to him. "Sorry, my Baas. I don't know what I did with your rifle. I was carrying it when the elephant charged, and lost it after that." "Well, while you two get out of that tree, I'll backtrack and look for it."

I headed off towards where the drama began. As I started down the sand bank there was my rifle, with only the butt sticking out of the soft sand.

In his panic, Clever had stuck the barrel into the sand to help get momentum up the sandy slope. I couldn't blame him. His life was worth more than my rifle. I pulled it out of the sand, expecting the barrel to be blocked all the way through to the bullet chamber. I walked over to a tree and tapped the barrel against it a few times and hardly any sand came out. Also, no sand had got into any of the breach mechanism. The rifle was undamaged.

By this time, my arm and ribs were aching, even though the bleeding had almost stopped. I heard footsteps behind me and with my nerves still on edge, I spun around, pointing the rifle at where the sound was coming from. My fear told me the elephant had returned to finish what he had started. Fortunately the safety catch was on. No shot was fired. Aaron and Clever who had come up from behind me had both dropped to the ground holding their hands on their heads.

"Hey, I'm sorry guys. I heard your footsteps and thought it was the elephant." Greatly relieved, they got back on their feet, dusting sand off their bodies. "I'm also sorry I forced you guys to come with me. I was warned about that elephant before we moved in here. I should have known better and been more sensible. Thankfully we are all alive. Now let's head back to camp." "Well, Baas," said Aaron, "you would have been killed if it wasn't for Major. He distracted the elephant long enough for you to get to the river. He ran back and forth, barking, right in front of his front legs and just out of reach. This made the elephant follow him instead of you."

On hearing this, and realising that once again Major had saved my life, I got emotional. I dropped down to my knees and gave him another hug. As I released him and stood up he went tearing off, running in large circles and barking into the empty bushveld as if to say: '*Anyone else want to try me? Well, you just bring it on.*' We all laughed and to my surprise Aaron said, "Where are those hippos you were going to show us, Baas? We are close by. Let's go and see them." I looked at him dubiously.

"Wait 'till I tell Mr. Peter how close to them we were when you were frightened off by an elephant," he added. I laughed.

"Yes, of course we'll go and see the hippo. The elephant has gone to join his herd and won't trouble us again." My enthusiasm was rising again as the terror drained from my painful body.

So we set off once again in the direction we had been going before the elephant attack happened. This time we walked on the bank of the stream where we had a better view, and would see more quickly any new surprises that might come our way.

A little way ahead was a sand bank. When we reached the top we were confronted by a view of the pool with masses of wallowing hippo. A few of them had climbed out of the water, getting ready for their night feed. While hippo have been seen eating during the day, they usually spend the day wallowing in water and mud, and then come out at night to eat tons of grass.

We were, all three, overcome by the stunning view. None of us had ever seen so many hippos in one place at one time. Unfortunately, we couldn't stay long. A spectacular sunset, blazing orange and deep blue, reminded us that we needed to get back to camp before dark.

I was relieved to find our vehicle intact, where we had left it. Without wasting any more time, we climbed in and she fired up on the second spin of the starter motor. I turned the Land Rover around and slowly we made our way back to camp, arriving at around 8.00pm. We had a story to tell the guys who were waiting for us back at the site.

Chapter 62

Mid-morning on Thursday Peter arrived. "Hi, Trevor, I saw the new site. You guys have worked your butt's off." he said sounding satisfied and pleased.

"Yes. Hi, Peter. We're ready to go." On relating to him our encounter with the elephant on our way to see his hippo pool and showing him my wounds from the dive onto the rocks, he was at first shocked and incredulous, but that soon wore off, changing to laughter. When disaster has been diverted, the funny side is always there.

"By the way," he said, on being reminded, "I was never sure whether or not to believe your story about the rhino, but, funnily enough, we saw two rhino in the same area you talked about on our way out here. Wow! They were two large animals. We decided not to get out of our vehicle and investigate like some people I know. We stayed in the Landy with engine running - just in case." "I'm glad you got to see them. It's good to know they run free down here without a worry in the world." I said. "That's not quite true. I called someone I know who is in conservation, to tell him what we had seen. He said he knew about all the rhino down here and that there is a concern for them, as they are being poached for their horns."

He said they were planning a rhino rescue in the dry season the following year. "They'll come in and dart and load them up and take them to a safer place where they can be closely monitored. With this area devoid of humans, poachers could have a field day, without any risk of being apprehended."

"That's great news," I said. I'd love to be on that rescue mission, but by then I'll be drilling on the other side of Rhodesia "Talking of drilling elsewhere," Peter replied, "the reason I'm so pleased you've exceeded the target depth is because Head Office has asked for this hole to be drilled an extra forty five feet beyond our original E.O.H.[8] depth. If there is no intersection we're going to call it a day, for now anyway."

Seeing my confused expression, he continued: "Yes. If we fail to find an intersection, we're going to pack up and pull out of here." "We are already fifteen feet past the original estimate," I responded. "Are you saying there's only another thirty feet to drill?"

I was happy and excited by the prospect of getting out of here sooner than expected. "I hope you told my head office to organise themselves to send a truck down to us so we can load up." I was sure there would not be a big ore zone intersected, and I hoped there would not be one. I really wanted to go home.

"Yes, Trevor. I spoke to Gus myself, and he said he'd have a truck here by the weekend. You and your guys will be out of here by next week at the latest," he said, smiling. "That news is music to my ears!" I shouted to the others, telling them the good news. They were all as pleased as I was.

"I'm sorry," said Peter. "You may have worked on the new site for nothing. It will probably not be used." "We'll all be so happy to be going home, we won't care about the time wasted preparing the new site."

By the following night, the extra drilling had been done. There was no change in the formation. By early Saturday morning we had completed the final survey with the acid bottle tests. I rigged down by lowering the shear legs to the ground and started loosening each section for ease of loading them back onto the truck and had the guys start filling in all the old water sumps.

This was an essential part of tidying up when a contract was completed. If not done, animals could fall into the sumps and die a slow and agonising death. Aaron and I began hauling the rig, timbers and water pump down to the ramp which had already been dug. We trusted that the eight-ton Morris truck was already well on its way from Salisbury. By lunch time we had the Bedford truck fully loaded with the lighter but bulkier equipment - water tanks, rolls of plastic water hose and camping gear.

Once I was satisfied that everything was ready and in order, I went down to the river to catch some bream for our last meal in this beautiful valley. After organising two of the guys to clean up the rig which was not looking great after all the hard work it had done day-in-and-day-out,

---

[8] E.O.H. End Of Hole

Aaron joined me on the river bank. We weren't looking good either, after all our hard work and long hours. But I was feeling good, and tremendously satisfied that we had not only completed the contract, but had finished up before the rains arrived. After the spectacular thunderstorm Mike and I had witnessed, there had hardly been another cloud in the sky.

In a short time I caught eight bream. As I handed them over to Clever to cook for breakfast, I heard the welcome rumbling of a truck coming up over the pass. Soon Gus and his Land Rover rolled in. He climbed out and came over to shake hands.

"Peter tells me you guys are keen to get out of here.""He's right," I laughed. "With a bit of luck, if we can finish loading by this afternoon and reach the Mozoe River before dark, we can camp there for the night. Then part of the trip will be done. That will give us the whole day tomorrow to get through the pass and as far as John's farm by Sunday night."

It was a good plan. By 4.30pm everything was loaded. All the vehicles were loaded higher than their cabs. On board the Morris truck was the rig, timbers casing, drill rods, shear legs, camping gear, paraffin deep freeze, water tanks, diesel drums and four large rolls of plastic piping. As soon we were ready to go we told the drivers to head off with my faithful driver, Piet, commandeering the old, but also faithful, Bedford truck.

Gus said it would be slow-going for the trucks that had already left to grind their way up the pass. He suggested we relax and give them a half-hour head-start. From his cooler box he took out a beer for himself and an ice cold Coke for me. It felt like civilization already. We listened as the sound of the trucks eventually died away, then we climbed into our respective Land Rovers and headed off in pursuit.

To our dismay, when we arrived at the first dangerous pass, the Morris was standing at the base of the slope. We climbed out and walked over to the driver to find out what had gone wrong. I had visions of the clutch plate being burned out, or a similar mechanical disaster. He told us he had tried to get up the pass, but ran out of power because of the heavy load. He'd had a scary time reversing back down to the bottom. He said we'd have to lighten the load, as the truck would not make it over the pass with the weight it was carrying.

"Gus!" I exclaimed, "It's not possible to offload and do a second trip. We have to get the truck up the pass!" I was very frustrated. "Just how do you propose we do that?" Gus asked, as frustrated as I was.

"Bring your vehicle around to the front of the truck and we'll connect the two with a chain I have. With your pulling power in front, and me driving the truck on full power up behind you, together with some luck, we could make it," I said. I think trying to convince myself more than Gus.

"What happens if we almost reach the top, and can't go any further?" asked a worried Gus. "You'll pull me backwards down the pass with you." "Let's cross that bridge if we get to it. I think we'll make it. We did the same thing on our way in here. It was touch and go, but I managed to coax it up and over. There was no Land Rover pulling me from the front then, so I believe we can do it." I was trying to sound confident.

"Remember though, that once we get going there's no turning back. We must both push full power, and once up there on the top, on that short level strip before going down the other side, we must stop to check out the two vehicles." We tied the chain from the tow hitch of Gus's vehicle to the front chassis ring on the truck. The chain was strong. It would not break, and there was no chance of it slipping.

"I'll need to build up air pressure as the truck has been standing for a while," I said. "In the meantime, you take up the slack on the chain and when I hoot we go." "Shit, Trevor, I can't say I'm happy about this plan of yours, said a somewhat worried Gus, but if we can make it, we'll save loads of time. So - what the hell. Let's do it."

It took a couple of minutes to build up the air pressure in my truck, and with a hoot, off we went up the mountain with the driver following behind in my Land Rover. With engines roaring, dust flying, and hearts full of hope, we crawled up the pass. As it is with mountain passes, there are tight bends all the way up. Negotiating these with the heavy loads on board is dangerous. There were times when the front bumper of the truck either scraped, or was inches away from scraping the side wall on the apex of the bend. There was no chance of stopping. If we did that, we would not be able to get going again.

The Land Rover pulling up front got around the corner seconds before I got there and pulled the chain at an oblique angle, tugging the front of the truck sideways. This helped me to make the tighter turns. We were almost at the top and I should be starting to relax. But on the last and final steep section, just yards from the crest, I felt the powerful engine on the truck losing revs.

"Come on." I coaxed, "Come on! We're almost there. Don't die on me now." But the engine was about to quit. All I could do was ride the clutch to get the revs back up again. By doing that, we just made it to the top. Dust and stones flew from under the spinning wheels of Gus's Landy as he tried to gain traction on the loose rocky surface.

We reached the short flat section at the top. Gus, excited that we'd made it over the top, continued pulling full power and began the descent. With the strong smell of burnt clutch in my nostrils, I tried putting on my brakes to stop him pulling me over the ridge.

Before setting off, we had agreed that when we reached the top of the pass we would stop and check the vehicles for mechanical faults. Their loads would also need to be re-secured. Once we were satisfied with both, we would begin the descent. For some reason, this agreement had slipped Gus's mind. To compound the problem, the truck I was driving had no brakes!

It flashed through my mind that I might have depleted the air in the system by jumping and riding the clutch and the air needed to build up again. Although in theory, this doesn't make any sense. A safety mechanism on the braking system locks the wheels if the air reservoir looses pressure. But, whatever the reason, there was no way of stopping, and we were about to make a steep descent. I wondered if this would be where my life would end, out here in this remote wilderness.

Gus was already on his way down the first steep section on the other side. It was dusk. In Rhodesia, twilight is short, and the light fades fast. I held my hand on the hooter trying to alert him to the danger, and to get him to stop - to no avail. I had no option, but to follow him down the other side.

As I started on the downward spiral, the truck picked up speed. I had nothing but the gear box to slow me down. Immediately the engine revs were way up again in the red line area. The gap between the two trucks began to close. I shouted and screamed, holding one hand on the hooter as I came closer and closer to changing the shape of his Land Rover by pushing him over the side. All kinds of thoughts flew around my head. If I were to crash into him and he went over the side, our connecting chain would ensure I followed. How could he not hear and see what was happening? The sound of engine revs and hooter was deafening. Now, at last, only seconds away from smashing into the back of his vehicle he turned his head to look through the back window.

His eyes turned into saucers. His head swung back to look forward and he accelerated away from me until he felt the restraining jar from the chain.

Here I was again, in the same situation we had when first going down into the valley. There was no way for either of us to stop. I had no brakes, and any attempt he made to stop would send me crashing into the back of his vehicle. All we could do was ensure a gap between the two vehicles and continue careering down the pass much faster than either of us found comfortable. Not only was the surface of the road extremely rough and with loose boulders everywhere, but the road itself was a series of sharp bends. Gravity ruled.

This was quite different to the struggle on the other side, to get to the top. How would we stop safely at the bottom? Could we keep the two vehicles, their loads, and the two of us, intact? If we needed an adrenaline rush, this was one hell of a way to get it!

Down we hurtled, bend after bend, bump after bump, with bits and pieces of the load flying off the back and sides of the trucks. We had tied everything down as well as we felt was necessary. We hadn't anticipated anything quite this dramatic. The truck bounced wildly. It was almost impossible to hold onto and control the steering wheel. There were times when my head was an inch away from banging into the roof as I jolted down the pass. It must have taken less than ten minutes to reach the bottom, but it felt like ten hours. The relief when we eventually coasted to a stop at the bottom of the pass was immense.

"What the hell were you doing, apart from trying to kill both of us?" I shouted as Gus came over to me. "I clearly remember telling you to stop at the top so we could check the vehicles. If we had stopped we would have discovered that my vehicle didn't have any brakes!" I barked angrily.

"Hell, Trevor! I'm sorry! You did tell me to stop at the top, but I was on such a high having made it to there I just kept on going!" he said.

While the guys were collecting all the equipment that had fallen off the truck on our bumpy descent, I climbed under the truck. It was now so dark I couldn't see anything under there. Needless to say there was no torch available. I shut the engine down on the truck to give it a rest. It was beyond my comprehension how the con-rod hadn't broken and smashed through the engine block, considering the RPM.

By the time the equipment had been reloaded and secured, a whole hour had elapsed. The engine of the truck had cooled down, everyone's blood pressure had returned to normal, and we were all ready to continue. Seeing that we were down in the valley, and had a flat and easy ride to the river, I suggested to Gus that we proceed slowly. I could control the truck with the gear box. In the morning when it was light, I'd see what I could do to fix the problem.

This we did and it worked well. Then Gus, who was driving about 100 yards ahead of me, suddenly braked, and came to a slow standstill, giving me time to stop. By force of habit I touched the brake pedal and the truck stopped! I eased forward again slowly and once again touched the bake pedal, with the same result. For whatever reason, the brakes were operating again. What a relief.

"Hey, Gus, you won't believe this. I don't know how or why, but the brakes are working again! Now why have you stopped here, when we are still a long way from the river?" I asked, as he came over to the truck. "That's great news about the brakes, but the bad news is that there are some elephant up front. I don't think we can go on!" he said. Surprised, I asked, "What makes you think there are elephants?" "There are a few sets of eyes shining, and they're high off the road. It can only be elephant." It may have seemed obvious to him, but I had never seen elephant eyes shining at night. I thought to myself that if they were to shine we would only be able to be seen one at a time as they were so far apart. I walked up to his Land Rover and, sure enough, there were the eyes reflecting in his head lights.

"Wow, Gus!" I began sarcastically, "those look very dangerous. You're right. We should camp right here for the night. It would be dangerous to try and get past those killers!" Then I burst out laughing, and told him they were the eyes of nightjars sitting on a branch up in a tree. Gus was only slightly embarrassed.

"Well they could have been elephant. I wasn't going to take any chances! I'm not as experienced as you are with the wild life down here." With a sheepish smile he climbed back into his Land Rover.

Chapter 63

When we arrived at the river, Clever immediately set about lighting a fire to cook us a fish supper. Gus had brought some potatoes so we were going to have chips with our fish. What a treat. We were excited at the prospect. We put up our tents to give us some security from the wandering hippo. There would certainly be some around during the night as new green grass had sprouted after the rains a few weeks ago.

By 9.00pm we had all eaten and gone to bed. It had been a long, hard day. We really needed sleep. In the morning we had to negotiate the pass out of the Mazoe River Valley and we all knew how difficult that could be.

In the early hours of the morning we were woken by a loud crunching sound. The hippo had arrived, and they were happily eating the grass all around our makeshift camping area. It crossed my mind that one of them could be the one Major had swam out to, and I grinned to myself at the memory.

Major was also wide awake, sitting alert and tense in the opening of the tent. But he made no sound. He knew that the best way to avoid aggressive behaviour from hippo was to remain silent. He and I were going to miss this natural, comfortable communion with wild life. I sat with him for about fifteen minutes, scratching his head and watching the huge animals eating, before climbing back into bed.

Because of the size of a hippo it would be logical to think that each one would need to eat a fully grown buck every day to stay alive. But in reality all they eat is tons of vegetation.

The dawn light woke us, we stumbled out of our tents. Apart from foot prints, there was no sign of the hippo. As always, Clever had the fire going with our tin kettle resting on its little stand merrily blowing steam from the spout. We made coffee and warmed up some meat I had left over in a cool box. It wasn't a meal for a king, but it put some energy into our bodies for the tough drive out. When we had finished eating, I lit my first cigarette for the day and walked over to the trucks to check them over.

To my dismay, the Bedford truck had a cracked brake pipe. Piet had mentioned his brakes weren't good coming in last night. I removed the broken pipe by loosening the Ferrule at the 'T' junction where the pipe was split to send brake fluid off to both wheels. The only thing we could try was to close the pipe off, allowing only the other three wheels to be bled. If this was successful, it would mean that only the back right hand wheel would have no brakes. I broke off a thin branch and using my pocket knife, I shaved it down until it fitted into the opening of the brake pipe on the Ferrule side. I forced it in as far and as tightly as possible. Then I flattened the broken end of the brake with a small hammer, bent it over and hammered it again. Then, for good luck, I bent it one more time and one last time hammered it tightly closed. I tightened the Ferrule back from where I had removed it and filled the brake master cylinder with brake fluid. Between what Gus had brought with him, and what we had with our vehicles, we had enough brake fluid to bleed through into the slave cylinders of the three wheels. This in turn, once pressurised, would force the brake shoes to open causing friction through the brake pad contacting the inside of the brake drum and with a bit of luck stop the truck.

By this time the tents had been folded and packed wherever there was space for them. We were ready to continue on into the climb out of the valley. On our way into the valley, we had almost lost the truck, when the temporary road work completed by Peter and his crew on the same pass had broken away. But additional repair work done since then made the road safe for our journey out.

Gus drove his Land Rover up to the truck and we once again joined the two vehicles using the chain. I was not sure this was necessary, in spite of the pass being steep and long. But we were in agreement that it was better to be safe than sorry.

The old Bedford truck set off, leading the way. With Gus in front, pulling with his Land Rover and me behind pushing the Morris truck to its limits, we moved slowly but surely towards the top of the pass. As my wheels crossed over the section of road that had broken away on the way down, I felt myself lifting my body up off the seat as if to keep as much weight as possible off the wheels. I laughed at my involuntary response, knowing that it would make no difference. But it made me feel more in control.

It was a slow climb, but we arrived at the top without incident. We drove on a few hundred yards to ensure we were well over and pulled up and stopped. Everyone cheered. In one trip, we had managed to get everything up and out of the valley.

Standing there, looking down into the valley, I thought sadly to myself that I would never go down there again. It felt so final, so incomplete. I had left something important down there. The memories of the months in the valley would remain with me forever, but I was leaving behind the physical space in which those events took place. It had been a life changing experience. I had grown up. I was more confident and had learned there was no limit to what I could achieve.

We were relieved and happy to be up there on the top of the pass, safe and sound. To celebrate, Gus brought out the Cokes from the back of his truck and we all drank to the end of a memorable and incredible experience.

Not to be outdone, Major wandered off to the side on the road, sniffed around, then squatted. With a satisfied look on his face he left his mark by depositing his characteristic brown mound. He made sure it was a good one.

When the short, impromptu celebration was over, I climbed under the Bedford truck once more to check whether there were any leaks on the repaired brake pipe. It was dry. Everything appeared to be in order on both trucks. The only blemish on the truck after all the hell it had just been through was that the 'M' of the Morris sign on the front of the truck had fallen off somewhere.

Because of the heavy loads we were carrying, we knew we still had a few tricky sections to navigate. But we also knew they were not nearly as bad as what we had just been through. The worst was over.

Chapter 64

We set off again towards the farm, passing my water spot and the turn off to the original project we had undertaken, drilling the two angled holes into both sides of the kopje. This had yielded the same negative results as deeper into the valley. We also passed the place where I had had the experiences with the leopards and, as we continued, other familiar spots brought back other memories.

This had been a tough contract. I doubted that any other contract would ever come as close to this one for experiences with wild animals, or the remote ruggedness of the area. For the rest of my life, I would remember everything that happened down here. I felt privileged to have been the one to have been chosen to drill here. I was satisfied with our performance. We had completed the contract, on a tight schedule. All of our equipment was in good order, and the personnel were coming out of the valley, healthy and safe.

We arrived at the farm by mid-afternoon. John was there to greet us. It was good to see him. He had been a real friend, sometimes under difficult circumstances. Sally came out, giving both Gus and me a hug. She invited us in for tea and cake. Before the tea and cake, though, I wanted to feed the guys, so that they could move on in advance with the trucks. Gus and I would follow later in the Land Rovers. We were all anxious to get home and it didn't make sense keeping the truck here while we visited. After a meal, the Morris and Bedford trucks trundled off, heading for Salisbury.

Gus and I spent an hour with John and Sally. I talked non-stop. There was so much to tell since last seeing them. Also, my incessant chatter delayed the inevitable sad goodbyes. Once again I apologised for what had happened to his dogs, and John, understanding again, said life has to go on, and that while Major was acting in self defence, it was just sad that it had been his dogs. I can't come close to writing about how sad an occasion this was. They had become two special people in my life. They gave me a friendship I would cherish for all time. They had helped me in every way they could and I owed them a lot. They said I should be sure to come back and visit, and I said for them to be sure to look me up through the head office sometime. In the drilling game you don't know where you'll be going, and right then I had no idea of the where I would be next.

Gus wrote out a company cheque to cover the last statement Sally had made up for us for goods purchased through them. Shaking hands with John and giving Sally a hug, holding her tight for longer than I should have, I gave her a kiss on the cheek. Sadly, we set off to catch up with the trucks. I gave a hoot on the horn and a last wave as I turned onto the main road, knowing that the chances of ever seeing them again were slim. The great feeling of loss that I'd had at the top of the pass overwhelmed me again. I was leaving something behind, never to be encountered again. It was late on Sunday afternoon when we arrived back in Salisbury. We parked the trucks and the two Land Rovers in the yard for safe-keeping, and planned to offload the following day. Gus drove Major and me home in the spare Landy and said he would pick me up in the morning at around 7.00am. My Mom and sisters were excited to see me, but were concerned at how thin I had become. I joked with them saying, "Well, it doesn't say much for my cooking." After unloading the trucks, I spent the rest of the week going over the machine and repairing whatever needed attention, and replacing the valves on the pump. When that was done the guys cleaned and sanded the rig, ready for re-spraying the standard Boyles blue colour. Gus had successfully tendered for a contract at Umvuma, which would be my next assignment, starting in less than a week.

I spent as much time as possible with Les. We had been engaged for four and a half months and in that time had spent only four days together. We needed to make up for lost time, and we began planning our wedding in December. We decided that 20th December 1969 would be our big day. There had been times when I made wrong decisions, but marrying Les was not one of them. We let both sets of parents know that we had set a date. They had fears that we were too young to get married. I was 21 and Les was 20. We understood their concerns, but we knew what we wanted. On seeing that our minds were made up, they gave us their blessing and we began to plan in earnest. As I would be heading back into the bush, I had to leave all the wedding plans to Les and the two families. In any case, organising weddings was not one of my strong points. I would not have been much use, anyway. The best thing for me to do was to make money for us to live on.

Chapter 65

The same crew had been assigned to work with me on the new project. I was pleased. We loaded up the trucks on a Monday morning with all the drilling equipment. This time, along with the water tanks, we were also taking a five-hundred-gallon diesel tank. We would be drilling just ten miles outside the small town of Umvuma which is on the road to Fort Victoria, which continues on through to South Africa. Due to the close proximity of a town, the company we used for our diesel supply had agreed to deliver to our camp, and would even supply the diesel tank. This would save a lot on trips in and out of town to collect diesel supplies.

First thing on Tuesday morning we sent the trucks off. I was excited as I had been given a caravan to tow out and use as my accommodation. Gus knew I would soon be married, and joined by my new wife. I was sure that was the reason for this kind offer. A caravan would be a lot more comfortable than the little tent I had lived in down in the valley.

I hooked it up onto the tow hitch of the Land Rover, inserted the power plug into the vehicle socket, and checked that the tail, brake and indicator lights worked. Then I was ready to go. As usual, the trucks had gone on ahead. If they encountered a problem along the way, I was following behind and hopefully would be able to get them going again.

As I drove out the gate I was relaxed and excited about being on my way to mobilize to a new contract. This one would be tame compared to our experience in the Ruangwa Valley. My companion, Major, was beside me. I gave him a hard scratchy rub on his head and he replied with a loud bark. He hadn't been happy cooped up at the house for a few days, and seemed to know we were once again heading off into the bushveld.

The two trucks had a uneventful trip. I caught up to them just before they arrived in Umvuma. That seemed to be a sign that this would be a good contract. We drove into town and found the fuel station where we met up with Peter, the geo we had worked with down in the valley. He had been assigned to this new project, while he waited for the results of the samples that had been sent in from the valley. This could take several months. The laboratories laboured under a heavy backlog. Ore samples were coming in daily from all over Rhodesia. The site geologist who had undertaken the original groundwork on the Umvuma project had done masses of trenching and sent off hundreds of soil samples. Now he had gone away on extended leave.

I was happy to be working with Peter again. We got on well. In the valley we had a lot of fun together out in the bush. This time his wife, Sandy, was joining him. She was happy to hear I was getting married and would be bringing Les out to stay with me. There would be two women in camp with us.

In the town we had lunch together – ordering the famous Rhodesian steak rolls, with ice cold Coke to wash them down. After that, we headed out, in close convoy, to the new site.

The terrain was flat, and there were many big trees. Having just spent many months in an unbelievably beautiful, wild and diverse area, this new place, by comparison, was very ordinary. There were no mountains, or valleys teaming with game. But I was not deterred. I knew we were going to have a good experience here. Life is what you make it, and I was going to make it good.

Chapter 66

The trucks were moved close to the first drill site and offloaded. We began to set up the site and our camps, and the empty trucks were sent back to Salisbury. Peter had parked his caravan under a huge tree. There was another one of similar size just twenty yards away. We decided to set up a duel camp, with shared cooking area and toilet. I reversed the caravan as close to the tree as possible, unhitched it from the vehicle and lowered the levelling jacks down onto a few old bricks I had found. I was pleased with the position. I was going to make our camp as attractive and comfortable as possible, ready for Les's arrival in January.

She had spent her whole life in the city. Her life had been sheltered and safe. This was going to be a wake-up call for her. No fancy bathroom and toilet. In fact, there were no upmarket features at all. I hoped she wouldn't take one look, and run back home.

One of the first things to set up was a long-drop toilet. About fifty yards from our living space, the hole was dug. We also dug holes for the gum poles that would surround it. They would support the tightly pulled two yard high hessian material secured with fencing nails to the gum poles. Using large brushes, the hessian was covered with a sloppy mix of cement, and left to set. The following day, to complete the construction, we painted the cemented hessian with white-wash. Once completed, we had very effective walls around the long-drop toilet.

We made a toilet-seat platform from thick branches cut from the local trees. On the opening at the top, over the deep hole, I nailed a plastic toilet seat. For me, after months of using a shovel for a toilet, this was high tech indeed. It was close to being a "modern toilet." But for someone who had only ever used an indoor flush toilet, in a tiled bathroom with chrome fittings – well, my concern was warranted.

I also set about building the bathroom, right next to the caravan, and using the same building technique. Once it was complete I installed my large tin bath into it. Using sticks and reeds, my new cook, Kenneth, made a shelf for storing shampoo and other girl-stuff. To finish it all off with some flair, I hung a mirror above the tin hand basin which fitted snugly into an opening made on the shelf. The basin was almost level with the top of the shelf. I stood back and admired what we had made. It had walls, a shelf, a wash hand basin, a mirror and for good measure I tied a length on nylon rope across one side for a towel rail. What woman in her right mind would not be impressed with this masterpiece? I felt proud of my creation.

By this stage, the rig was up and we had started drilling. We were accustomed to drilling the hard gneisses down in the Ruangwa valley. Now we were drilling into Talc Schist which is a soft, soapy formation. Trying to penetrate it with a normal surface set bit was a problem. It kept mudding up, and shutting off the coolant water flow at the bit face. Penetration rates were therefore slow.

To rectify this problem I changed to what are called 'Hand Set Drill Bits. These had larger diamonds inserted into the tiny holes drilled for this purpose. Then, to tightly secure each diamond firmly in place a small centre punch and hammer were used to centre pop around each stone individually. Generally this operation has been performed by women who, I'm informed, are more patient for this kind of operation which is done entirely by hand, hence the name 'Hand Set Drill Bit'

Changing to these bits tripled our penetration rates and at the same time tripled our production. If we had the same conditions down in the valley we would have completed the work in less than half the time. But then I would have missed out on some memorable experiences.

One of the challenges that comes with drilling is the need to maintain a full, or, as it later turned out, even a partial water return. This was a problem at the new site. There were serious delays caused by the slow delivery of water by the water truck. It was frustrating to have good drilling conditions, but being forced to spend hours each day waiting for the next load of water.

Another difficulty was the inconsistency of the formations. Some sections were softer and even more slippery and soapy. This meant that sometimes, when withdrawing the rods to retrieve the core, we found that the complete ten foot length of core was often left behind in the hole. This then entailed the time-consuming job of lowering the rods again, and gently drilling and pushing the drill bit and core barrel over the core to retrieve it in as pristine condition as possible. Once it was retrieved it was interesting to see the grooves scratched out by the core spring cutting through the soft and soapy Talc Schist formation.

A technique that helped in this regard was to shut down the pump, or by-pass it, to stop the flow of water to the bit when we started filling the core barrel. This allowed the drill cuttings to settle down around the core spring, thus – theoretically - giving it more grip. We still had some failures, but usually this method helped.

The drilling progressed well and our production through to the Christmas break was excellent. With our wedding date set for 20th December 1969 I had to work in a few Sundays to get the extra few days off to enable me to get back to Salisbury and organise my life for the biggest day of my life so far.

Chapter 67

Before leaving for Salisbury, I stripped the batteries, starter motors, and generators off the rig for safe-keeping. The water pump was small enough to load onto the Land Rover and be brought back to head office. I arranged for a watchman to stay on site to look after the equipment and the camp for the period that I would be away.

I organised for the guys to collect their salaries with leave pay and Christmas bonuses, and they all left by bus to their various homes to spend Christmas with their families. I briefed Gus on our progress and gave him the stores list we would need once we got started in the New Year. He seemed pleased with the production and wished me luck for the wedding. He gave me my paycheque and I drove off home.

My two younger sisters knew and loved Les, to the extent that they warned her not to marry me. They told her I was really wild with the girls and was best left alone for a few more years to settle down. Don't get me wrong, my sisters also loved me. In their defence they knew me better than most and up to that stage of my life they were right. However I was ready to settle down and get married to the only girl I had ever really loved up to that time, and told them so.

The night before the big day, my Dad took me off down to the golf club where he had arranged for some of our close friends to join us for my bachelor party. I didn't drink alcohol at all and was told that would have to change for that night. I was compelled one way or another to have far too many beers, until I was eventually drinking voluntarily and even starting to enjoy myself. I think I might have been making a fool of myself, but it was my bachelor party, so why not?

This continued late into the night, and eventually I went home with my Dad to spend the night at his house. The following morning waking up and getting out of bed seemed an impossible task. My head was falling off my shoulders. In the few moments that I could think straight, these thoughts went through my head. 'How could I have had that kind of party the night before my wedding? Would I sober up in time to make it to the church? Why was the roof of the bedroom going round and round?'

My Dad found this amusing and actually phoned Les, telling her he was sorry, but he thought the chances of my getting to the church on time were slim. He made it sound so convincing that I wondered whether he could be right. My head throbbed as he handed me a strong cup of coffee. This was the biggest day of my life, and now, instead of being excited, I was a wreck. I thought to myself, "This is going to be one hell of a long day."

Fortunately, after a few more cups of strong coffee, my head began to clear. I managed to get myself into a borrowed suit. The owner of the suit had longer legs than I. So the trouser legs had a crinkly bulge around my ankles, as they rested heavily on my shiny shoes.

Putting on a tie was a mission. I couldn't remember when I last wore one. After at least eight attempts the knot was good enough by my standards. Through perseverance, commitment, and love for Les, I managed to get to the church on time.

It was a small wedding, with just our close friends and family present. My new in-laws had given us the choice of small wedding and a decent cash gift or a large, lavish wedding. To us there was no choice. We needed the money.

Les looked stunning in her long flowing white dress. I knew I was a lucky man to be standing there ready to be joined together as husband and wife with this vision of loveliness. When the moment came, and it was time to take our vows, my head was clearer, and I successfully bumbled my way through what I needed to say.

The reception at the home of Les's parents was small, but we had all the necessary frills. There was a beautiful wedding cake, and champagne. After the usual toasts to the bride had been made, I was surprised when I was asked to make a speech. Nobody had told me about this part. It made me wonder what kind of friends I had.

The only speeches I had ever made were when collecting golf prizes. Had I known this was going to happen I might have postponed the wedding for a few more years. I had prepared nothing. I bumbled my way through my wedding vows but that was nothing compared to my speech. At the end of my saying all the silliest of things that came into my head there were a couple of polite claps, and a lot of not so polite laughter. Like I say, it made me realise who my friends were. I imagined Les's parents, whom I so much wanted to impress, wondering to themselves '*Why us, why does it have to be us?*'

At the end of the day though, everything, apart from my blundering and pathetic speech, had gone off well. We did the garter thing, and Les threw her bouquet over her shoulder and it was caught and tightly embraced by a good friend of hers.

For our honeymoon, we went to the place where we first met – Mermaid's Pool. I assured my friends I would get this part right. We had booked the beautiful Greek room. We had a sunken bath, and all the other trimmings. I told Les, jokingly of course, that the bathroom I had built for her in the bush was similar, except that the bath wasn't sunken. We had a wonderful time and neither of us had any idea or even cared what the weather was like for the three days we were there.

Cutting the cake on the big day

Chapter 68

On New Year's Eve, with a bunch of friends, we let our hair down and partied through until the golden glow in the eastern sky heralded the first day of a new decade, the 1970s. For us, it was the beginning of a new era. I had a partner beside me, to share all my experiences, good and bad. Until now, I had only my faithful dog to talk to. Now I had the best girl in the whole world as my wife.

To be honest, though, I was apprehensive about how Les would settle down into our new life style in the bush. More than anything in the world I wanted her to be happy. I was seldom anxious about anything, but this was different. It had even crossed my mind that I should look for another career in the city, where I could provide Les with a proper house, as opposed to the rough, tough conditions I was taking her into..

After all the wedding and New Year celebrations were over, we loaded up with everything we had, which wasn't much, and set off together into our new destiny. On our arrival in Umvuma, I took Les around the little town to show her where she could shop. Being a really small town, within an hour she had seen everything there was to see, including the bottle store for my constant supply of Cokes. I had no problem getting through a case of Coke a day. It was all I ever drank, as I never touched alcohol (except at my bachelor party). Les, on the other hand, mainly just drank water. One of the few things she insisted on though, was a good supply of oranges. She didn't eat much else. It was a woman thing. After having been a little over weight in her growing up years, she was now looking stunning and she intended to stay that way.

I dilly-dallied around town a little longer than we needed to, trying to hold off for as long as possible, our inevitable arrival at the site, and our home. Hell. So far, we were happily married. Why spoil it now?

"Are we ever going out to the camp?" asked Les. "I want to unpack and sort out our caravan."

"The problem is," I admitted at last, "I'm nervous about taking you out there. I've told you everything about it, but I'm still worried about how you'll feel when you see it all for the first time."

"Oh, don't be so silly!" she scolded, "I'm going to love it out there and what I don't like I will do my best to fix. Now come on, let's go out to our new home!" What a girl!

With that, off we went, with Major in the back of the Landy also becoming restless and needing a good run after the trip. Nature had conspired to be on my side and to give us a great wedding gift. There had been good rains in December and everything had turned green.

Just that made a big improvement to the appearance of the camp. The leaves on the big tree above the caravan had all come out throwing shade over the awning room outside the caravan and bathroom area. There was even a carpet of green grass leading up to the caravan.

In no time at all, my fears were turned to joy. Les was relaxed and perfectly happy - and impressed with the camp. "Wow!" she exclaimed, "This is so much better than you told me. I'm going to love it here. It's so quiet. I will enjoy being away from the city noise."

Major, by this time, was tearing around hunting out all the new animal smells that might have invaded his territory over the Christmas break.

We got going with offloading and packing into the limited space we had. I got the old paraffin fridge and deep freeze up and working. They are very sensitive and once the wick has been lit and the glass wind protector lowered, the adjustment of the flame is critical. If there is any smoke whatsoever the compartments won't get cold. The flame needs to be turned up until smoke comes out the exhaust, then, ever so slowly, turned down again until the smoke stops. The other trick is that it has to be perfectly level, I used a spirit level to do that. If both of these procedures are married up perfectly, the fridge and deep freeze work well and were perfect for keeping my Cokes cold.

I had loads of experience with paraffin. When in the Ruangwa Valley, the glass protector of the flame broke making it useless, and I didn't have a spare one. Through sheer desperation, however, I hollowed out the insides of an old torch battery and found the outer case fitted perfectly. This got the fridge working well, but the downside was that I couldn't see the flame. Instead, I held my hand over the exhaust. If there was heat, I knew the flame was burning.

Les was terribly organized and in no time, she had everything looking like a home. Our bed had new linen, and she had hung the new curtains she had made from measurements I had taken. Not having had any curtains before, these alone were a big improvement. Yes, our new life had started.

While Les turned our caravan into home, I sorted out everything down at the rig, ready to get going first thing in the morning. There was no point starting the drilling this late in the day. We wouldn't get much done. In any case, the guys needed to sort out their camp before dark.

Between Les and the camp cook, they sorted out supper for us, and later Les was introduced to the first of her hundreds of tin tub baths. The hot and cold water were brought into the bathroom in five-gallon tins and then poured in until the water was to her liking. To really be flash and impress Les, I had completely enclosed the bathroom - even giving it a roof. On the roof, before thatching, I tied some thick plastic sheeting tightly across to help with water proofing. The pitch of the roof was too flat and there would be negative run off. The negative pitch was as a result of my original plan to make it an open air bathroom. Had I given it the pitch required, the low side would have been at head banging height even for the shortest person.

I placed some candles on the little shelf and lit them. I poured in some bubble bath into the hot water. Les's towel was hung up over the rope towel rail, I had hammered in a few nails into the wooden posts to be used as clothes hangers whilst bathing, shaving or whatever. It might not have made five star status, but for a bush camp, it was at least a one star.

I then ushered Les into the masterpiece designer bathroom and pointed out all the mod cons. She was happy with everything and I left her to have her bath. I was sitting under the awning of the caravan listening to her splashing around happily when suddenly she let out a blood curdling scream.

Knocking my chair over backwards in my haste to get up, I raced around the caravan tripped over one of the guy ropes and eventually half stumbling, raced into the bathroom with the ever present Major close on my heels, to kill what could only be a huge snake for which this area was renowned. I could think of nothing else that could cause such an hysterical scream.

"Where is it?" I shouted

Les, still in the bath, never said a word. With a terrified look on her face she gingerly pointed up to the plastic sheet. At the same time there was a rustling sound from up there and I nearly broke my neck swivelling my head up to see how big the snake was. There was not much that scared me in the bush, but snakes, spiders and scorpions hit my horror spot quite well.

To my utter astonishment, there, clearly visible between the plastic and the grass thatch above was a large rat. Major spotted it too, and barked loudly with excitement. I suspected that he also found the situation amusing. Nobody in their right mind is fond of rats, but at the end of the day a rat is a whole bunch better than a large snake.

"Shame," I soothed. "That gave you a big fright. But you don't need to be worried. It's above the plastic so it can't fall on you. As horrible as they are, you'll have to get used to them as there are hundreds around here, They are the reason there are so many snakes." She was watching me with growing horror on her face. Unwisely, I continued. "Rats, to most snakes, are like rump steak is to most humans. As long as they are around, there will also be snakes. "

"Are you trying to tell me this will be a common occurrence? Me lying in the bath tub watching rats running around above me, being chased by snakes?" she finally asked.

I just burst out laughing. "Welcome to bush life! There are very few women who have the pleasure of these unique experiences."

Les was not impressed. Shaking her head indignantly she said, "I would rather be one of the few that don't have that pleasure." Still laughing, I assured her she would get used to it and within a year or so would not worry about things like rats. She managed a weak smile.

"Well, isn't that reassuring? I see the rat has now disappeared, Maybe it wasn't as serious as I thought it was."

To be sure she had no more scares on her first night, I stayed in the bathroom until she was finished, handing her the towel when she needed it. Once she was dry and dressed in her night clothes I walked her around to the awning to sit, relax and have dinner. In the mean time, while waiting for Johnson to bring the food through, I carried Major's blanket into the caravan.

Chapter 69

"Why are you taking his blanket inside?" asked a surprised Les. "When I was down in the valley he always slept in the opening of my tent as protection for me," I answered, "and since coming out here with the caravan he has been sleeping in the open doorway, so we can't change that now."

"Oh yes, we can!" she declared. "He has to sleep out here under the awning. He'll be quite happy and he can still protect us. He'll have his own awning over his head."

"That's not a good idea. He's always been with me at night and will scratch on the door all night. The chances of us getting any sleep will be nil."

"Well, I'm not happy about him being in the caravan and leaving the door open for him. Who knows what might come in at night?" Les said, trying to put an end to the subject.

"That's the point," I tried to explain. "There is no way that Major would allow anything into the caravan. The safest I have ever been is when Major is on guard. In any case, it's tame around here, compared to where I've been for the last few months. But if you'll be happier with him under the awning, we can try it and see what happens. Who knows, he just may settle down and be fine."

When we finished eating we cleaned our teeth, sorted Major's bed out as comfortably as we could in the outside awning and retired into our caravan closing and locking the door. We climbed into bed, both needing a good night's sleep. We switched off the lamp and within fifteen minutes were falling off into a deep sleep. Then all hell broke loose.

There was an almighty crashing sound and the mosquito gauze and frame holding it in place across the large front window came flying into the caravan closely followed by Major. It goes without saying that Les was not impressed by this episode, But it did convince her that it might be a good idea to have Major sleeping in the caravan at night.

After her exciting first day, Les settled down fast, taking like a duck to water to becoming a bush wife. Soon she had a vegetable garden going. Johnson taught her how to turn an ant hill into an oven and she was baking fresh bread in the bush-style oven. All my concerns for her enjoying the bush life evaporated.

The drill rig wasn't far from the caravan, so every time I needed a Coke, which was often, I would give a loud sharp whistle. When needing a new packet of cigarettes I would give two sharp whistles. Within minutes Johnson would arrive at the rig with the order.

Les cooked a great breakfast and at 10am every morning she would arrive at the rig carrying the bacon and eggs with the accompanying ice cold Coke. This was the life! Sometimes, on her way to the rig with my breakfast, she would come across a snake on the path, but soon became so bush-wise that without batting an eye lid she would hop over it and continue on her way. For some reason she was more comfortable with snakes than she ever was with rats.

She did have one really uncomfortable and frightening experience on one of her walks with Major. They came across a large troop of baboons, some making their loud barking sound to warn the rest of the troop of danger around. Les was terrified. I had warned her how dangerous baboons could be, especially when they had young hanging tightly under the body of their mothers, or on their backs. She feared as much for Major as for herself, because she didn't think his chances would be good should he choose to protect her.

Slowly she turned and sprinted back to the camp with Major close at her side. Generally a baboon will not attack without provocation. But they are extremely powerful animals and with longer front fangs than a lion, they could cause serious injuries. She got back to camp safely but this was the beginning of many more similar experiences.

The drilling was going exceptionally well, and Les was well into the system of collecting rations from town. She had become friendly with the shop owners who all got to know her. We had opened an account at the local butchery for our meat and they could also supply us with mealie meal, and fresh vegetables. Cabbage was a particular favourite with the staff. We were surrounded by privately owned farmland and to shoot anything for the pot was out of the question. It would have been poaching.

Drilling results were looking promising, so, to speed up the operation, the Mining House asked us to mobilise a second rig on the site. Having been given notice of this well in advance, Gus had managed to find a youngster who was interested in going into the drilling world.

Rob Brown was energetic, enthusiastic and willing to learn - and was as much a Coke-alcoholic as I was. Drillers are generally known to be big drinkers – but usually of alcohol. He had been sent out to me as my learner driller and I was to teach him all I could in the short time before the new rig arrived.

Rob was a fast learner and a perfect apprentice in the drilling game. He really wanted to learn, and to excel at everything. He had a natural talent for drilling, and an uncommonly good attitude. So he did excel at everything. He somehow moulded in with the drill rig, with an uncanny ability to handle and understand machinery. In the three weeks I had him on site prior to the new rig's arrival he had advanced so quickly that I told Gus not to worry about sending an operator out for the machine. Rob was already doing a great job. If there were any problems I was on hand to help.

Unsurprisingly, our production doubled over night and, as the results still looked good, the project was extended. It had turned into a good drilling contract, with not only a large amount of feet to be drilled, but our production was good, drilling was easy, and our drilling costs were kept down to a minimum. We were making a dream come true, as far as drilling contracts go. Rob was producing great results on his rig both in production and also with the quality of core. His rig was neat and clean. We were all happy, including the Mining House, which is not always easy to please.

Chapter 70

We were well into the season of rains. One day in the mid-afternoon massive cumulous clouds drifted in from the North east. A storm was building up. The air was heavy and oppressive, with an ominous sense of expectation as the clouds grew larger and darker. Eventually the sun was shut out, and a dusky gloomy atmosphere set in. We were heading for a downpour.

Around 2.00pm Les had gone into town to collect rations and at 3.30pm the angry sky was split by forked lightning followed immediately by rolling thunder. There was just an instant between the lightning flash and the thunder clap. We were in the centre of the brewing storm. I decided to close down both rigs and told everyone to head for cover.

Our drill masts were lightning attractors. A direct strike could kill anyone close to the machine at the time. I waived frantically for Rob to cut the engine on his rig and get the hell away from it by drawing my hand across my throat

I ran back to my caravan to close all the windows. As I arrived I shouted to Johnson to run around the back and push the window closed so that I could secure the latch from inside. We closed the first window and then he moved to the second one which was closer to the huge tree. I was kneeling on the bed inside waiting for him to push it closed when there was an explosion and a blinding light. I found myself lying dazed on the floor, wondering what had happened.

As soon as I managed to clear my head and stand up, I realized it must have been a bolt of lightning. Where was Johnson? I stumbled out of the caravan and in a daze ran around the back to where he had been standing. He was lying still on the ground. The huge tree just behind him had a gaping split right up the middle with smoke pouring out.

There was no ways he would have been able to survive a direct strike that close. Could he be alive? I dropped down onto one knee next to him and felt for a pulse. He neither moved nor resisted and felt terribly limp. My heart sank. Then, there it was, the unmistakable beat of his heart pumping in his wrist.

Calling for help I rolled him over onto his back and ran into the caravan to fetch water and a face flannel. I had no idea what I was supposed to do, but remembered when boxing and I was badly dazed by a solid punch, my corner man would throw water onto my face to clear my head, so that I could continue.

I wet the flannel and started dabbing his face gently all over with cold water. After some minutes his eyes opened. He had a faraway look, with his eyes going round and round, unable to focus after the serious blast his body had endured. I was so relieved he was alive, but at the same time still concerned. I had no idea how serious his injuries could be.

Fortunately the comforting sound of the Land Rover's engine broke through the sound of crashing thunder all around us, and pounding of the torrential rain. Les had returned safely from her shopping spree. Her timing could not have been better. Now I had transport to take Johnson into the small medical clinic in town.

I helped him to stand up, and by supporting him I managed to get him around the caravan to the protection of the awning. The lightning and thunder claps continued. I asked Johnson if he could get to the Land Rover so that I could get him to medical help.

To my surprise, he stood up, walked around in small circles under the awning, then said he was fine and didn't need to go anywhere. He asked if he could just go and lie down for a while in his tent.

"You just sit and relax here on this chair," I said. "When the rain eases a bit we will get you across to your tent. Then you can lie down for the rest of the day. I really thought you were dead when I first found you." With bewildered relief on his face he replied that I must also have been hit by the explosion from the lightning strike, and he was relieved that I too was alive.

Chapter 71

Our exceptional progress with the contract continued. Around 11.30 one morning, Mr. Longstaff made one of his surprise visits. Out of nowhere he arrived at the camp where Les was busy hanging up the washing on our makeshift washing line. As always he had brought some really good rump steak, a case of Cokes and two pockets of large juicy oranges. Les was still strictly on an orange diet. Somehow she managed to survive and looked great having them for breakfast lunch and supper. I always used to joke about how easy it was for me to prepare a meal for her. Apart from cooking a piece of meat over the fire, I was clueless in the catering department, and had no natural aptitude in that direction. There was always someone to cook for me. First my Mom, then I had Clever, my cook down in the valley. Now I had Johnson and my wife.

After dropping off the supplies he had kindly brought through for us, Mr. Longstaff drove over to the staff camp to offload mealie meal, ration meat, salt and veggies. He then walked down to the rig to see how things were going. It was always good to see him.

"Hi, Trevor, married life hasn't done you any harm. You have put on some weight," he said, with a firm hand shake.

"Hi, Mr. Longstaff, it's so good to see you. Married life suits you too," I joked. "You're looking great."

We talked together while the rig's chuck was spinning and boring its way down into the rock formation below. He was surprised to see how good the penetration rate was, and said he could now see how we were achieving the high monthly production. In no time the core barrel was full and we needed to pull the rods to remove the core. I explained to him why I shut the water flow off for a few minutes to help hold the core in the core spring.

"You are the guys on site, and you must do whatever works," he said. "Every hole you drill will be different and only you, the operators, with hands on experience, can find the most efficient way to deal with each situation."

After I had lowered the rods and started drilling again, he dropped the bomb shell.

"I'm going to take a few months leave and go overseas. Mrs. Longstaff and I have talked about it many times and are now going to do it." he stated.

"This will cause a huge increase and travel load for Gus to cope with, so we need you and Les to move back into town to help with running the business and looking after all the rigs scattered around the country."

I was gob-smacked, feeling honoured to have been asked to do such a thing, but on the other hand, we were happy out here in the bush. I was my own boss out here, and was fully responsible for the efficient running of the drilling programme. It was going well. Also, Les had settled in so well, and was happy out here in the bush with me.

We went back up to the caravan to discuss it with Les who was not overjoyed with the idea, but she reluctantly agreed to move back into the city. Rob, although still much a beginner was to take over my position out here which included the caravan to which Les and I had become attached. There was no question it was a move up the ladder for me, but somehow it had a hollow feeling to it. I had as much respect for Mr. Longstaff as I have had for any man, and so ultimately I would do anything he asked, and would always give him my 100% best effort.

Chapter 72

Within a week of Mr. Longstaff's visit we were back in Salisbury and looking for a place to stay. We eventually found a small duplex flat. The rent would be covered by the company. It was sparsely furnished with the bare minimum. For us, accustomed to roughing it out the bush it was comfortable. We certainly had no funds, so couldn't consider buying new furniture. We were quite content with what we had.

But the new accommodation presented us with a problem regarding Major. The complex didn't allow pets, not even small dogs, let alone a 'brute' like Major. Besides that, Major would not be happy cooped up in a small place in the city. I would be permanently on the road helping Gus to manage all the drilling contracts throughout Rhodesia. It would not be possible for him to join me on those trips.

We were really at a loss as what to do. I knew we were going to be in Salisbury for quite a few months and we couldn't put him in kennels for that amount of time. It would kill him. He was so devoted to me and had been such a faithful companion and protector to me. How on earth were we going to solve this awful predicament?

Then I remembered a good friend of mine who lived out on his parent's farm out on the other side of Mount Hampton. Michael loved animals and had often mentioned to me that he would love to have a big dog. I phoned him and told him we would be coming out to see him over the weekend.

I didn't want to tell him I was bringing Major with me as I wanted to see his natural reaction to having him running around the farm while we were out there. The two of them seemed to get on immediately. Dogs have a sixth sense and know when they're welcome. Michael and Major got on like a house on fire.

We spent the day there fishing in his dam with Major trying to catch the fish as we reeled them into the shallows. All in all we had loads of fun. Eventually it was time to go, and not wanting to force

Major onto him, I was not sure whether I should say anything or not. Thankfully he asked me where I had got Major from as he would love to have a dog like him. This made everything so much easier for all of us. I told him the full story. Much to my joy, he was so excited and promised to look after Major as though he was his own brother. We told him we would come out as regularly as possible, not to check on him, but to visit Major and let him know that although he had a new home we would never forget him.

Sadly, with tears in our eyes, we gave Major hugs and tried to tell him why we had to do this. As we drove off, Michael stroked Major and he sat watching the Land Rover with a puzzled look on his face. I knew he was with someone who would love him, care for him, and give him the run of the farm. He needed to be free and not cooped up in a town house. For my own sake, I had to believe he felt that way. Major and I had become so bonded, and had so many experiences together. But now for his sake I had to leave him with my good friend Michael on the farm,.

Life has many twists and turns. Some are good, some are hard. I really felt I had abandoned my best friend. But in reality I had given him a chance to be happy. To be free on the farm with someone who would love him and treat as part of the family as I had. I on the other side I felt sure I would find it more difficult to adapt without him than he would to his new surroundings. Dogs in particular need tender loving care and will return it two-fold. This probably applies to most animals and to life in general.

Over the next few months we went out to see him on a regular basis and were thrilled at how he and Michael had bonded. The two of them, like Major and I, had become inseparable. Michael promised me faithfully he would keep him happy on the farm for the rest of his life and I believed that would happen.

Chapter 73

My new responsibility involved lots of travelling. Apart from weekends, I was seldom home. Usually I would leave first thing on Monday morning with a full load of supplies required by the rig I was visiting. The contracts were widespread, so I almost covered Rhodesia by road each week. First, there was a rig at Rasendie Mine close to Umtali, then we moved onto the lowveld via Birchenough Bridge that spans the Sabi River, about 85 Miles south of Umtali.

Birchenough Bridge is an impressive piece of engineering, way out in the remote bush of Rhodesia. From far off, it rises mysteriously like a spider web out of the shimmering dusty heat among thorn bushes and baobab scrub. It's a single arch suspension bridge closely resembling the Sydney Harbour Bridge. The two bridges were designed by the same structural designer, Ralph Freeman.

The area is also known for the flowering shrub called the Sabi Star which resembles a baby baobab tree when it loses all its leaves. It's rare and hard to find, so it's greatly rewarding to find one when it's flowering, which it does when the rest of the velt around is dry and barren. The flowers burst out on the tips of its bare branches and are tuberous, with five frilly white petals edged in red, forming a perfect star.

www.morningmirror.africanherd.com/bulawayo.../SABI[9]

From there I continued on down to Chiredzi where we had two rigs running. This contract was a really difficult one with a fractured formation that caused countless drilling problems. Production was low. The drilling team spent more time pulling and lowering drill rods to remove the jammed core from the core barrel than actually drilling. The formation being drilled was serpentine and when it was solid, it was easy to drill, as it is not a hard rock.

---

[9] Photo's of the flower can be seen on this link.

At the Chiredzi rig, the formation had many thin stringers of asbestos running through the core in all directions. This resulted in fracturing of the core causing blockage in the core barrel inner-tube. Being a soft formation, special care had to be taken once the core blocked. Any attempt to drill the blockage away led to loss of ground core. This was not acceptable to the Mining House, nor should it be, as they paid for the core, not for a hole in the ground

I spent a day or two at a particular site. I needed to be satisfied that it was progressing as well as possible. I also had to ensure that all the supplies needed were on site and do my best to solve any in-hole problems.

From Chiredzi I would head off via Fort Victoria to Bulawayo. From there on to the Turk Gold mine where there were two drill rigs to be serviced.

Turk Mine is small mining village in Matabeleland about 35 miles north-east of Bulawayo. The village grew up around a gold mine of the same name and serves as an administrative centre for the surrounding mining and ranching area. The Streak family, including Heath and Denis who both represented Rhodesia in cricket, have been farming in the area for over a century. Denis Streak even created a cricket oval on his farm at Turk Mine.

The drilling in this area was distinctly easier, with solid formations making drilling production significantly higher.

I enjoyed my visits there. The people, as they usually were in the smaller centres, were friendly and accommodating. There were usually not many drilling problems to solve. I felt more like a supplier ensuring that drill bits, core springs, reaming shells and such were on hand along with the supply of food rations.

This would normally take more than a morning to check out. I would also pay a courtesy visit to the geologist to find out if he was satisfied with the work being done, and also to see if there were any changes to the current contract.

On the few occasions I stayed out on site for the night, where possible, I would take the geologists for a meal at the local club. Country clubs had the most wonderful atmosphere and some of the nicest people you could ever wish to meet anywhere in the world. They consisted mostly of the local farmers in the area.

Something most Rhodesians were well known for, and even respected for was their ability to swallow a beer or six. Somehow they managed to empty pint bottle after pint bottle at constant and regular intervals without showing any signs of inebriation. I was always made to feel welcome, and within a short space of time felt like part of the furniture.

From the Turk Gold Mine, we had some drill rigs scattered between Bulawayo and Salisbury at a place called Battle Fields.

Then there was the famous Great Dyke, which ran through Rhodesia. Parts of the range are rich in vast mineral deposits, including platinum, gold, chromium, silver, asbestos and nickel. This led to many Mining Houses carrying out extensive and expensive exploration projects on The Great Dyke in the hope of reopening some of the old workings, or starting up newly found mines. It's thought to have been formed when molten rock forced its way into existing rock formations and it extends from north to south through the centre of Rhodesia, passing just to the west of Salisbury. It consists of a band of short, narrow ridges and hills spanning for approximately three hundred and forty miles.

Rhodesia had everything going for it as far as minerals were concerned. There was Chrome, Nickel, Copper, Platinum, Coal and Gold to mention a few. Also, there was fertile farming country which produced, for example, maize, tobacco, cotton and tea. At that time, the country was known as the bread basket of Africa. It was almost completely self-sufficient, with enough of everything to be in a position to export and help the foreign exchange flow into the country

Sadly, today, in Zimbabwe, the majority of these mines are not producing and have been put on ice. There has also been a collapse of agriculture due to the take-over of the farms by individual peasant farmers who don't have the expertise or the equipment to use the land effectively. The population has fallen into starvation. The potential for the country remains huge. One day it will surely return to its former glory. The millions of friendly and hard-working people who live in that country have suffered enough. It's time for prosperity and happiness to reward them in a country that has everything to offer.

Those who know it, and who live there, call it God's own country. It also has a near perfect climate and vegetation. We were all happy, as were the majority of local black Rhodesians. The Rhodesian indigenous peoples have a reputation for being the most intelligent and hardest working force in Africa. They were known to be honest, pleasant, and friendly, and always gave one hundred percent to whatever job they undertook.

If things went well, I would be back in Salisbury by Friday night after my round trip. But more often, I would get home sometime on Saturday. This would give me the weekend with Les and then first thing Monday the whole cycle began again. The hours of driving didn't bother me. I enjoyed seeing so much of the Rhodesian countryside, and to make it even more enjoyable, I was being paid to see it.

Chapter 74

After eight months living in the city and travelling around the country, a new drilling contract came up in Filabusi, a tiny town with one fuel station, one store and butchery, and a few houses. In all the small towns of Rhodesia, no matter how small the population, there was always a sports club, with tennis, golf, badminton and most importantly, a bar.

Rhodesians were good at whatever they put their minds to, but when it came to alcohol consumption, they were hard to beat, and were proud of this reputation. As is the case in all the rural clubs scattered around Rhodesia, this sports club was popular with the local farmers. There was a great atmosphere in the bar and you could be sure of a good experience on every visit.

Gus needed someone to go out and get the contract up and running and I was to be that someone. Initially two rigs would be sent to the site and to start drilling as soon as possible. Les and I were happy with the new assignment. We longed to be out of the city, and we would be together again for seven days a week. Fortunately, we had not bought much for our little flat. We didn't want to waste any cash, when we knew that this kind of move was always possible. Packing up and moving back to the bush was not complicated. We were excited about the move.

Within a week all the equipment required to go out to the site was loaded and on its way out to what would be our new home. We had packed all we felt we would need into the Peugeot pickup I would be using out there and the caravan was hooked to the tow-hitch. On my rounds the previous week I had stopped in at the shop and the petrol station in Filabusi to open accounts for fuel and food supplies.

On both occasions the owners were accommodating, especially considering they had never dealt with us before. There was so much trust back in those days. There was very little crime. Rhodesians were natural business people. They could spot a possible opportunity to boost sales.

We had a comfortable journey to Umvuma, with no mechanical problems in our own vehicle, nor with the trucks transporting the drilling equipment. Immediately on arrival we offloaded the trucks on site and sent them back to Salisbury to reload the second rig and equipment. That too went off without a hitch. Within four days of the first load leaving Salisbury we had everything on site.

The whole process of building a camp started all over again. We both knew what we needed and how to make improvements on what we had done in our last camp in Umvuma. I left two guys with Les during the day to build the camp under her supervision and concentrated all my attention on getting the rigs up and drilling on their first sites as fast as possible.

Within a few days it was evident this was going to be another high production contract. Once again the formation was Talk Schist which varies in hardness on a scale of one to ten somewhere in the range of 4-6. The same formation we drilled in Umvuma I would rate a six, while this formation we were drilling into was around 4. It was soft and solid, so the side walls on the sections drilled held up with no collapsing whatsoever.

Using the same hand set bits as in Umvuma the penetration rates were good. But to some extent they tended to mud up on occasions. This slows penetration rates and can shut the water off from flowing through the waterways that are cut on the bit, to ensure continuous water flow. I had spoken to our bit supplier in Salisbury about this problem, and asked them to design a couple of test BXM bits with fine tungsten chips instead of the hand set diamonds. Although fine, the chips were larger than the diamonds and once the supplier had delivered the bits to the site we ran them into the hole not really knowing if they would cut the formation or not. They not only cut beautifully, with high penetration rates, but they also gave us a good mileage. From that time on I kept some diamond handset bits in stock in the event we drilled into a harder formation, but only ordered our new design tungsten bits which were half the price of the diamond bits.

We completed the first two holes successfully. They intersected good looking nickel mineralisation. These would be sent away to the laboratory to be analysed, but from both sides, we were excited.

The next four holes all had similar intersections. By this time, high grade nickel results from the first two had come back from the laboratory. The geologist on site was very happy, and wanted to hit this bonanza hard and fast, He asked us to send a further rig out to the site to speed up the operation. Similar ore zones were intersected again, and it wasn't long before we had five drill rigs running on the site. I was no longer operating one of the machines, as the supervision required for the five rigs was too demanding. It wasn't possible to supervise all five rigs, and run one of them. One of the company's Botswana contracts had been cut back, and there was a spare operator so he was brought in to take over my rig.

Our production rate was so high that the Mining House arranged with the university for four student geologists to come out and do their practicals on our site, logging core. This is a painstaking job and one of the reasons I always give for not ever wanting to go into geology when asked if I would like to. Each and every foot drilled has to be precisely logged and recorded. On the site there were now five geologists working nonstop from 6.00am to 6.00pm, to keep up with the drilling production. Although there was a small lean-to on site it was too small to accommodate all the activity going on. Only two people could use the space at one time, so there was a rotation programme and they took it in turns to improve their sun tans. I didn't envy them. No sooner had they completed the logging of one hole there was a new batch of core waiting to be logged.

Don't get me wrong, I believe geology is a great career and at times can be rewarding, as it was in this case where we were drilling into these beautiful ore zones every day. But there are times when it can be devastatingly disappointing.

For recreation, we travelled into Filabusi at least twice a week in the evening to play badminton. It was popular with the younger people in town and we all looked forward to those nights. The standard of our play at the start was average, but steadily we all improved with practice and we were able to have wonderfully competitive games.

It was good for us to have a break from drill sites, and we very much enjoyed mixing with new people. Bar none, they were all friendly, happy people. Yes. Those were happy times that I will never forget. On our weekends off we once again set off for Filabusi to play golf or to go fishing. A few times, we drove all the way to the big city of Bulawayo. If you knew where to go, accommodation there was cheap, so we spent the night there. In the day the women could all go shopping, and for those of us who played, we would have a round of golf.

Chapter 75

Not only was the drilling project turning into a great success. We had still more to celebrate. Les was pregnant with our first child. He had been conceived in our flat in Salisbury around August, and it was now the beginning of March. Les was huge and very uncomfortable. But she never once complained.

At night, after work, we used to go "hunting" with The Bird Man as he was known. Roger was one of the geological field assistants. He had an aptitude for bonding with and training birds of prey. At that time he owned an eagle and spent many hours with it.

I never tired of watching him exercise his majestic bird. He would carry the eagle on his arm into an open section of the bush. There would be a hood over the bird's head to subdue him. His arm was protected by a thick elbow-length leather glove. Once the bird was settled he would gently pull the hood off and release him.. The eagle would take off flapping its wings until he picked up a thermal that would lift him high into the sky, and all we could see was a small speck floating effortlessly above. Roger would let him circle up there for a while and then give a loud sharp whistle. As loud as it was, it seemed there was little chance of a bird that high hearing it. But there would be an immediate reaction and the bird became a missile, descending in fast sweeps. In no time at all the eagle swooped in and was back sitting on the gloved arm waiting for his reward, which he knew was in the pouch Roger had hanging on his belt. From the pouch Roger pulled out a chunk of raw rabbit or possibly dove meat, which was a day or two past its sell-by date, held it in one hand and took a bite, pulling off a piece which he held out for the eagle, who swallowed it in one gulp. To ensure that the raptor maintained his hunting ability so essential for survival, we would go night hunting.

We drove in the old Land Rover, with a very pregnant Les beside me. Behind the cab and standing in the open back would be Roger with his leather glove and the hooded eagle. The hood was a necessary accessory. When its eyes were covered and it had no vision, the bird was completely relaxed.

We drove along narrow country roads, shining a bright torch into the bush on either side, searching for the eyes of a rabbit. When we spotted one, we turned off the road and bounced our way towards the prey. Many times there would be a severe jolt as one of the wheels ran into a log or rock hidden in the long grass, as we drove through the dark.

Once close enough, Roger tapped lightly on the roof, and I stopped with headlights trained on the unsuspecting rabbit. The hood was removed. As soon as the eagle spotted the rabbit it took off from Roger's arm, and swooped down over the windscreen, with talons outstretched. Watching this display from inside the cab was a marvellous experience. The eagle flew right over us, showing off its beautiful under-feathers before it grasped its prey.

On one of the times we went out, we came across a spring hare. They look almost like a baby kangaroo. As the eagle took hold of him we were surprised to see the power in its long back legs. It took off, and ran into a thorn bush, dragging the bewildered bird along with it. The hare escaped, but the poor eagle was caught in the thorn bush, with its wings widely spread. It took Roger some time to free the bird. Needless to say, after that experience, we ignored spring hares.

We all enjoyed these hunting trips, including Les. But considering her advanced stage of pregnancy, it was probably not a good idea for her to go bumping and bashing through the bush. It was probably these hunting trips that caused the premature birth of our first son. We were young and ignorant, and didn't realise the possible consequences of our actions.

There were no good hospitals in the area. Our baby was due at the end of April We decided that Les would return to Salisbury and stay with her parents until the birth. They would keep me informed, and when things started to happen, I would make a dash for Salisbury.

On a weekend, I drove Les into Salisbury, just before the end of March. I had to return immediately to Filabusi on Sunday afternoon to be on site for an early morning start to drilling on Monday. Every morning I drove into the little town where I could make a call from a call box at the Post Office. There was no way for Les or her parents to contact me, to let me know how things were going. Les assured me that things were progressing smoothly and we were on track for the end of April.

Then, on 7th April 1971, when I called, Les' Dad answered the phone. On hearing my voice he said, "Congratulations. You are a father!" This was too much for me to comprehend. I thought I had dialled the wrong number. I couldn't speak.

"Hello! Are you there? You have a baby son and all is well," he assured me. "That can't be! The baby was due at the end of the month!" I stammered, with my head in turmoil. "Seriously, how is Les? Please let me talk to her?" I said, laughing, realising that this was a joke. My father-in-law had quite a sense of humour, and now he was pulling my leg. "That's not possible. She's in The Lady Chancellor Hospital with your son who arrived three weeks early and he needs to be monitored closely." he said, with an amused tone.

This time I believed him. I thanked him for the news, and shot off back to camp to throw some clothes into an overnight bag. After arranging for Paul, the driller who had come through from Botswana, to look after things while I was away, I raced off to Salisbury to meet my son, and to see how Les was doing. I very much wanted to be there for the birth, and had made arrangements to be away from the site at the end of the month, to be present at this momentous occasion, which had now already happened.

On my arrival I went straight into the Lady Chancellor Hospital and asked to see my wife and baby. They said it wasn't really visiting hours, but after I explained to them what had happened, I was whisked up to the first floor and into the post-delivery ward.

I was so excited. I had even stopped and bought flowers and champagne to celebrate. It was the first time in our life together I had bought flowers for Les. Les was amazed to see me walk in. "Wow, you got here quickly." she said as I walked in.

"Yes. When I called early this morning and Dad told me the news, I left immediately. I'm so glad to see you! Well done!" I kissed her and asked, "How are you? Tell me everything went well?" She told me all that had happened. However, her labour had been a nightmare. It started when she got out of bed the day before. Eventually, around midday, her Mom drove her to the Lady Chancellor Hospital, which happened to be the same hospital where I had been born. Poor Les was in intense pain, which she endured for many hours. Eventually at 18h45 that night our 6lb 14oz little boy arrived into the world.

Throughout her pregnancy we had nick-named him Joshua, but now that he had arrived we needed to find him a real name. Eventually, after throwing loads of names around and a whole week after the event, we settled on Darrin. Why Darrin? I have no idea as neither of us had a Darrin anywhere in our family tree, but we both liked the name.

I had to return to the site the next day. Les spent a week with her Mom in Salisbury, learning the ropes of caring for our tiny baby. Then I drove back to Salisbury to fetch my family, to bring them back to the camp site.

We had purchased a 1958 Ford Fairlane. It was in immaculate condition. It was a large vehicle, powered by a 302 V8 engine. We could almost fit our house in the boot. But even with this much space, there were still odds and ends that we had to push into little spaces here and there all over the inside of the car. The large rear seat was packed solid.

"We need a bigger car," I joked. "Just imagine our predicament if we owned a Mini Minor."

Eventually, with a wave goodbye, off we went down the driveway feeling like a removals company, with a nervous Mommy holding our tiny son snugly wrapped in his blue blanket. She was terrified of the responsibility of caring for this fragile little baby. Not only was it nerve-wracking in the city for a first time Mom, but we were heading into the bush, away from hospitals, Mother or any other kind of help. One of the things that pushed her into this nervous state knowing that not only did she not know what to do with a small baby, but I knew ten times less than she did. I could fix engines, pumps and any kind of hole drilling problem. But when it came to babies, or any other household chores, on a scale of ten, I came in on minus one.

In spite of her fears, Les did a great job as a Mom. We quickly settled into our new life with little Darrin out in the bush in our caravan. During the night when she had to get up to either feed or change nappies, it entailed her climbing over me to fetch him from his cot. She somehow managed to do this several times every night without ever waking me. I was working from sun up to sun down so by the end of the day I dropped into a deep sleep, and was never witness to the nightly events between Darrin and his Mom.

Each day, after Mom had played with, fed and winded little Darrin he would be placed in his pram, a screen net pulled right over the top to keep out flies and other insects, and pushed out into a shady spot under the trees around the caravan. There he slept until his next feed. Some of the Moms in town were horrified on hearing this, yet he absolutely flourished. He put on weight, had rosy chubby cheeks, was full of smiles and never sick. The fresh air did him the world of good. Whether or not

Les's method of looking after a baby tied in with the baby books, trust me, it worked and I would recommend it to anyone.

At first, after being placed under the tree, he would sometimes wake and give a little cry. Les, knowing he had been fed and winded left him. She knew there was nothing he needed. He slept from feed to feed. He was a happy baby, always laughing and alert.

Mother and child were happy at home in the camp. This helped me put my best into the drilling activities. These were peaceful and happy months.

Chapter 76

The day came when Gus arrived on site to inform us that there was an urgent drilling contract to be done at the Gwaai River Mine in the North West of the country.

One thing about being in the exploration drilling game is that you never know where or when you could be sent off to another contract, somewhere else in the country.

The Gwaai River Mine was a classic case of under-drilling at the start. The Mining House had awarded the original tender to one of our opposition companies. Many months of hard work had been spent on the usual geological work and eventually, due to promising soil sampling results, five proposed vertical drill holes were marked out. The drilling company came in and drilled the holes. All five showed high-grade copper ore. Not only was the grade exceptional in all the holes, but each hole made the intersection at almost exactly the same depth. The Mining House couldn't believe their luck. They believed they had a bonanza mine there. If only they had drilled one or two more infill holes between any of the five holes they would have seen a different picture.

One of the best organised housing schemes I have seen on any mine was built for the top management, and also for the supervisors, miners, blasters and also top quality accommodation for the black mine workers. There was also a club house with tennis courts, a swimming pool, and a snooker room with full-size table.

At the start, there was a grand opening ceremony organised. The Rhodesian Prime Minister, Mr. Ian Smith, was invited to officially open the mine. Catering was arranged at great expense through a large hotel chain based at Victoria Falls at huge expense. No expense was spared.

The head-gear was installed, the shaft was sunk, and the mining operation began in earnest. Production was going well until reaching the 'pay dirt'. The results were shattering. Each ore zone intersected proved to be a pocket of high-grade ore. In between each pocket was a thin low-grade ore zone joining them all together.

It was a chance in a million that each of the five holes intersected with similar high grade ore, and that the depths all tied in with strata dip - yet each one was proved to be just a pocket. It was a horrible coincidence. The odds against a geologist ever hitting such a seeming jackpot again have to be slim to non-existent. Suddenly, after spending millions on infrastructure and mining operations the question had to be asked: Was the mine actually viable? This was the point at which our head office in Salisbury were contacted to see if we had a rig available to urgently drill to find out what was really happening. Was the ore-body there or was it not?

When we arrived we were impressed to see how well established the mine was, and were pleased to have the chance to live in a comfortable environment with all amenities, including a hospital, on hand. The hospital was important, because Les was pregnant with our second child.

We settled into the camping area with a tiny caravan. I had been instructed to leave the larger one back in Filabusi. On our first visit to the club, we met a wonderful couple who, after hearing of us living in a tiny caravan with a baby, offered us a place to stay in their home. We were overwhelmed by their generosity, and appreciated their trust in us after just one meeting. We were concerned though, that this could be an inconvenience for them to have a family move into their house. This wasn't a short term project. It would take a few months to complete the drilling programme. But our new friends insisted and assured us that they would enjoy the company.

The following day we moved in, and spent the next eight months with them. They were wonderful people, and we became close friends.

Chapter 77

The first hole marked out for drilling was on the side of a mountain. The rig and equipment had to be transported on a winding, steep road that had been recently bulldozed, for this purpose. It took three days to level the area, and deal with bulldozer problems. Eventually we got started with the drilling.

Tension was running high. Negative results were feared. We were drilling on an infill hole between holes four and five of the originally collared holes. The mining operations had not reached this area, because of what they thought they had discovered on the first three intersections underground.

The chief geologist was pressurized by top management for results. He visited the site at least twice a day. In spite of the urgency, we had been instructed not to run a night shift. We worked from first light until it was too dusky to see. The drilling progressed well and production was good. One day, when the geologist arrived, we had reached the presumed intersection depth, and I was pulling rods. After climbing from his vehicle he walked over, with an enquiring look on his face, giving me the thumbs up sign at the same time. I smiled returning the same sign back to him. His eyes lit up.

"I take it you have intersected?" "Yes, six to eight inches of massive sulphides." I said with a smile. "It was towards the end of the run. Unfortunately the black water indicating the strike cleared after about eight inches, but who knows what the next run could pick up. This one could be a stringer above the real thing. I should only be another half an hour pulling rods so sit down and relax. Soon you can have a look at this one."

I continued pulling rods. Eventually I had them all out of the hole and the core placed neatly in the core box. Two feet from the end of the run was an eight-inch section of what looked like a copper pipe. It was high grade ore and the geologist was much encouraged by what he saw. He was now desperate to see what came up in the following run. I told him to come back in a couple of hours and hopefully I would have good news for him.

Within half an hour he was back, accompanied by the Mine Manager. They had decided to come and watch while I drilled the important run. They wanted to be there when it happened, to experience the thrill of the moment, when the water turned black indicating a strike. The results would change the life of the mine, and their futures, and they wanted to be there.

Unfortunately, I drilled that run and the next and the next, with no further sign of ore. To say this was a disappointment was an understatement. Having well exceeded the expected intersection depth with only the eight-inch intersection to show for our concerted efforts, it was accepted that that was it, the hole was terminated. I drilled a further four holes all coming up with the same devastatingly disappointing results.

The Land Rover I used at the start of the contract was needed elsewhere, and I was limited to mine transport when it was available. This was inconvenient, and embarrassing. We were one of the largest drilling companies in the country and I felt we shouldn't have to rely on the goodness of our clients for my transport, and for the transport of supplies around the mine. Gus was a real professional, and there must have been something of this nature written into the agreement. But I felt disempowered and guilty every time I had to look for help with transport.

To solve the problem and ease the problem of getting to work and back each day, I purchased an old 500cc Matchless four stoke single motor bike from Theuns, the friend with whom we were staying. He had not used it for a long time as it needed repairs done. It was old and well worn. The kick start lever had completely stripped all the splines both on the shaft and inside the housing of the kick start arm that attached to the shaft. I made various attempts at rectifying the problem, but they all proved to be temporary. Ultimately, I resigned myself to the fact that a running start was the only way to fire her up. I had to run down the road pushing the bike, jump on kick it into gear, let out the clutch to spin the motor and with a bit of luck it would burst into a deafening roar. The exhaust baffles were blown through long ago. It would sometimes take up to six attempts before she would fire, and doing this at 5am each morning had become a bit of a standing joke on the mine. The accompanying roar, when she eventually fired into life guaranteed that everyone within two miles would be woken up on time to get to their various jobs on the mine. There was no need for anyone to set their alarm clocks.

We were then moved across the Gwaai River to drill one exploration hole in the hope the one-body could have been separated by a major fault zone and possibly recur on the East side. To get to the site was an experience on its own. There was a section of the river that ran over smooth flat rock. At this point the water was shallow. This ensured a solid but narrow base. If anyone making the crossing were to wander off the line even slightly, there was every chance of a swim.

Every day, to get to site and back, I had to ride through the river on the faithful old Matchie. I had devised a method of carrying five-gallon tins of either diesel or hydraulic oil on the top of my fuel tank. Although it looked dangerous and was the popular subject of humour around the club bar, it worked well.

All my guys stayed on the rig in their tents, and I even transported their ration meat on the Black Bomber as I fondly named my transport. Once a week, I made use of the geologist's Land Rover to bring in a forty-five-gallon drum of diesel.

Chapter 78

At 10.00am on 4th April 1972, while drilling on this particular hole, I had a premonition. Something told me Les was in labour, giving birth to our second child. How could I be so certain of this? She was 500 miles away. Yet I knew it was true. The premonition was mysteriously compelling.

To ensure there would not be a repeat of the kind of surprise that happened when Darrin was born, we had decided that she should go to stay with her Mom once again. She packed her things, and a month before the due date she left for Salisbury. There was someone from the mine going through to the city, and we gratefully accepted the offer of a ride for her. It saved me taking off from work and the long two-day drive there and back.

This time around, however, everything was going to plan and the baby was due anytime now. Knowing this, and having had this overwhelmingly strong feeling that the baby was on the way, I made my decision there and then. I told the guys on the rig that I was going to be away for a few days and they would have to look after everything. I told them that, on my return, I expected the machine to be spotless. They had just received their rations so were set up for the next week.

I rushed off on the black bomber to the house, threw some clothes into a bag and told Theuns of my plans. I rushed out the house, leapt into the old Fairlane and set off for Salisbury. I drove right through, arriving there in the early evening. I went straight into the Lady Chancellor Hospital. At the reception desk I asked if my wife had come in. The receptionist laughed and said that she had arrived at 10.00am that morning (which was the same time I had the premonition). She was on the first floor, waiting for the baby to arrive. I was thrilled to hear that Les had not yet given birth.

I raced up the stairs two at a time, so excited to see her. The sister on duty was a big lady and genuinely looked like she was in charge. She was waiting for me at the top of the stairs.

"Where do you think you're going?" she asked in a husky, authoritative voice. She wasn't happy about me being there. "Who do you think you are just rushing up here. I think I should call security."

"I'm here to see my wife who was admitted this morning." I said, a little out of breath, both from the run upstairs and the excitement of arriving on time to support Les through the birth.

"What is your wife's name?" By her tone of voice, I knew she was not as excited as I was. I gave her Les's name. "Who would you like to see first, your wife or your son?" Needless to say, once again, I was gob-smacked.

"Well, firstly my wife hasn't given birth yet. Secondly we're having a girl this time. You have confused me with someone else." I said, feeling terribly confused myself.

"Well, aren't we just the clever one, knowing more about what happens in my ward than I do?" she said sarcastically. "Maybe you should take over my job." "Sorry, sister, but the lady downstairs assured me that the baby had not yet been born. And we are both convinced that this time we are having a baby girl."

I was feeling sheepish, and went on to explain the day's events and the distance I had driven to get here, without any confirmation that anything had even happened. She softened.

"Well, your son was born some hours ago and is well, and so is your wife. Now, if you would like to just slow down, I'll take you through to see your son and then your wife." With that, she spun around and I followed after her like a lost sheep.

I was told to stand behind a window looking into the baby care room. In no time she was back standing in front of me with what had to be the ugliest baby I have ever seen.

"Wow." I exclaimed, "He's not pretty. Are you sure he is mine?" I blurted it out without thinking. She smiled.

"He's only a couple of hours old and being as busy as we are in the maternity ward we haven't yet combed his hair."

We both burst out laughing and the tension between us vanished, and my new-born baby looked prettier.

Les was so surprised to see me. She couldn't believe I had got there so fast. Her Dad had only just managed to get a message through to the mine to pass on to me. I told her what had happened and she was as amazed as I had been when the premonition came.

Throughout my life I have had many unexplainable premonitions or visions or whatever-you-may-call-them. They are a mystery and puzzlement. This time it was an indicator of something good. That has not always been the case. More often, it has been a foreboding.

Within a week, our enlarged family of four, left for the mine to start our new life. Dion was no longer the ugly little guy I had seen through the inspection window. He was as cute as Darrin had been. We hoped he would be as happy and easy to manage as his bigger brother had been.

It's incredible how different children can be! It soon became clear that Dion was his own person. He was on a mission to be as different to his brother as he could be. Boy oh boy! Was he successful! Les had her hands full with him and there were no problems with his vocal cords. He exercised them with both vigour and determination. Anyone listening from outside must have wondered what we were doing to the poor child. I comforted Les by telling her that it was impossible for it to get worse, so it could only get better from here on.

With two babies, just three days under a year apart, Les's life had become far more hectic. Apart from that, nothing else had changed. The drilling continued, generally yielding disappointing results.

Chapter 79

I was still working on the other side of the river when one of the guys came running over, shouting that he had a snake in his tent. I asked my assistant to look after the rig and went over to see how big the snake was.

It was a harmless grass snake with yellow lines running parallel all the way down its back. I fetched the thick leather gloves I used to ride to work each day, and easily caught the snake with the help of a forked stick. I placed it in the tog bag that I wore to carry my lunch and drinks. It was the type that had the draw strings on the top. The reason I decided to keep the snake was because Theuns had a snake pit at the house. He was always happy to add a snake to his collection.

Happy that the snake was safe and snug, and feeling sure he would go to sleep in the darkness of the bag, I walked back to the rig. I had just taken over the controls again when the same guy ran up with the same story of a snake in his tent. I honestly thought he was joking. But he assured me that there was another snake in his tent. Once again, I set off, armed with my gloves and the forked stick, to catch the new intruder which I thought must be the mate of the original snake.

As I entered the tent, sure enough, there was another snake. This time however, it was a brilliant green colour with small flecks of black along the side and back. It was really a stunning looking snake. I was amazed at just how different the male and female were. The other difference I noticed was the size of the eyes. This one had much bigger eyes that its mate. I caught it, and dropped it into the bag, reuniting it with its loved one.

Late that afternoon, I shut down the rig down for the day and organised the bag with the two snakes, balancing it safely half on my lap and half on the fuel tank. The guys gave the bike a good push and it fired into its deafening roar and I set off for home. Just after negotiating my way over the river I noticed out the corner of my eye there was a movement of sorts in the bag. Looking down and seeing about a quarter of the green snake poking through the hole at the top of the bag, I came to a stop, gave the bag a good shake with the head of the snake flapping around until he fell, or retreated, back into the bag. From there I kept a close watch on the bag and to my relief had no further incidents.

Theuns loved standing outside in the early evening to watch the spectacular sunsets, and that is where I found him on my return. As soon as I climbed off the bike I called excitedly for him to come and see the surprise I had for him. When hearing what was in the bag he carried it over to his inspection pit and dropped the two snakes into it. To my utter surprise he killed the green one with the black flecks and beautiful eyes almost as it emerged from the bag.

"What are you doing?" I exclaimed, in shock. I was shattered by what he had done.

"You obviously don't know what kind of snake that is!" he shouted back, looking at me like I was an idiot. Up to that point I was standing proud, thinking I was a wise snake charmer of sorts for having caught them and brought them home alive.

I told him how they were mates, and had been caught in the same tent within fifteen minutes of each other.

"That, my friend, is a Boomslang. Although back-fanged, it's one of the most venomous snakes around. The serum would take a week to get here, but by that stage you would be pushing up daisies." For some reason he found this amusing. I was shocked.

"Well!" I retorted, "From now on you can find your own snakes!" From then on, in the bar I became known as the 'Snake Hunter'. Living in such a small community, there was nothing anyone could do without the whole town knowing about it, almost before you yourself knew.

Chapter 80

On 6th June 1972 shattering news filtered through to the mine. A massive methane gas explosion had ripped through the nearby Wankie Coal Mine. Many deaths were reported. The force of the explosion caused the cable car from No. 2 shaft to be shot out of the ground like a giant cannonball. It came to rest fifty yards away, taking out a row of trees and killing four men instantly. That was the first sign of the disaster.

An explosion, possibly ignited by a dynamite magazine which, in a chain reaction, ignited the ever-present coal dust in the air, together with the methane gas, ripped through the whole section. The No. 2 shaft was the major shaft of the Wankie Colliery. It's destruction instantly killed all the people who were down there, and crippled the mine that produced all of Rhodesia's coal.

For fifteen hours rescue operations were tragically hampered by gas seeping from the mineshaft, making access impossible. Any attempt to go in immediately with a proto team would have been suicidal and would have caused further loss of life. It was eventually decided to clear the shaft of these deadly gasses by pumping air into the shaft and pushing the fumes deeper into the mine. This decision permitted the rescue effort to begin, but it also reduced the chance of finding anyone alive.

Around the opening of the shaft were literally hundreds of wives and family members of miners down below. Some were sitting where they could find space and the rest of them were standing or milling around and wailing for their loved ones, trapped far below. They wanted to be as close as possible to the shaft, but their presence hampered the work of the rescue teams. The police had their hands full trying to urge them to move back.

A group of us from our mine rushed through in the hope of offering assistance. Seeing the gasses pouring from the shaft, and the faces of the families who were holding onto a hopeless hope of that their husband, brother or father was alive, was painful. Many of the women were pregnant.

The sight of those frightened, suffering people will remain the saddest, most tragic sight I have witnessed. I was overwhelmed with helplessness, knowing there was nothing that could be done to relieve their distress. How could this happen? How could anyone allow such suffering to befall these good people? Events like these have puzzled and distressed me. How and why is life that cruel?

After three days of around-the-clock rescue work, and all possible efforts exhausted, there was no sign of life in the three-mile long tunnel. On the third day, the mine manager announced that all hope was lost, adding as a small comfort, that indications were that the missing men had died instantly and would not have known what happened.

The final death toll was expected to exceed 430 men, making the Wankie coal mine disaster the fifth worst in history. At the mine-head, the wailing of women permeated the air as they cried out the pain of losing their loved ones.

Chapter 81

The drilling programme at the Gwaai River Mine was coming to an end. There was great despondency from management level all the way through to unskilled employees. Everyone knew that the writing was on the wall for the new mine still in its infancy, and for their employment. We had ultimately proved that there was no viable ore-body. Apart from a couple of holes left to drill, to all intents and purposes the drilling contract was complete, soon to be followed by the closure of the mine.

The South African Sunday Times newspaper was delivered and sold on the mine. When reading it one day, my eye was drawn to an advert for a vacancy for a Diamond Driller at the Messina Mine in the Northern part of South Africa. What caught my interest in a big way was that staff housing was one of the perks. Les had been a one-in-a-millions wife and Mom, living in a small caravan in a remote area. Theuns and his wife had been generous and kind beyond words, giving us space in their home during the last eight months of our stay. But now we longed to bring up our sons in our own home.

Gus had informed us that when this contract was complete we would be transferred back to Filabusi and be given an even smaller caravan. The advertisement in the newspaper could not have come at a more appropriate time. It was a big decision to make, as it would mean uprooting my family and moving out of our home country, away from friends and immediate family. But it would be far more stable and comfortable. Les and I talked for many hours, weighing up the pros and cons of such a move. Eventually deciding to go for it, and I applied for the position.

I sent off my CV. Within a week, the job was mine. All I had to do was give them confirmation of my acceptance of the appointment.

To be sure, I again discussed with Gus the matter of our accommodation in Filabusi.

He gave the same response. Our accommodation would be the tiny caravan. I was deeply disappointed and told him how much this would affect my family. I then had to tell him that this situation had forced us to make a difficult decision. I dropped the bombshell, telling him that as soon as he could arrange for an operator to take over from me, I would be leaving, but that I was not prepared to stay beyond the end of the month.

I told him I would be moving to South Africa to work on the mines there. Living in the bush was fine before we had children. But now things had changed. I told him of my successful application for a new job. I also told him that the main reason for my leaving was concern for the security for my family, medical aid, a pension scheme, and most importantly a stable roof over our heads.

Sadly, a few months later, with little money or possessions to take with us, we left Rhodesia and our family and friends whom we would dearly miss. We headed off to what was to become a completely new life for the four of us. What would that new life bring? Would we be happy? Only time would tell.

The end

(sequel to follow)

www.ingramcontent.com/pod-product-compliance
Lightning Source LLC
Chambersburg PA
CBHW070629290526
45790CB00001B/55